OXFORD PAPERBACK REFERENCE

The Oxford Dictionary of
Musical Works

Oxford Paperback Reference

The most authoritative and up-to-date reference books for both students and the general reader.

ABC of Music
Accounting
Allusions
Animal Behaviour*
Archaeology
Architecture
Art and Artists
Art Terms
Astronomy
Better Wordpower
Bible
Biology
British History
British Place-Names
Buddhism
Business
Card Games
Catchphrases
Celtic Mythology
Chemistry
Christian Art
Christian Church
Chronology of English Literature
Classical Literature
Classical Myth and Religion
Computing
Contemporary World History
Countries of the World
Dance
Dates
Dynasties of the World
Earth Sciences
Ecology
Economics
Encyclopedia
Engineering*
English Etymology
English Folklore
English Grammar
English Language
English Literature
Euphemisms
Everyday Grammar
Finance and Banking
First Names
Food and Drink
Food and Nutrition
Foreign Words and Phrases
Geography
Humorous Quotations
Idioms
Internet
Islam

Kings and Queens of Britain
Language Toolkit
Law
Linguistics
Literary Quotations
Literary Terms
Local and Family History
London Place-Names
Mathematics
Medical
Medicinal Drugs
Modern Design*
Modern Slang
Music
Musical Terms
Musical Works
Nicknames*
Nursing
Ologies and Isms
Philosophy
Phrase and Fable
Physics
Plant Sciences
Plays*
Pocket Fowler's Modern English Usage
Political Quotations
Politics
Popes
Proverbs
Psychology
Quotations
Quotations by Subject
Reverse Dictionary
Rhyming Slang
Saints
Science
Shakespeare
Slang
Sociology
Space Exploration*
Statistics
Synonyms and Antonyms
Weather
Weights, Measures, and Units
Word Games*
Word Histories
world History
World Mythology
World Place-Names*
World Religions
Zoology

*forthcoming

The Oxford Dictionary of

Musical Works

EDITED BY
ALISON LATHAM

OXFORD
UNIVERSITY PRESS

OXFORD

UNIVERSITY PRESS

Great Clarendon Street, Oxford OX2 6DP

Oxford University Press is a department of the University of Oxford.
It furthers the University's objective of excellence in research, scholarship,
and education by publishing worldwide in

Oxford New York

Auckland Cape Town Dar es Salaam Hong Kong Karachi Kuala Lumpur
Madrid Melbourne Mexico City Nairobi New Delhi Shanghai Taipei Toronto

With offices in

Argentina Austria Brazil Chile Czech Republic France Greece
Guatemala Hungary Italy Japan South Korea Poland Portugal
Singapore Switzerland Thailand Turkey Ukraine Vietnam

Oxford is a registered trade mark of Oxford University Press
in the UK and certain other countries

Published in the United States
by Oxford University Press Inc., New York

British Library Cataloguing in Publication Data
Data available

Library of Congress Cataloging-in-Publication Data
The dictionary of musical works / edited by Alison Latham.
    p. cm. — (Oxford paperback reference)
  Includes index.
  ISBN 0-19-861020-3
  1. Music—Dictionaries. I. Latham, Alison. II. Series.
  ML100.D561 2004
  780'.3–dc22

                                                            2004021940

ISBN 0-19-8610203

1

Typeset in Swift and Frutiger by Kolam Information Services Pvt. Ltd, Pondicherry, India
Printed in Great Britain by Clays Ltd, St Ives plc.

Preface

This dictionary provides essential information about a range of the most frequently performed and recorded musical works, from medieval times to the present day: operas, ballets, choral and vocal music, orchestral, chamber and instrumental pieces, nicknamed works, collections (e.g. the '48' preludes and fugues of J. S. Bach), national anthems, traditional tunes, and hymn tunes. Song cycles are included but, for practical reasons, individual songs generally are not. Catalogues of composers' works (e.g. that of Köchel for Mozart) are also described because they provide a standard system for identifying a work in a composer's output. Entries specify a work's genre, the author of a libretto, text, or scenario, with any literary source, the date of its composition or, for staged works, the place and date of first performance, dates of any subsequent revisions, and any other important information that puts a work in historical context (an event for which it was commissioned, for example). French, German, Italian, and Spanish works are listed under their original titles, with cross-references from their English titles where appropriate; Slavonic works appear under the titles by which they are known in English (though their original titles are also given). There is an appendix listing composers whose works are included.

The titles of articles to which useful further reference may be made are marked with an *asterisk if they occur in the text of an entry; otherwise the reader is directed to 'see also' one or more entries listed at the end.

A dictionary of this kind embodies a certain eccentricity: a work can be included only if it was given a title or has acquired a nickname. Thus those composers whose works are identified solely by their genre (e.g. Symphony no. 1, String Quartet no. 10) may be misleadingly underrepresented in terms of the size and significance of their musical output. Although there are 17th- and 18th-century examples of instrumental pieces with fanciful titles, the majority of the works defined here date from the 19th century to the present day, the period when music became increasingly influenced by literature and the visual arts and composers gave their programmatic orchestral works (symphonic poems, tone-poems, etc.) descriptive titles.

I am grateful to Pam Coote of Oxford University Press, who initiated this book, and to her colleagues Joanna Harris and Lisa Begley, who have overseen its production. Andrew Clements made helpful suggestions as to which 20th- and 21st-century works should be included, enabling me to make this dictionary as up to date and topical as possible. Polly Fallows's meticulous copy-editing, as always, has been invaluable.

Alison Latham
Pinkneys Green
July 2004

Contents

Abduction from the Seraglio, The. *See* ENTFÜHRUNG AUS DEM SERAIL, DIE.

Abegg Variations. Schumann's op. 1 (1829–30), for piano; it is dedicated to his friend Meta Abegg, whose name is represented by the notes A–B♭–E–E–G–G (German B = English B♭) at the beginning of the theme.

Abencérages, ou L'Étendard de Grenade, Les ('The Abenceragi, or The Standard of Grenada'). Opera (*tragédie lyrique*) in three acts by Cherubini to a libretto by Victor Joseph Étienne de Jouy after Jean-Pierre de Florian's novel *Gonzalve de Cordou* (Paris, 1813). It was revised in two acts. The title refers to the Moorish Abenceragi warriors.

Aberystwyth. Hymn tune (1879) by Joseph Parry, to which the words 'Jesu, lover of my soul' are sung; Charles Wesley wrote the words in 1840 for his *Hymns and Sacred Poems*.

Abide with me. Hymn of which the words were written in 1820 by the Revd Henry Francis Lyte (1793–1847) after he had been at the deathbed of a friend at Pole Hore, near Wexford. It was first published in Lyte's *Remains* (1850). The organist William Henry Monk (1823–89) composed the tune *Eventide* for these words for *Hymns Ancient and Modern* (1861) and Vaughan Williams wrote it a descant (in *Songs of Praise*, 1925). It is now particularly associated with the FA Cup Final, at which the crowd sing it.

Abraham and Isaac. 1. Britten's Canticle II (1952) for alto, tenor, and piano, a setting of a text from the Chester miracle play.
   2. Sacred ballad by Stravinsky (1962–3), for baritone and chamber orchestra; to a Hebrew text, it is dedicated to the people of Israel.

Abschiedsymphonie. *See* 'FAREWELL' SYMPHONY.

Abu Hassan. *Singspiel* in one act by Weber to a libretto by Franz Carl Hiemer after Antoine Galland's story *Le Dormier éveillé*, a version of a tale from the *Thousand and One Nights* (Munich, 1811).

Academic Festival Overture (*Akademische Festouvertüre*). Brahms's op. 80 (1880), dedicated to Breslau University in slightly ironic acknowledgment of an honorary doctorate conferred on the composer; it incorporates four German student songs, notably *Gaudeamus igitur*.

Accompaniment to a Film Scene (*Begleitmusik zu einer Lichtspielszene*). Schoenberg's op. 34 (1929–30); it was not written for a real film but is a programmatic piece illustrating a sequence of emotions, its movements being 'Drohende Gefahr' ('Danger Threatens'), 'Angst', and 'Katastrophe'.

Acis and Galatea. Masque, or serenata, in one, later two, acts by Handel to a libretto by John Gay and others after Ovid (Cannons, 1718); it was revived in London in 1732 incorporating new material, principally from Handel's cantata *Aci, Galatea e Polifemo* (Naples, 1708). Lully (1686), Literes (1708), and Haydn (1762) are among the composers who also wrote operas on the subject.

Actus tragicus. The name by which J. S. Bach's church cantata *Gottes Zeit ist die allerbeste Zeit* ('God's time is the best time') BWV106 is known; it was written for a funeral, probably in 1708.

Adagio. Work by Samuel Barber for strings, originally the slow movement of his String Quartet op. 11 (1936). Toscanini suggested that he orchestrate it (1938) for full string orchestra. It came to prominence as a memorial to the Americans killed in World War II and has since been played at numerous solemn and state occasions in the USA. Barber arranged it (1967) for chorus, with or without organ, setting the Latin text of the 'Agnus Dei'.

Adam Zero. Ballet in one act by Bliss to a scenario by Michael Benthall, choreographed by Robert Helpmann (London, 1946).

Adelaide. Song for voice and piano, op. 46 (1794–5), by Beethoven, a setting of a poem by Friedrich von Matthisson.

Adélaïde Concerto. A violin concerto falsely ascribed to Mozart, who was said to have written it when he was ten and to have dedicated it to the Princess Adélaïde, daughter of King Louis XV of France; it was first performed in Paris in 1931 by Marius Casadesus, who in 1977 admitted he had written it himself.

Adeste fideles ('O Come, all ye Faithful'). Hymn on the prose for Christmas Day, now ascribed to John Francis Wade (1711–86), a Latin teacher and music copyist of Douai. The words first appeared in *Evening Offices of the Church* (1760 edition) and the tune was first printed in *An Essay on the Church in Plain Chant* (1782) by Samuel Webbe.

Adieux, Les. The French title (in full 'Les Adieux, l'absence et le retour') given by the publisher to Beethoven's Piano Sonata no. 26 in E♭ major op. 81*a* (1809–10), which Beethoven called *Das Lebewohl (Abwesenheit und Wiedersehn)*; he dedicated it to his patron Archduke Rudolph on his departure from Vienna for nine months.

Admeto, re di Tessaglia ('Admetus, King of Thessaly'). Opera in three acts by Handel to a libretto adapted anonymously from Ortensio Mauro's *L'Alceste* (1679) after Antonio Aureli's *L'Antigona delusa da Alceste* (1660) (London, 1727).

Ad ora incerta—Four Orchestral Songs of Primo Levi. Work ('At an Uncertain Hour'; 1994) by Simon Bainbridge for mezzo-soprano, bassoon, and orchestra, a setting of four poems by Levi.

Adriana Lecouvreur. Opera in four acts by Cilea to a libretto by Arturo Colautti after Eugène Scribe and Ernest Legouvé's play (Milan, 1902).

Adventures of Mr Brouček, The. *See* EXCURSIONS OF MR BROUČEK, THE.

Adventures of the Vixen Bystrouška, The. *See* CUNNING LITTLE VIXEN, THE.

Africaine, L' ('The African Woman'). Grand opera in five acts by Meyerbeer to a libretto by Eugène Scribe (Paris, 1865). It was begun in 1837 but Meyerbeer was constantly interrupted by changes to the libretto and died the year before it was staged; subsequent alterations were made to both libretto and score, notably by François-Joseph Fétis, who made cuts to reduce its six-hour duration.

African Sanctus. Work by David Fanshawe for two sopranos, piano, organ, chorus, percussion, amplified lead and rhythm guitars, and tape-recordings made in Africa (London, 1972; revised Toronto, 1978).

Afternoon of a Faun. *See* APRÈS-MIDI D'UN FAUNE', PRÉLUDE À 'L'.

After the Requiem. Work (1990) by Gavin Bryars for electric guitar, two violas, and cello.

Age of Anxiety, The. Bernstein's Symphony no. 2 (1949) for piano and orchestra, inspired by W. H. Auden's *The Age of Anxiety: A Baroque Eclogue* (1946); it was choreographed as a ballet in six scenes by Jerome Robbins, to his own scenario (New York, 1950).

Age of Gold, The (*Zolotoy vek*). Ballet in three acts by Shostakovich to a scenario by Aleksandr Ivanovsky; it was choreographed by Semyon Kaplan and Vasily Vainonen (Leningrad, 1930). Shostakovich arranged an orchestral suite from it (op. 22*a*).

Age of Steel, The (*Stal'noy skok*). Ballet in two scenes by Prokofiev; it was choreographed by Leonid Massine (Paris, 1927). Prokofiev arranged a four-movement orchestral suite from it (op. 44*bis*).

Agincourt Song. An English song commemorating the country's victory at Agincourt in 1415, when it was probably written; it is for two voices and three-part chorus. The tune has been included in some modern hymnbooks and Walton used it in his film music for *Henry V* (1944).

...agm.... Work (1979) for chorus and three instrumental ensembles by Birtwistle to Fayum fragments of Sappho, translated by Tony Harrison.

Agon (Gk., 'Contest'). Ballet in three sections by Stravinsky; it was choreographed by George Balanchine (New York, 1957).

Agrippina. Opera (*drama per musica*) in three acts by Handel to a libretto by Vincenzo Grimani (Venice, 1709).

Ägyptische Helena, Die ('The Egyptian Helen'). Opera in two acts by Richard Strauss to a libretto by Hugo von Hofmannsthal (Dresden, 1928; revised Salzburg, 1933).

Aida. Opera in four acts by Verdi to a libretto by Antonio Ghislanzoni after a scenario by Auguste Mariette (Cairo, 1871; Milan, 1872); it was not, as is often supposed, written for the opening of the Suez Canal in 1869, nor commissioned by the Khedive of Egypt to open the new Cairo Opera House, which was inaugurated in 1869 with *Rigoletto*.

Aiglon, L' ('The Young Eagle'). Opera (*drame musical*) in five acts by Honegger (Acts II, III, and IV) and Ibert (Acts I and V) to a libretto by Henri Cain after Edmond Rostand's play (1900) (Monte Carlo, 1937).

Airborne Symphony. Symphony (1945) by Blitzstein, for narrator, tenor, baritone, chorus, and orchestra, to his own text on the evolution of flying.

Air on the G String. The title given to an arrangement (1871) for violin and piano (or strings) by August Wilhemj of the second movement (Air) of J. S. Bach's Orchestral Suite no. 3 in D; in the arrangement the melody is transposed to C major so that it can be played exclusively on the lowest (G) string of the violin.

Akhmatova: Requiem. Work (1979–80) by Tavener for soprano, baritone, and orchestra, to a text combining poems of Anna Akhmatova and prayers for the dead from the Orthodox liturgy.

Akhnaten. Opera in three acts by Philip Glass to a libretto by the composer, Shalom Goldman, Robert Israel, and Richard Riddell (Stuttgart, 1984).

Akrostichon-Wortspiel ('Acrostic Wordplay'). Work (1991) by Unsuk Chin for soprano and ensemble, to texts from Lewis Carroll's *Through the Looking Glass* (1872) and Michael Ende's *The Endless Story*; the texts are deconstructed and reassembled so that consonants and vowels are randomly juxtaposed, and the instruments are tuned microtonally.

Alassio. *See* IN THE SOUTH.

Albert Herring. Chamber opera in three acts by Britten to a libretto by Eric Crozier adapted from Guy de Maupassant's short story *Le Rosier de Madame Husson* (1888) (Glyndebourne, 1947).

Alborado del gracioso ('The Fool's Morning Song'). Piano piece by Ravel, the fourth of his *Miroirs* (1905); he orchestrated it in 1918.

Album für die Jugend ('Album for the Young'). Schumann's op. 68 (1848), for piano, a collection of pieces for young players.

Alceste. 1. Opera (*tragédie en musique*) in a prologue and five acts by Lully to a libretto by Philippe Quinault after Euripides' *Alcestis* (Paris, 1674); its full title is *Alceste, ou Le Triomphe d'Alcide*.

2. Opera (*tragedia*) in three acts by Gluck to an Italian libretto by Ranieri Calzabigi after Euripides (Vienna, 1767); Gluck made a revised French version with a libretto translated by Marie François Louis Gand Leblanc Roullet (Paris, 1776). In the preface to the score of the Italian version, Gluck outlined his ideas for operatic reform. Euripides' story was also used for operas by Strungk (1693), Handel (1727), Anton Schweitzer (1773), and Wellesz (1924).

Alcina. Opera in three acts by Handel to an anonymous libretto after Ludovico Ariosto's *Orlando furioso* (1516) (London, 1735).

Aleko. Opera in one act by Rakhmaninov to a libretto by Vladimir Ivanovich Nemirovich-Danchenko after Pushkin's *The Gypsies* (1824) (Moscow, 1893).

Alessandro. Opera in three acts by Handel to a libretto by Paolo Antonio Rolli adapted from Ortensio Mauro's *La superbia d'Alessandro* (1690) (London, 1726); it was revived as *Rossane* (London, 1743).

Alexander Balus. Oratorio (1748) by Handel to a text compiled by Thomas Morell.

Alexander Nevsky. Cantata (1939) by Prokofiev, for mezzo-soprano, chorus, and orchestra, a setting of a text by the composer and Vladimir Lugorsky; it is a reworking of the music Prokofiev wrote for Sergey Eisenstein's film of the same name (1938).

Alexander's Feast. Handel's setting (1736) of John Dryden's *Ode for St Cecilia's Day* (1697) with additions from Newburgh Hamilton's *The Power of Music*; Mozart later reorchestrated it.

Alfonso und Estrella. Opera (*romantische Oper*) in three acts by Schubert to a libretto by Franz von Schober (Weimar, 1854). Its overture was also used for *Rosamunde* but is not the piece known as *Rosamunde* overture (which was composed for *Die Zauberharfe*).

Alfred. Masque by Arne to a libretto by James Thomson and David Mallett (Cliveden, now in Berkshire, 1740); it contains the song 'Rule, Britannia!'. Arne expanded it from two to three acts and revised it; it was performed as an oratorio and several times during the 1950s on the London stage.

Al gran sole carico d'amore ('In the Bright Sunshine Heavy with Love'). Opera (*azione scenica*) in two acts by Nono to a libretto by the composer and Yuri Lyubimov after texts by Bertolt Brecht, Tania Bunke, Fidel Castro, Ernesto Che Guevara, Georgy Dimitrov, Maxim Gorky, Antonio Gramsci, Vladimir Lenin, Karl Marx, Louise Michel, Cesare Pavese, Arthur Rimbaud, Celia Sanchez, and Haydée Santamaria, and popular sources (Milan, 1975; revised, Milan, 1978).

Alhambra Fantasy. Work (2000) for 15 players by Julian Anderson.

Allegro barbaro. Work (1911) by Bartók for solo piano; it was transcribed for orchestra by Jenő Kenessey in 1946.

Allegro, il Penseroso ed il Moderato, L' ('The Cheerful, the Thoughtful, and the Moderate Man'). Choral work (1740) by Handel to a text by Charles Jennens partly after John Milton.

Alleluiasymphonie. Haydn's Symphony no. 30 in C major (1765), so called because part of an Easter plainchant alleluia is quoted in the first movement.

All Through the Night. The tune of the Welsh folksong *Ar Hyd y Nos*; it is known outside Wales by this title.

Almira (*Der in Krohnen erlangte Glücks-Wechsel, oder Almira, Königin von Castilien*; 'The Change of Fortune Gained with a Crown, or Almira, Queen of Castile'). *Singspiel* in three acts by Handel to a libretto by Friedrich Christian Feustking after Giulio Pancieri's *L'Almira* (1691) (Hamburg, 1705).

Alpensinfonie, Eine ('An Alpine Symphony'). Tone-poem, op. 64 (1911–15), by Richard Strauss; in 22 sections, it describes a day in the mountains and is scored for an orchestra of over 150, including wind and thunder machines.

Also sprach Zarathustra ('Thus Spake Zoroaster'). Tone-poem, op. 30 (1895–6), by Richard Strauss, based on Friedrich Nietzsche's poem of the same name. Delius set 11 sections of the poem in A **Mass of Life*.

Altenberglieder (*Fünf Orchesterlieder nach Ansichtskartentexten von Peter Altenberg*). Five songs for voice and orchestra, op. 4 (1912), by Berg to picture-postcard texts by Peter Altenberg (pseudonym of Richard Englander, 1862–1919). Schoenberg conducted the first performance of two of them in Vienna in 1913 but they caused such a hostile disturbance that the rest of the programme had to be abandoned; they were not performed complete until 1952, in Vienna.

Alto Rhapsody. The name by which Brahms's Rhapsody op. 53 (1869), for alto voice, male chorus, and orchestra, is known; the text is from Johann Wolfgang von Goethe's *Harzreise im Winter* ('Winter Journey through the Harz Mountains').

Alzira. Opera (*tragedia lirica*) in a prologue and two acts by Verdi to a libretto by Salvadore Cammarano after Voltaire's play *Alzire, ou Les Américains* (1736) (Naples, 1845).

Amadigi di Gaula ('Amadis of Gaul'). Opera in three acts by Handel to an anonymous libretto adapted from Antoine Houdar de Lamotte's libretto *Amadis de Grèce* (1699) (London, 1715).

Amadis (*Amadis de Gaule*). Opera (*tragédie en musique*) in a prologue and five acts by Lully to a libretto by Philippe Quinault after Nicolas Herberay des Essarts's adaptation of Garcí Rodríguez de Montalvo's *Amadís de Gaula* (Paris, 1684). J. C. Bach wrote a *tragédie lyrique* (1779) on the same subject.

Amahl and the Night Visitors. Opera in one act by Menotti to his own libretto; it was the first television opera (NBC, New York, 1951; staged Bloomington, IN, 1952). The night visitors are the Magi.

Amelia Goes to the Ball (*Amelia al ballo*). *Opera buffa* in one act by Menotti to an Italian libretto by the composer, translated into English by George Meade (Philadelphia, 1937).

America: A Prophecy. Work (1999) by Thomas Adès for mezzo-soprano, optional chorus, and large orchestra, settings of Mayan and 16th-century Spanish texts.

American in Paris, An. Tone-poem (1928) by Gershwin.

'American' Quartet. The nickname of Dvořák's String Quartet in F major op. 96 (1893), so called because he composed it in America incorporating African-American tunes.

America the Beautiful. American patriotic song to a poem by Katharine Lee Bates (1859–1929). No one tune is consistently associated with it but the one by Samuel Augustus Ward (1847–1930), of 1913, is the most common.

Amériques. Orchestral work (1921) by Varèse; it includes parts for cyclone whistle, fire siren, crow-call, etc.

Amfiparnaso, L'. Madrigal comedy in a prologue and 13 scenes by Orazio Vecchi to his own texts (possibly in collaboration with Giulio Cesare Croce); for five voices, it was not intended to be staged and was first performed in Modena in 1594 (published 1597).

Amico Fritz, L' ('Friend Fritz'). Opera (*commedia lirica*) in three acts by Mascagni to a libretto by P. Suardon (pseudonym of Nicola Daspuro) after Erckmann-Chatrian's novel *L'Ami Fritz* (1864) (Rome, 1891).

Amid Nature. *See* NATURE, LIFE, AND LOVE.

Amor brujo, El ('Love, the Magician'). Ballet in one act by Falla to a scenario by Gregorio Martínez Sierra after an Andalusian Gypsy tale (Madrid, 1915); it includes songs, originally intended to be sung by the ballerina, and the famous *Ritual Fire Dance. Falla arranged an orchestral suite from it (1916).

Amore dei tre re, L' ('The Love of Three Kings'). Opera (*poema tragico*) in three acts by Italo Montemezzi to a libretto by Sem Benelli after his own verse tragedy (1910) (Milan, 1913).

Amour de loin, L' ('Love from Afar'). Opera in five acts by Kaija Saariaho to a libretto by Amin Malouf after Jaufré Rudel's *La vida breve* (12th century) (Salzburg, 2000).

Ancient Voices of Children. Work (1970) by George Crumb for soprano and treble with instrumental ensemble, to words by Federico García Lorca.

Andante favori. A piano piece by Beethoven, originally written as the slow movement of his Piano Sonata in C major op. 53 (1803), 'Waldstein', but detached and published as a separate work.

Andante spianato. The title of Chopin's op. 22 for piano (1834), composed as an introduction to his Grand Polonaise in E♭ major (1830–1) for piano and orchestra.

An der schönen, blauen Donau ('By the Beautiful Blue Danube'). Waltz, op. 314 (1867), by Johann Strauss (ii). It is known in English simply as *The Blue Danube*.

An die ferne Geliebte ('To the Distant Beloved'). Song cycle, op. 98 (1815–16), by Beethoven; the six songs, for voice and piano, are settings of poems by Alois Jeitteles. The cycle is not to be confused with Beethoven's songs *Lied aus der Ferne* and *Der Liebende* (both 1809), to words by Christian Ludwig Reissig, and *An die Geliebte* (1811, revised ?1814), to words by J. L. Stoll.

Andrea Chénier. Opera (*dramma istorico*) in four acts ('tableaux') by Giordano to a libretto by Luigi Illica (Milan, 1896).

And Suddenly it's Evening. Work, op. 66 (1966), by Lutyens for tenor and 11 instruments, a setting of Salvatore Quasimodo's *Ed è subito sera* (1942), translated by Jack Bevan.

Angel of Light. Subtitle of Rautavaara's Symphony no. 7 (1995).

Anima del filosofo, L' (*L'anima del filosofo, ossia Orfeo ed Euridice*; 'The Spirit of the Philosopher, or Orpheus and Eurydice'). Opera (*dramma per musica*) in four or five acts by Haydn to a libretto by Carlo Francesco Badini (Florence, 1951).

Anna Bolena. Opera (*tragedia lirica*) in two acts by Donizetti to a libretto by Felice Romani after Ippolito Pindemonte's *Enrico VIII, ossia Anna Bolena* and Alessandro Pepoli's *Anna Bolena* (Milan, 1830).

Anna Magdalena Books. Two collections of keyboard music by Bach (from his **Clavier-Büchlein*), presented to his second wife, Anna Magdalena, in 1722 and 1725.

Années de pèlerinage ('Years of Pilgrimage'). Three volumes of piano pieces by Liszt, composed between 1835 and 1877. Book 1 (published 1855), on Swiss subjects, includes many pieces composed in 1835–8, published as *Album d'un voyageur* and later revised; book 2 (1858) is on Italian subjects; book 3 (completed in 1877) is a more heterogeneous collection and several of the pieces have titles relating to Liszt's stay at the Villa d'Este, near Tivoli.

Anon in Love. Song cycle (1959) by Walton for tenor and guitar, settings of six anonymous 16th- and 17th-century love poems; Walton arranged it for tenor and small orchestra in 1971.

Antar. Orchestral work, op. 9 (1868), by Rimsky-Korsakov, originally described as his Symphony no. 2; he revised and reorchestrated it in 1876 and 1897 and again in 1903, when it was designated 'oriental suite'. It is based on an oriental tale by Osip Senkovsky.

Antarctic Symphony. Symphony (2001) by Maxwell Davies, his eighth.

Antigone. Plays by Sophocles and Euripides that have been used as the subject of several operas, notably by Hasse (1743), Gluck (1756), Zingarelli (1790), Honegger (1927), and Orff (1949); Mendelssohn (1841) and Saint-Saëns (1894) wrote incidental music to Sophocles' play.

Antony and Cleopatra. Opera in three acts by Barber to a libretto by Franco Zeffirelli after Shakespeare's play (1606–7) (New York, 1966). Malipiero wrote an opera (1938) on the subject.

Apartment House 1776. Work (1976) by Cage for mixed media.

Apollo. *See* APOLLON MUSAGÈTE.

Apollon musagète (*Apollo musagetes*; 'Apollo, Leader of the Muses'). Ballet in two scenes by Stravinsky, choreographed by Adolph Bolm (Washington, DC, 1928) and later the same year by George Balanchine (Paris); it is scored for strings. Stravinsky revised the work in 1947 and it is now known as *Apollo*.

Apostles, The. Oratorio, op. 49 (1903), by Elgar, for six soloists, chorus, and orchestra, to a biblical text compiled by the composer; Elgar composed a sequel, *The* *Kingdom.

Appalachia. 'Variations on an Old Slave Song' (1903) by Delius, for baritone, chorus, and orchestra, a reworking of his *American Rhapsody* for orchestra (1896).

Appalachian Spring. Ballet in one act by Copland, choreographed by Martha Graham (Washington, DC, 1944); it is scored for 13 instruments. Copland arranged a suite (1944), then orchestrated it (1945). The whole ballet was also orchestrated (1945).

Apparitions. Orchestral work (1958–9) by Ligeti.

'Appassionata' Sonata. The publisher's apt title given to Beethoven's Piano Sonata no. 23 in F minor op. 57 (1804–5) when it was published in an arrangement for piano duet (1838).

Apprenti sorcier, L' ('The Sorcerer's Apprentice'). Symphonic scherzo (1897) by Dukas based on Johann Wolfgang von Goethe's ballad *Der Zauberlehrling*, which, in turn, is based on a dialogue in Lucian (2nd century AD). In the Disney film *Fantasia* the apprentice was represented by Mickey Mouse.

Après-midi d'un faune', Prélude à 'L' ('Prelude to "The Afternoon of a Faun"'). Orchestral work by Debussy (1894), an 'impression' of a poem by Stéphane Mallarmé; it was choreographed and danced by Vaslav Nijinsky for Serge Diaghilev's Ballets Russes (Paris, 1912). Debussy intended to compose a *Prélude*, *Interlude*, and *Paraphrase finale*, but completed only the *Prélude*.

Arabella. Opera (*lyrische Komödie*) in three acts by Richard Strauss to a libretto by Hugo von Hofmannsthal after his novel *Lucidor* (Dresden, 1933).

Arbre des songes, L' ('The Tree of Dreams'). Violin concerto (1979–85) by Dutilleux.

Arcadiana. String quartet, op. 12 (1994), by Thomas Adès.

Arcana. Orchestral work (1925–7) by Varèse.

'Archduke' Trio. Nickname of Beethoven's Piano Trio in B♭ major op. 97 (1810–11), dedicated to his patron the Archduke Rudolph of Austria.

Architectonics I–VII. A series of chamber works (1984–94) by Erkki-Sven Tüür for different combinations of instruments.

Arden muss sterben ('Arden must die'). Opera in two acts by Goehr to a libretto by Erich Fried after an anonymous play *Arden of Faversham* (1592) (Hamburg, 1967).

Ariadne auf Naxos ('Ariadne on Naxos'). Opera in one act by Richard Strauss to a libretto by Hugo von Hofmannsthal; the first version (Stuttgart, 1912) was performed with a condensed version of Molière's *Le Bourgeois gentilhomme* (1670), for which Strauss had written incidental music, but it was subsequently staged as an independent work, with a new prologue (Vienna, 1916).

Ariane et Barbe-bleue ('Ariane and Bluebeard'). Opera (*conte musical*) in three acts by Dukas to a libretto by Maurice Maeterlinck after a fairy tale by Charles Perrault (Paris, 1907).

Arianna, L'. Opera (*tragedia*) in a prologue and eight scenes by Monteverdi to a libretto by Ottavio Rinuccini (Mantua, 1608); the score is thought to be lost, the only surviving section being *Lamento d'Arianna*. Goehr composed an opera to the same Rinuccini libretto (London, 1995).

Ariettes oubliées ('Forgotten Ariettas'). Six songs (1885–7) by Debussy for voice and piano, settings of poems by Paul Verlaine.

Ariodante. Opera in three acts by Handel to a libretto adapted anonymously from Antonio Salvi's *Ginevra, principessa di Scozia* (1708) after Ludovico Ariosto's *Orlando furioso* (1516) (London, 1735). Méhul wrote a three-act opera *Ariodant* on the subject, to a libretto by François-Benoît Hoffman (Paris, 1799).

Arlecchino ('Harlequin'). Opera (*theatralisches Capriccio*) in one act by Busoni to his own libretto (Zürich, 1917).

Arlésienne, L' ('The Woman of Arles'). Incidental music by Bizet for Alphonse Daudet's play (Paris, 1872); it consists of 27 items, some of which Bizet incorporated into the ballet of *Carmen*. There are two orchestral suites, one arranged by Bizet (1872), the other posthumously by Ernest Guiraud (1879).

Arme Heinrich, Der ('Poor Heinrich'). Opera (*Musikdrama*) in three acts by Pfitzner to a libretto by James Grun and the composer after the medieval poem by Hartmann von Aue (Mainz, 1895).

Armide. Opera in five acts by Gluck to a libretto by Philippe Quinault after Torquato Tasso's poem *Gerusalemme liberata* (1581) (Paris, 1777). There are nearly 50 operas based on Tasso's story, notably those by Lully (1686), Handel (*Rinaldo*, 1711), Traetta (1761), Jommelli (1770), Salieri (1771), Haydn (1784), Rossini (1817), and Dvořák (1904).

Aroldo. Opera in four acts by Verdi to a libretto by Francesco Maria Piave after his libretto *Stiffelio (Rimini, 1857).

'Arpeggione' Sonata. Schubert's Sonata in A minor D821 (1824), originally written for arpeggione (a six-stringed bowed fretted instrument) and piano but now usually played by a cello or viola.

Artaxerxes. Opera in three acts by Arne probably to his own libretto after Pietro Metastasio's *Artaserse* (London, 1762). There are many operas on the subject, for example by Hasse (1730), Gluck (1741), Piccinni (1762), Paisiello (1771), and Cimarosa (1784).

Art de toucher le clavecin, L' ('The Art of Playing the Harpsichord'). Treatise by François Couperin, published in Paris in 1716 and revised in 1717. An influential harpsichord method, known to have been used by J. S. Bach, it covers many aspects of technique and performance and includes eight pieces as teaching material.

Art of Fugue, The (*Die Kunst der Fuge*). A collection of fugues and canons by J. S. Bach, BWV1080, composed in the 1740s to display a wide variety of contrapuntal techniques using the same simple subject; the medium is unspecified but almost all the movements are playable on a solo keyboard instrument. It has survived unfinished and the intended order of the numbers is uncertain but it consists of 14 fugues ('contrapuncti') for different voices, four canons, a pair of mirror fugues, and an incomplete quadruple fugue. Completions of the final fugue have been made by Donald Tovey, and by Busoni in his *Fantasia contrappuntistica*.

Ascanio in Alba. Serenata in two acts by Mozart to a libretto by Giuseppe Parini (Milan, 1771).

Ascension, L' ('The Ascension'). Orchestral work (1933) by Messiaen, arranged for organ (1934).

Ash Grove, The. A Welsh harp melody to which (since 1802) a variety of English and Welsh words have been set, the most common being the anonymous Welsh 'Down yonder green valley'.

Ashoka's Dream. Opera in two acts by Peter Lieberson to a libretto by Douglas Penick after a Buddhist legend (Santa Fe, NM, 1997).

Aspern Papers, The. Opera in two acts by Dominick Argento to his own libretto after Henry James's novella (1888) (Dallas, TX, 1998).

Asrael. Suk's Symphony in C minor, op. 27 (1905–6). It was begun in 1904 as a memorial to Dvořák, Suk's father-in-law, but it also became a memorial to Suk's wife, who died 18 months after her father. Asrael is the Angel of Death.

Assassinio nella cattedrale ('Murder in the Cathedral'). Opera in two acts and an intermezzo by Ildebrando Pizzetti to his own libretto, shortened and adapted from Alberto Castelli's translation of T. S. Eliot's play *Murder in the Cathedral* (1935) (Milan, 1958).

Assedio di Corinto, L'. *See* SIÈGE DE CORINTHE, LE.

Asyla. Orchestral work (1997) by Thomas Adès in four movements played continuously.

At First Light. Work (1982) for 14 players by George Benjamin.

Athalia. Oratorio (1733) by Handel to a text by Samuel Humphreys after Jean Racine.

Atlántida (*Atlantis*). 'Scenic cantata' in a prologue and three parts by Falla to a text based on Jacint Verdaguer's Catalan poem (1877); it was completed by Ernesto Halffter (Milan, 1962).

Atlas. Opera in three parts by Meredith Monk to a libretto by the composer (Houston, TX, 1991).

Atlas eclipticalis. Work (1961) by Cage for any ensemble from 86 instruments; contact microphones are attached to the instruments and the sound is distributed to several loudspeakers.

Atmosphères. Orchestral work (1961) by Ligeti.

At the Boar's Head. Musical interlude in one act by Holst to a libretto by the composer based on the tavern scenes from Shakespeare's *King Henry IV* Parts I and II (*c*.1597) (with two of Shakespeare's sonnets and some traditional songs) (Manchester, 1925).

Attila. Opera (*dramma lirico*) in a prologue and three acts by Verdi to a libretto by Temistocle Solera and Francesco Maria Piave after Zacharias Werner's play *Attila, König der Hunnen* (1808) (Venice, 1846).

Atys ('Attis'). Opera (*tragédie en musique*) in a prologue and five acts by Lully to a libretto by Philippe Quinault after Ovid's *Fasti* (St Germain-en-Laye, 1676). Piccinni wrote an opera (1780) on the subject.

...au delà du hasard ('Beyond Chance'). Work (1958–9) by Barraqué for soprano, women's voices, and 20 instruments in four groups, using texts from Hermann Broch's *Der Tod des Vergil* (1945; translated by Albert Kohn) and by the composer.

Auf einer Gondel ('On a Gondola'). Title given by Mendelssohn to three of his *Lieder ohne Worte*: op. 19 no. 6 in G minor (book 1, 1834); op. 30 no. 12 in F♯ minor (book 2, 1835); and op. 62 no. 29 in A minor (book 6, 1845).

Aufforderung zum Tanz ('Invitation to the Dance'). Weber's *Rondo brillant* in D♭ major for piano (1819), which consists of an introduction (the 'invitation'), a waltz, and an epilogue; it was orchestrated by Berlioz (1841) and, much altered, by Felix Weingartner, and was used by Serge Diaghilev's Ballets Russes as music for *Le Spectre de la rose*.

Aufstieg und Fall der Stadt Mahagonny ('Rise and Fall of the City of Mahagonny'). Opera in three acts by Weill to a libretto by Bertolt Brecht (Leipzig, 1930).

Augenlicht, Das ('Eyesight'). Webern's op. 26 (1935), a setting for chorus and orchestra of a text by Hildegard Jone.

Auld Lang Syne. A ritual song of parting used in England and Scotland. The tune first appeared in the overture to William Shield's opera *Rosina* (1782), played by bassoons in imitation of the bagpipe, and acquired Robert Burns's words in 1794. This origin has been disputed by some Scottish authorities, who argue that the tune can be found in Scottish publications of the period and that Shield, who lived not far from the Scottish border, may well have heard it and copied it.

Aura. Orchestral work (1994) by Magnus Lindberg.

Aurora's Wedding. The divertissement from the last act of The *Sleeping Beauty*, supplemented by extra numbers based on Serge Diaghilev's 1921 London production, performed as a separate ballet (Paris, 1922).

Aus den sieben Tagen ('From the Seven Days'). 15 works (1968) by Stockhausen for different ensembles of three or more instrumentalists; each piece has a verse or text to suggest a mood the players must create or a manner of playing.

Aus Italien ('From Italy'). Symphonic fantasy, op. 16 (1886), by Richard Strauss, inspired by his visit to Italy.

Ausklang. Work (1985) for piano and orchestra by Helmut Lachenmann.

Aus meinem Leben. *See* FROM MY LIFE.

Ave Maria (Lat., 'Hail, Mary'). The salutation of the Virgin Mary by the Archangel Gabriel (Luke 1: 28). Schubert's song of that title (D839, 1825) is a setting of a German translation of Walter Scott's poem from The *Lady of the Lake* (1810). The 'Bach–Gounod' *Ave Maria* is the first prelude from Bach's *The *Well-Tempered Clavier* with Gounod's *Méditation* (1853) as a counterpoint and words added by someone else.

Aventures; Nouvelles Aventures. Works by Ligeti to his own texts for three solo voices and seven instruments; they were composed in 1962 and 1962–5 and arranged for performance in 1966; later that year they were expanded and combined for the stage as *Aventures & Nouvelles Aventures* (Württemberg, 1966).

Baa Baa Black Sheep. Opera in three acts by Michael Berkeley to a libretto by David Malouf after Rudyard Kipling's short story *Baa Baa Black Sheep* (1888) and *The Jungle Book* (1894) (Cheltenham, 1993).

Babiy-Yar. The subtitle of Shostakovich's Symphony no. 13 in B♭ minor op. 113 (1962), a setting of five poems by Yevgeny Yevtushenko for bass, male chorus, and orchestra; Babiy-Yar was the site of the grave of thousands of Russian Jews murdered by the Germans during World War II. *Babi Yar* is an orchestral work (1983) by Steve Martland.

Bacchus et Ariane. Ballet in two acts by Roussel to a scenario by Abel Hernant, choreographed by Serge Lifar (Paris, 1931). Roussel arranged two orchestral suites from the score (no. 1, 1933; no. 2, 1934).

Bachianas brasileiras. Nine works (1930–45) by Villa-Lobos, for various combinations of voices and instruments, exploring affinities between the spirit of Bach's counterpoint and Brazilian folk music; each is a suite with two titles, one reflecting the Baroque influence, the other referring to a Brazilian popular form. The best known is no. 5, for soprano and at least eight cellos.

Baiser de la fée, Le ('The Fairy's Kiss'). Ballet in four scenes by Stravinsky with a scenario after Hans Christian Andersen's *The Ice Maiden*, based on piano pieces and songs by Tchaikovsky linked by passages Stravinsky composed in a similar style; it was choreographed by Bronislava Nijinska (Paris, 1928).

Balcon, Le ('The Balcony'). Opera in ten scenes by Peter Eötvös to a libretto by Françoise Morvan after Jean Genet (Aix-en-Provence, 2002).

Ballad of Baby Doe, The. Opera in two acts by Douglas S. Moore to a libretto by John Latouche (Central City, CO, 1956).

Ballet mécanique ('Mechanical Ballet'). Work by Antheil, conceived as a film score, originally for 16 player pianos and percussion; synchronizing it with the film was impossible, so Antheil arranged it for two pianos, one player piano with amplifier, three xylophones, electric bells, three propellers, tam-tam, four bass drums, and siren, and it was performed in Paris in 1926.

Ballo delle ingrate, Il. Dance entertainment by Monteverdi (Mantua, 1608).

Ballo in maschera, Un ('A Masked Ball'). Opera (*melodramma*) in three acts by Verdi to a libretto by Antonio Somma after Eugène Scribe's libretto (for Auber) *Gustave III, ou Le Bal masqué* (Rome, 1859).

Bandar-log, Les. Orchestral work (1946) by Koechlin after Rudyard Kipling.

Bánk bán. Historical dramatic opera in three acts by Ferenc Erkel to a libretto by Béni Egressy after József Katona's play *Bánk bán* (1814) (Pest, 1861).

Banquet céleste, Le ('The Celestial Banquet'). Organ work (1928) by Messiaen.

Barbe-bleue ('Bluebeard'). *Opéra bouffe* in three acts by Offenbach to a libretto by Henri Meilhac and Ludovic Halévy (Paris, 1866).

Barbiere di Siviglia, Il ('The Barber of Seville'). Opera (*commedia*) in two acts by Rossini to a libretto by Cesare Sterbini after both Beaumarchais's play *Le Barbier de Séville* (1775) and the libretto often attributed to Giuseppe Petrosellini for Paisiello's opera of the same name (Rome, 1816); it was originally called *Almaviva, ossia L'inutile precauzione*, presumably to differentiate it from Paisiello's opera (St Petersburg, 1782), which was the most successful of the several other operatic versions of the play.

Barbier von Bagdad, Der. Opera (*komische Oper*) in two acts by Peter Cornelius to his own libretto after a story from *The Thousand and One Nights* (Weimar, 1858). Most performances since 1884 have been of the version revised and shortened by Felix Mottl for a production that year at Karlsruhe.

Bard, The (*Barden*). Orchestral tone-poem, op. 64 (1913), by Sibelius; he revised it in 1914.

Bartered Bride, The (*Prodaná nevěsta*). Opera in three acts by Smetana to a libretto by Karel Sabina (Prague, 1866); Smetana made five versions of it, expanding it from two acts to three, the fifth and commonly performed version having its premiere in 1870.

Bassarids, The. *Opera seria* with intermezzo in one act (four movements) by Henze to a libretto by W. H. Auden and Chester Kallman after Euripides' *Bacchae* (Salzburg, 1966).

Bastien und Bastienne. *Singspiel* in one act by Mozart to a libretto by Friedrich Wilhelm Weiskern and Johann Müller revised by Johann Andreas Schachtner, after Marie-Justine-Benoîte Favart and Henry de Guerville's opera *Les Amours de Bastien et Bastienne*; it was first performed at Friedrich Anton Mesmer's house (Vienna, 1768).

Bat, The. *See* FLEDERMAUS, DIE.

Battaglia di Legnano, La ('The Battle of Legnano'). Opera (*tragedia lirica*) in four acts by Verdi to a libretto by Salvadore Cammarano after Joseph Méry's play *La Bataille de Toulouse* (1828) (Rome, 1849).

Battalia ('Battle'). Sonata (1673) by Biber for solo violin, strings, and continuo, an early example of a work depicting the sounds of battle.

Battle Hymn of the Republic. Song with the words of a poem (1862) by Julia Ward Howe (1819–1910), of which the first line is 'Mine eyes have seen the glory of the coming of the Lord'; it is sung to the tune of

John Brown's Body. The last verse, beginning 'He is coming like the glory of the morning on the wave', is not in the original poem and is of unknown authorship.

Battle of the Huns. *See* HUNNENSCHLACHT.

Battle of Victoria. *See* WELLINGTONS SIEG.

Battle Symphony. *See* WELLINGTONS SIEG.

Bauerncantate. *See* PEASANT CANTATA.

Bayadère, La (*Bayaderka*; 'The Temple Dancer'). Ballet in four acts by Léon Minkus to a scenario by Sergei Khudekov and Marius Petipa, who choreographed it (St Petersburg, 1877).

Bear, The. *See* OURS, L'.

Béatitudes, Les ('The Beatitudes'). Oratorio, op. 53 (1869–79), by Franck, for soloists, chorus, and orchestra, to a text based on the Sermon on the Mount (Matthew 5: 3–12).

Beatrice di Tenda. Opera (*tragedia lirica*) in two acts by Bellini to a libretto by Felice Romani after Carlo Tedaldi-Fores's play *Beatrice di Tenda* (1825) (Venice, 1833).

Béatrice et Bénédict ('Beatrice and Benedick'). Opera in two acts by Berlioz to his own libretto after Shakespeare's *Much Ado about Nothing* (?1598–9) (Baden-Baden, 1862).

Beautiful Maid of the Mill, The. *See* SCHÖNE MÜLLERIN, DIE.

Bees' Wedding, The. Nickname of Mendelssohn's *Lied ohne Worte* no. 34 (op. 67 no. 4) in C major (book 6, 1845) for piano, also entitled 'Spinnerlied'.

Beggar's Opera, The. Ballad opera in three acts arranged and partly composed by Pepusch to a libretto by John Gay (London, 1728). It was reworked several times in the 20th century, notably by Frederic Austin (1920), Edward Dent (1944), Britten—who virtually created a new work (1948), Bliss (1953), and Dominic Muldowney (1982). Weill's *Die *Dreigroschenoper* sets the libretto to new music.

Behold the Sun (*Die Wiedertäufer*, 'The Anabaptists'). Opera in three acts by Goehr to a libretto by John McGrath and the composer, translated into German by Bernhard Laux (Duisburg, 1985).

Belisario. Opera (*tragedia lirica*) in three acts by Donizetti to a libretto by Salvadore Cammarano after Luigi Marchionni's adaptation of Eduard von Schenk's *Belisarius* (1820) (Venice, 1836).

'Bell' Anthem. Purcell's verse anthem *Rejoice in the Lord Alway* (*c*.1682–5); its name, which dates from the composer's lifetime, alludes to the pealing scale passages of the instrumental introduction.

Belle Hélène, La ('The Fair Helen'). *Opéra bouffe* in three acts by Offenbach to a libretto by Henri Meilhac and Ludovic Halévy after classical mythology (Paris, 1864).

'Bell' Rondo. *See* CAMPANELLA, LA.

Bells, The. Choral symphony, op. 35 (1913), by Rakhmaninov, for soprano, tenor, and baritone soloists, chorus, and orchestra, a setting of a text by Konstantin Balmont adapted from Edgar Allan Poe's poem.

Bells of Aberdovey. A song assumed to be by Dibdin and published in 1785, when it was sung in his opera *Liberty Hall*. It is not a Welsh folksong, as has been claimed.

Belshazzar. Oratorio (1745) by Handel to a biblical text by Charles Jennens.

Belshazzar's Feast. Cantata by Walton for baritone, chorus, and orchestra, to a text compiled from biblical sources by Osbert Sitwell (Leeds, 1931).

Benvenuto Cellini. Opera (*opéra semi-seria*) in two acts by Berlioz to a libretto by Léon de Wailly and Auguste Barbier, assisted by Alfred de Vigny, loosely based on Cellini's memoirs (Paris, 1838); Berlioz revised it twice in 1852, the second time into three acts, but withdrew it because of its failure. He used some of the music from it in the overture *Le Carnaval romain*.

Berenice (*Berenice, regina d'Egitto*; 'Berenice, Queen of Egypt'). Opera in three acts by Handel to a libretto anonymously adapted from Antonio Salvi's *Berenice, regina d'Egitto* (1709) (London, 1737); the well-known minuet is from the overture.

Bernarda Albas Haus ('The House of Bernarda Alba'). Opera in three acts by Aribert Reimann to a libretto by the composer after Enrique Beck's German translation of Federico García Lorca's play *La casa de Bernarda Alba* (1936) (Munich, 2000).

Besuch der alten Dame, Der ('The Visit of the Old Lady'). Opera in three acts by Einem to a libretto by Friedrich Dürrenmatt after his tragicomedy (1956) (Vienna, 1971).

Betrothal in a Monastery (*Obrucheniye v monastïre*; *Duen'ya*). Opera in four acts by Prokofiev to a libretto by the composer and Mira Mendelson (Prokof'yeva) after Richard Brinsley Sheridan's opera libretto *The Duenna, or The Double Elopement* (1775) (Prague, 1946).

Bettelstudent, Der ('The Beggar Student'). Operetta (*komische Operette*) in three acts by Millöcker to a libretto by F. Zell (Camillo Walzel) and Richard Genée after Edward Bulwer-Lytton's *The Lady of Lyons* and Victorien Sardou's *Les Noces de Fernande* (Vienna, 1882).

Biches, Les ('The Hinds'; 'The Little Darlings'). Ballet in one act by Poulenc to his own scenario, incorporating choral settings of 17th-century texts; it was choreographed by Bronislava Nijinska (Monte Carlo, 1924). Poulenc arranged a suite from the score (1939–40).

Bikini. *See* THREE TALES.

Bilitis, Chansons de. *See* CHANSONS DE BILITIS.

Billy Budd. Opera by Britten to a libretto by E. M. Forster and Eric Crozier after Herman Melville's unfinished story (1891); it was originally in four acts (London, 1951) but Britten made a two-act version (broadcast 1961; staged London, 1964).

Billy the Kid. Ballet in one act by Copland to a scenario by Lincoln Kirstein, choreographed by Eugene Loring (Chicago, 1938).

'Bird' Quartet. Nickname of Haydn's String Quartet in C major op. 33 no. 3 (1781), so called because the grace notes in the main subject of the first movement and the violin duet in the trio of the Scherzando suggest birdsong.

Birds, The. *See* UCCELLI, GLI.

Birthday odes. Several Restoration composers wrote works for soloists, chorus, and orchestra to commemorate royal birthdays, the most famous being Henry Purcell, who wrote six for Queen Mary II (1689–94); they include *Come ye Sons of Art.

Black Angels (Thirteen Images from the Dark Land). Work (1970) by George Crumb for amplified string quartet; conceived as a response to the Vietnam War, it depicts a 'voyage of the soul' in three stages—Departure, Absence, Return—and makes much use of diabolic imagery and number symbolism.

'Black Key' Étude. Nickname of Chopin's *Étude* in G♭ major for piano op. 10 no. 5 (1830), so called because the right hand confines itself to the black keys.

Black Knight, The. Symphony, op. 25 (1893), for chorus and orchestra by Elgar, a setting of H. W. Longfellow's translation of Ludwig Uhland's ballad.

Black on White. Music-theatre work by Heiner Goebbels using texts from Edgar Allan Poe's *Shadow* (read by Heiner Müller), T. S. Eliot's 'That Corpse' (from *The Waste Land*), and Maurice Blanchot's *L'Attente l'oubli* (Frankfurt, 1996). Goebbels described it as 'a sort of farewell to Heiner Müller'.

Blessed Virgin's Expostulation, The. Song (1693) by Henry Purcell, a setting of a text by Nahum Tate that begins 'Tell me some pitying angel'.

Blest Pair of Sirens. Cantata (1887) by Hubert Parry to words from John Milton's *At a Solemn Music*.

Blond Eckbert. Opera in two acts by Judith Weir to her own libretto after Ludwig Tieck's *Der blonde Eckbert* (1796) (London, 1994).

Blood on the Floor. Suite (1996) for three jazz soloists and ensemble by Mark-Anthony Turnage.

Bluebeard. *See* ARIANE ET BARBE-BLEUE.

Bluebeard's Castle (*A Kékszakállú herceg vára*; 'Duke Bluebeard's Castle'). Opera in one act by Bartók to a libretto by Béla Balázs after a fairy tale by Charles Perrault (Budapest, 1918).

b

Blue Bells of Scotland. A song of unknown origin that was first sung by the London actress Mrs Jordan (an Irishwoman) at Drury Lane Theatre, London, at the end of the 18th century and the beginning of the 19th. (The title is properly 'Blue Bell of Scotland'.)

Blue Danube, By the Beautiful. *See* AN DER SCHÖNEN, BLAUEN DONAU.

B minor Mass. A Latin Mass by J. S. Bach, BWV232, for soloists, chorus, and orchestra, assembled between 1747 and 1749.

Boatswain's Mate, The (*Der gute Freund*). Comic opera in one act (two parts) by Ethel Smyth to her own libretto after William Wymark Jacobs's story (London, 1916).

Boeuf sur le toit, Le ('The Ox on the Roof'). Ballet by Milhaud to a scenario by Jean Cocteau (Paris, 1920); it was first performed as a music-hall spectacle, then as a ballet.

Bohème, La ('Bohemian Life'). **1.** Opera in four acts by Puccini to a libretto by Giuseppe Giacosa and Luigi Illica after Henry Murger's novel *Scènes de la vie de Bohème* (1849) (Turin, 1896).
    2. Opera (*commedia lirica*) in four acts by Leoncavallo to his own libretto after Murger's novel (Venice, 1897); it was revised as *Mimì Pinson* (Palermo, 1913).

Bohemian Girl, The. Grand opera in three acts by Balfe to a libretto by Alfred Bunn after Joseph Mazilier and Jules-Henri Vernoy de Saint-Georges's ballet-pantomime *La Gypsy* (1839), based on Miguel de Cervantes's story *La gitanilla* (1614) (London, 1843); it was given in Italian (London, 1858) as *La zingara* and in Paris (1869) as *La Bohémienne*.

Bohemia's Meadows and Forests. *See* FROM BOHEMIA'S WOODS AND FIELDS.

Boîte à joujoux, La ('The Box of Toys'). Ballet in four scenes by Debussy with a scenario by André Hellé, who choreographed it (Paris, 1919); Debussy began the orchestration but it was completed by André Caplet from Debussy's sketches.

Boléro. Ballet in one act by Ravel, choreographed by Bronislava Nijinska (Paris, 1928); it consists of the repetition of a theme, in C major almost throughout, in an unvarying rhythm and with a gradual crescendo. It has subsequently been choreographed by Serge Lifar (1941), Maurice Béjart (1961), and Leonid Lavrovsky among others.

Bolt, The (*Bolt*). Ballet (choreographic spectacle) in three acts by Shostakovich to a scenario by V. Smirnov, choreographed by Fyodor Lopokov (Leningrad, 1931). Shostakovich arranged an orchestral suite (1931) from the score.

Bomarzo. Opera ('gothic melodrama of sex and violence') in two acts (15 scenes with instrumental interludes) by Ginastera to a libretto by Manuel Mujica Láinez after his own novel *Bomarzo* (1962) (Washington, DC, 1967).

Bonne Chanson, La ('The Good Song'). Song cycle, op. 61 (1892–4), by Fauré, settings of nine poems by Paul Verlaine.

Boréades, Les (*Abaris*; 'The Descendants of Boreas'). Opera (*tragédie en musique*) in five acts by Rameau to a libretto attributed to Louis de Cahusac; it is not known to have been performed complete during the composer's lifetime but was probably given in concert at Lille in the 1770s.

Boris Godunov. Opera in seven scenes, or a prologue and four acts, by Musorgsky to his own libretto adapted from Aleksandr Pushkin's play *The Comedy of the Distress of the Muscovite State, of Tsar Boris, and of Grishka Otrepyev* (1826), supplemented in the revised version with extracts from Nikolay Karamzin's *History of the Russian Empire* (1829). The original version was rejected by St Petersburg Opera in 1870, so Musorgsky revised it (St Petersburg, 1874). Rimsky-Korsakov's first revision was given in St Petersburg in 1896 and his second revision (the version that has most often been performed) in Paris in 1908.

Boulevard Solitude. Opera (*lyrisches Drama*) in seven scenes by Henze to a libretto by Grete Weil after Walter Jockisch's *Boulevard Solitude*, itself based on Antoine-François Prévost's novel *L'Histoire du chevalier des Grieux et de Manon Lescaut* (1731) (Hanover, 1952).

Bourgeois gentilhomme, Le ('The Would-be Gentleman'). *Comédie-ballet* in five acts by Molière, for which Lully wrote the music for the first performance (Chambord, 1670). Richard Strauss wrote incidental music for Hugo von Hofmannsthal's adaptation of Molière's play (Berlin, 1918), later arranging it as a suite (1920).

Boutique fantasque, La ('The Fantastic Toyshop'). Ballet in one act arranged by Respighi from Rossini's *Soirées musicales* and other pieces to a scenario by André Derain; it was choreographed by Leonid Massine for Serge Diaghilev's Ballets Russes (London, 1919).

Bow Down. Music-theatre piece by Birtwistle to a libretto by Tony Harrison (London, 1977).

Boy Was Born, A. Choral variations, op. 3 (1932–3), by Britten, settings of 15th- and 16th-century carols for boys' voices and chorus, later (1955) arranged with optional organ.

Brabançonne, La ('Après des siècles d'esclavage'). Belgian national anthem. It was written in 1830 during the struggle with Holland for independence. The music is by François van Campenhout (1779–1848) and the original text was by Hippolyte Louis Alexandre Dechet (1801–30); the present words, by Charles Rogier, were substituted in 1860. The Flemish population had their own anthem until 1951, when they adopted *La Brabançonne*.

Brandenburg Concertos. Six concerti grossi by Bach, BWV1046–51 (1711–20), dedicated to Christian Ludwig, Margrave of Brandenburg; Bach described them as 'Concerts avec plusieurs instruments'. They are significant for their unusual combinations of instruments and textures and for the way in which Bach moved away from conventional concerto grosso form; for example, no. 3 is for three groups of strings (a violin, viola, and cello in each), and no. 4 is for a violin and two recorders in the concertino and strings and continuo in the ripieno.

Brandenburgers in Bohemia, The (*Braniboři v Čechách*). Opera in three acts by Smetana to a libretto by Karel Sabina (Prague, 1866).

Brautwahl, Die ('The Bridal Choice'). Opera (*musikalisch-fantastisches Komödie*) in three acts and an epilogue by Busoni to his own libretto after E. T. A. Hoffmann's *Die Brautwahl* (1820) (Hamburg, 1912).

Brigg Fair. Orchestral work (1907) by Delius; subtitled 'An English Rhapsody', it is a set of variations on an English folksong, to which Delius's attention had been drawn by Percy Grainger.

British Grenadiers. The regimental march of the Grenadier Guards. The origin of the tune is unknown but it may date from the second half of the 16th century. The original words are from the end of the 17th century (hand grenades, to which the words refer, were in use from *c*.1678). A later version, alluding to the Battle of Waterloo, is sometimes substituted.

Bronze Horseman, The (*Medniy vsadnik*). Ballet in a prologue and four acts by Glière to a scenario by P. F. Abolimov, choreographed by Rostislav Zakharov (Leningrad, 1949).

Brouček, The Excursions of Mr. *See* EXCURSIONS OF MR BROUČEK, THE.

Browning. The name given to a number of English 16th- and 17th-century instrumental compositions based on a tune associated with such texts as 'The leaves be greene, the nuts be browne', mostly elaborate sets of variations (e.g. those in five parts by Byrd).

Buch der hängenden Gärten, Das ('The Book of the Hanging Gardens'). Songs for voice and piano, op. 15 (1908–9), by Schoenberg, settings of 15 poems by Stefan George.

Buffoon, The Tale of the. *See* CHOUT.

Burning Fiery Furnace, The. Church parable, op. 77, by Britten to a text by William Plomer based on the book of Daniel (Aldeburgh, 1966).

'Butterfly' ['Butterfly's Wing'] **Étude.** Nickname of Chopin's *Étude* in G♭ major for piano op. 25 no. 9 (1834).

BWV. Abbreviation for Bach-Werke-Verzeichnis, an informal title given to the thematic catalogue of J. S. Bach's works drawn up by the German music librarian Wolfgang Schmieder (1901–90) and published in Leipzig in 1950. Bach's works are usually referred to by BWV number, though 'Schmieder' (sometimes abbreviated to S) is still occasionally used.

Cadmus et Hermione. Opera (*tragédie en musique*) in a prologue and five acts by Lully to a libretto by Philippe Quinault after Ovid's *Metamorphoses* (Paris, 1673).

Calife de Bagdad, Le ('The Caliph of Bagdad'). *Opéra comique* in one act by Boieldieu to a libretto by Claude de Saint-Just (Godart d'Aucourt) (Paris, 1800).

Calisto, La. Opera (*drama per musica*) in a prologue and three acts by Cavalli to a libretto by Giovanni Faustini after Ovid's *Metamorphoses* (Venice, 1651). It was probably not heard again until 1970, when it was given in Raymond Leppard's realization at Glyndebourne.

Calm Sea and Prosperous Voyage. *See* MEERESSTILLE UND GLÜCKLICHE FAHRT.

Campanella, La. Transcription for piano by Liszt of the 'Rondo alla campanella' ('Ronde à la clochette'; 'Bell' Rondo) from Paganini's Violin Concerto in B minor (1826). Liszt first used the theme in the *Grande fantaisie de bravoure sur La clochette* (*La campanella*) (1833). The most popular version is 'La campanella' from the *Études d'exécution transcendante d'après Paganini* (1851), itself a revision of a version dating from 1838–9.

Campbells are Coming, The. Popular Scottish tune which first appeared in print in 1745, when it was used as country dance under the title *Hob and Nob*; it is also found under its present title at about the same time. There are many contradictory statements as to its origins.

Campiello, Il ('The Small Venetian Square'). Opera (*commedia lirica*) in three acts by Wolf-Ferrari to a libretto by Mario Ghisalberti after Carlo Goldoni's play *Il campiello* (1756) (Milan, 1936).

Camptown Races ('Gwine to run all night'). Song (1850) by Stephen Foster.

Candide. Operetta in two acts by Bernstein to a libretto by Lillian Hellman after Voltaire, with lyrics by Richard Wilbur, John Latouche, Dorothy Parker, Hellman, and Bernstein, orchestrated by Bernstein and Hershy Kay (Boston, 1956); it was revised into one act to a libretto by Hugh Callingham Wheeler, with lyrics by Wilbur, Latouche, Bernstein, and Stephen Sondheim, orchestrated by Kay (New York, 1973).

Cantata academica, carmen basiliense. Choral work, op. 62, by Britten for soprano, alto, tenor, and bass soloists, chorus, and orchestra; it was composed for the quincentenary of Basle University, where it was first performed in 1960. Its Latin text, by Bernhard Wyss, is compiled from the university charter and from orations in praise of Basle.

Canticum sacrum (ad honorem Sancti Marci nominis) ('Sacred Song to the Honour of the Name of St Mark'). Choral work (1955) by Stravinsky, a setting of a biblical text for tenor and baritone soloists, chorus, and orchestra.

Canti di prigionia ('Songs of Imprisonment'). Work (1938–41) by Dallapiccola for chorus, two pianos, two harps, and percussion, to texts by Queen Mary Stuart, Boethius, and Savonarola; it was composed as a protest against Mussolini's adoption of Hitler's racial policies, which threatened Dallapiccola's Jewish wife.

Cantiones sacrae ('Sacred Songs'). A term used by many composers, including Byrd for two books of motets: the first (1589) contains 29 for five voices, the second (1591) 20 for five voices and 12 for six voices. Byrd and Tallis jointly published a volume of *Cantiones sacrae* (1575) for five to eight voices.

Cantique de Jean Racine ('Hymn of Jean Racine'). Choral work by Fauré; it was originally (1865) for chorus and organ, but Fauré revised it (1866) for chorus, harmonium, and string quintet, and much later (1906) he orchestrated it.

Cantus arcticus ('Arctic Song'). Concerto (1972) by Rautavaara for birds and orchestra; the birdsong is electronically taped.

Canyons aux étoiles, Des. *See* DES CANYONS AUX ÉTOILES.

Cappello di paglia di Firenze, Il ('The Florentine Straw Hat'). Opera (*farsa musicale*) in four acts by Nino Rota after Eugène Labiche and Marc Antoine Amédée Michel's *Un chapeau de paille d'Italie* (Palermo, 1955).

Capriccio. Opera (*Konversationsstück für Musik*) in one act by Richard Strauss to a libretto by the composer and Clemens Krauss (Munich, 1942).

Capriccio espagnol. *See* SPANISH CAPRICCIO.

Capriccio italien. *See* ITALIAN CAPRICCIO.

Capriol Suite. Suite for string orchestra (or piano duet) by Warlock, composed in 1926 and arranged for full orchestra in 1928; its six movements are based on old French dances from Thoinot Arbeau's *Orchésographie* (1588), a manual on dancing in which 'Capriol' is a character.

Capuleti e i Montecchi, I ('The Capulets and the Montagues'). Opera (*tragedia lirica*) in two acts by Bellini to a libretto by Felice Romani based on Italian Renaissance sources (Venice, 1830).

Caractacus. Dramatic cantata (1898) by Elgar, for soprano, tenor, baritone, and bass soloists, chorus, and orchestra, to a text by H. A. Acworth. Several composers have written works based on the story of the British king who, during the reign of Claudius, put up almost the last resistance to the Romans, and was eventually captured and taken to

Rome in AD 51, but whose nobility of spirit so impressed the emperor that he was set free.

Carceri d'invenzione. Four instrumental works (1982–6) by Brian Ferney-hough, three for ensemble and one (no. 2b) for solo flute.

Card Game, The. *See JEU DE CARTES.*

Cardillac. Opera in three acts by Hindemith to a libretto by Ferdinand Lion after E. T. A. Hoffmann's *Das Fräulein von Scuderi* (1818) (Dresden, 1926); Hindemith revised it in four acts, to his own libretto (Zürich, 1952).

Carmelites. *See DIALOGUES DES CARMÉLITES.*

Carmen. Opera (*opéra comique*) in four acts by Bizet to a libretto by Henri Meilhac and Ludovic Halévy after Prosper Mérimée's novel (1845) (Paris, 1875).

Carmina burana (Lat., 'Songs of Beuron'). Scenic cantata by Orff, for soprano, tenor, and baritone soloists, boys' choir, chorus, and organ, a setting of 24 Latin poems from the *Carmina burana* with optional mimed action (Frankfurt, 1937); it is the first part of his trilogy **Trionfi. Carmina burana* is the title given by J. A. Scheller to his edition (1847) of a 13th-century German manuscript containing over 200 Latin secular poems, found at the monastery of Benediktbeuren (where, however, it probably did not originate); it is now in the Bavarian State Library, Munich. Most are love poems (some obscene), some in French and German, and several are provided with music in neumatic notation.

Carnaval ('Carnival'). Schumann's op. 9 (1833–5), for piano; it is subtitled 'Scènes mignonnes sur quatre notes' ('dainty scenes on four notes'), the notes being A–S–C–H (A–E♭–C–B). Asch was the home town of Ernestine von Fricken, with whom Schumann was in love, and its four letters were the only 'musical' letters of his own name. Each of the work's 21 pieces has a descriptive name (e.g. 'Papillons'—'Butterflies'). An orchestral version of *Carnaval* by Glazunov and others was used for a ballet by Mikhail Fokine (St Petersburg, 1910).

Carnaval des animaux, Le ('The Carnival of the Animals'). 'Grand zoo-logical fantasy' by Saint-Saëns (1886), originally for two pianos, string quin-tet, flute, clarinet, glockenspiel, and xylophone, but also for two pianos and orchestra; it is in 14 movements, each representing a different animal, no. 13 being the famous *Le Cygne* ('The Swan'). Performance was forbidden in the composer's lifetime.

Carnaval romain, Le ('The Roman Carnival'). Overture, op. 9 (1844), by Berlioz; it uses material from his opera *Benvenuto Cellini*.

Carnival. *See NATURE, LIFE, AND LOVE.*

Carnival of the Animals, The. *See CARNAVAL DES ANIMAUX, LE.*

Carré. Work (1959–60) by Stockhausen for four choruses and four orches-tras, partly realized by Cornelius Cardew.

Cassandra's Dream Song. Work (1970) for solo flute by Brian Ferney-hough.

Casse-noisette. *See* NUTCRACKER.

Castor et Pollux. Opera (*tragédie en musique*) in a prologue and five acts by Rameau to a libretto by Pierre-Joseph Bernard (Paris, 1737); Rameau revised it, without the prologue and with a new first act (Paris, 1754).

Catalogue d'oiseaux ('Catalogue of Birds'). Piano work (1956–8) by Messiaen; each of the 13 pieces includes the notated song of a different bird.

Cathédrale engloutie, La ('The Submerged Cathedral'). Piano piece (1910) by Debussy, no. 10 of his *Préludes*, book 1; it is based on the legend of the Cathedral of Ys with its tolling bells and chanting under the sea. Debussy quoted from it in his Cello Sonata (1915).

Cat's Fugue. Nickname of the keyboard sonata in G minor K30 by Dome-nico Scarlatti, so called because the fugue subject consists of wide, irregular leaps, as though created by a cat padding over the keyboard.

Catulli carmina ('Songs of Catullus'). Scenic cantata by Orff for soloists, chorus, four pianos, four timpani, and up to 12 percussionists, a setting of 12 Latin poems by Catullus, with opening and closing Latin choruses by Orff (Leipzig, 1943); it is the second part of his trilogy *Trionfi.

Cavalleria rusticana ('Rustic Chivalry'). Opera (*melodramma*) in one act by Mascagni to a libretto by Giovanni Targioni-Tozzetti and Guido Menasci after Giovanni Verga's play (1884), based on his story (1880) (Rome, 1890).

Cave, The. Work by Reich for two solo sopranos, solo tenor, percussion, keyboards, string quartet, woodwind, and videotape; a 'documentary drama' lasting a whole evening in performance, it mixes fragments of interviews with Israelis, Palestinians, and Americans with purely musical material (Vienna, 1993).

Cello Symphony. Britten's op. 68 for cello and orchestra, composed for and dedicated to Mstislav Rostropovich, who gave its first performance in Moscow in 1964.

Celtic Requiem. Work (1969) by Tavener for soprano, children's chorus, chorus, and orchestra, to a text compiled from the Requiem Mass, poems by Henry Vaughan, Cardinal Newman, and Blathmac, and children's singing-games.

Cendrillon ('Cinderella'). Opera (*conte de fées*) in four acts by Massenet to a libretto by Henri Cain after Charles Perrault's fairy tale (Paris, 1899). Isouard (1810), Rossini (1817; see below), and Wolf-Ferrari (1900) wrote operas on the same subject.

Cenerentola, La (*La Cenerentola, ossia La bontà in trionfo*; 'Cinderella, or Goodness Triumphant'). Opera (*dramma giocoso*) in two acts by Rossini to a libretto by Jacopo Ferretti after Charles Perrault's fairy tale and librettos by Charles-Guillaume Étienne for Isouard's *Cendrillon* (1810) and

Francesco Fiorini's for Stefano Pavesi's *Agatina, o La virtù premiata* (1814) (Rome, 1817).

Central Park in the Dark (in the Good Old Summertime) (A Contemplation of Nothing Serious). Work (*c*.1909) for chamber orchestra by Ives; it is the second of *Two Contemplations*, the other being *The Unanswered Question*.

Century Rolls. Work (1996) for piano and orchestra by John Adams.

Ce qu'on entend sur la montagne ('What one Hears on the Mountain'; *Bergsymphonie*, 'Mountain Symphony'). Symphonic poem by Liszt after Victor Hugo's *Feuilles d'automne*, orchestrated by Raff in 1848–9 and revised in 1850, later revised again by Liszt in 1854.

Ceremony of Carols, A. Settings of carols, op. 28 (1942), by Britten, for treble voices and harp, in 11 movements; Julius Harrison arranged it for mixed chorus and harp or piano.

Chain. Three instrumental works by Lutosławski: *Chain I* (1983) is for 14 instruments, *Chain II* is a 'dialogue for violin and orchestra', and *Chain III* (1986) is for orchestra. For the composer, a 'chain' represented a new way of juxtaposing and connecting musical ideas: phrases overlap so that their beginnings and endings do not coincide but form a series of melodic 'links'.

Chairman Dances, The. Foxtrot for orchestra (1985) by John Adams. It uses material from a dance interlude in his opera *Nixon in China*; the chairman is Mao Tse-tung.

Chamber Symphony (*Kammersymphonie*). Title of two works by Schoenberg for small orchestra: no. 1 (op. 9) was composed in 1906 and arranged for full orchestra in 1922 and again in 1935; no. 2 (op. 38) was begun in 1906 and completed in 1939. Webern made a simplified arrangement of the first. Other composers have used this title, including Schreker; but many have preferred the term 'Chamber Concerto'.

Chandos Anthems. 12 anthems by Handel for soloists, chorus, and orchestra, on religious texts, composed in 1717–18 for James Brydges, Earl of Carnarvon, later the Duke of Chandos, at Cannons (his palace near Edgware, Middlesex).

Changes. Choral work, op. 17 (1966), by Gordon Crosse for solo voices, chorus, and orchestra, settings of poems by Thomas Browne, William Blake, Robert Herrick, Stephen Hawes, William Davenant, and an anonymous poet.

Chanson de matin; Chanson de nuit ('Morning Song'; 'Evening Song'). Two pieces by Elgar (?1897) for violin and piano; Elgar later orchestrated them, in 1899 and 1901 respectively.

Chansons de Bilitis. Three songs (1897–8) by Debussy for voice and piano to prose poems by Pierre Louÿs. Maurice Delage made an orchestral version of them in 1926. In 1900–1 Debussy arranged the music for two flutes, two harps, and celesta to accompany readings of the poems; the celesta part was lost but was reconstructed by Boulez (1954) and Arthur Hoérée (1971). Debussy recomposed the music as part of *Six épigraphes antiques* (1914) for piano duet.

Chansons madécasses ('Malagasy Songs'). Song cycle (1925–6) by Ravel, settings for voice, flute, cello, and piano of three texts by Évariste Parny, said to have been translated from the Malagasy.

Chant après chant ('Song after Song'). Work (1966) by Barraqué for soprano, piano, and six percussion instruments, using words and phrases from Hermann Broch's *Der Tod des Vergil* (1945; translated by Albert Kohn) interspersed with original material.

Chant du rossignol ('Song of the Nightingale'). Ballet in one act by Stravinsky to a scenario after Hans Christian Andersen's fairy tale, choreographed by Leonid Massine for Diaghilev's Ballets Russes (Paris, 1920).

Chantefleurs et chantefables ('Song-flowers and song-fables'). Song cycle (1989–90) for soprano and orchestra by Lutosławski, settings of nine poems by Robert Desnos (1900–45).

Chants d'Auvergne ('Songs of the Auvergne'). Traditional dialect songs of the Auvergne region of France which have become well known through four collections (1923–30) of arrangements by Canteloube from which a suite of nine songs for solo voice and orchestra (or piano) is frequently performed.

Chasse, La ('The Hunt'). Nickname of Haydn's Symphony no. 73 in D major (probably 1781), so called because of the style of its last movement.

Chasseur maudit, Le ('The Accursed Huntsman'). Symphonic poem, op. 44 (1882), by Franck, based on Gottfried Bürger's ballad *Der wilde Jäger*.

Checkmate. Ballet in one act by Bliss to his own scenario; it was choreographed by Ninette de Valois and first performed by the Sadler's Wells company (Paris, 1937). Bliss arranged a suite from the score (1939).

Chemins ('Paths'). A series of orchestral and ensemble works by Berio, many based on his *Sequenze* (see SEQUENZA); *Chemins I* dates from 1964, *Chemins V* from 1992.

Cherevichki ('The Slippers'). Comic-fantastic opera in four acts by Tchaikovsky to a libretto by Yakov Polonsky, amplified by Nikolay Chayev and the composer, after Nikolay Gogol's story *Noch' pered rozhdestvom* ('Christmas Eve') in *Evenings on a Farm near Dikanka* (ii, 1832) (Moscow, 1887); it is a revision of *Vakula the Smith*.

Cherry Ripe. Song by Charles Edward Horn, a setting of a poem by Robert Herrick (published in *Hesperides*, 1648), apparently first performed in 1826.

Chérubin. Opera (*comédie chantée*) in three acts by Massenet to a libretto by Henri Cain and Francis de Croisset after the latter's play (Monte Carlo, 1905).

Chevaux de frise. Orchestral work (1988) by Gerald Barry.

Chichester Psalms. Work (1965) by Bernstein for countertenor, chorus, and orchestra (originally organ, harp, and percussion), a setting of a Hebrew text; Bernstein composed it for Chichester Cathedral, where it was first performed.

Childhood of Christ, The. *See* ENFANCE DU CHRIST, L'.

Child of our Time, A. Oratorio (1939–41) by Tippett for soprano, alto, tenor, and bass soloists, chorus, and orchestra, a setting of his own text prompted by the persecution of Jews that followed the assassination in 1938 of a Nazi diplomat by Herschel Grynsban, a 17-year-old Jewish boy; in it Tippett uses spirituals in the same way that Bach used chorales in his Passions.

Children's Corner. Suite of piano pieces (1906–8) by Debussy; dedicated to his daughter, and with English titles, they are *Doctor Gradus ad Parnassum* (*see* GRADUS AD PARNASSUM), *Jimbo's Lullaby* ('Jimbo' is the composer's mistake for 'Jumbo'), *Serenade for the Doll*, *The Snow is Dancing*, *The Little Shepherd*, and *Golliwogg's Cake-Walk*.

Chocolate Soldier, The. *See* TAPFERE SOLDAT, DER.

Chopsticks (Fr.: *Côtelettes*, 'Cutlets'; Ger.: *Koteletten Walzer*). An anonymous quick waltz tune for piano, first published in London in 1877 as 'the celebrated Chop Waltz'. It is performed with two outstretched forefingers or with the flat hands held perpendicularly, the notes being struck with the outsides of the little fingers, with a tonic–dominant vamping bass part and an occasional *glissando*. The name therefore refers to chopping and to Chinese eating utensils. *Paraphrases* (1877) is a collection of pieces for piano duet based on the tune, by Borodin, Cui, Lyadov, Rimsky-Korsakov, and Liszt.

Choral Fantasia. 1. Beethoven's op. 80 (1808), for piano, chorus, and orchestra, a setting of a poem by Christoph Kuffner; it consists of variations on Beethoven's song *Gegenliebe* (1794–5), a melody that resembles that of the principal theme of the finale of his Ninth Symphony, for which this fantasia seems to have been a preliminary study.

2. Holst's op. 51 (1930), for soprano, chorus, organ, strings, brass, and percussion, a setting of words by Robert Bridges.

'Choral' Symphony. Popular name for Beethoven's Symphony no. 9 in D minor (1823–4), which includes a setting for chorus and soloists of Friedrich von Schiller's *An die Freude* ('Ode to Joy') in the last movement. Other symphonies using choral forces include Berlioz's *Roméo et Juliette*; Liszt's *Dante Symphony* (1856) and *Faust Symphony* (1854); Holst's First Choral Symphony (1923–4), a four-movement setting for soprano, chorus, and orchestra of four poems by John Keats; Mahler's Second ('Resurrection'), Third, Fourth (a solo soprano appears in the final movement), and Eighth symphonies; Vaughan Williams's *A Sea Symphony*; Britten's *Spring Symphony*; and Shostakovich's Second, Third, 13th, and 14th symphonies.

Chout (*Skazka pro shuta*; 'The Tale of the Buffoon'). Ballet in six scenes by Prokofiev to his own scenario after Nikolay Afanas'yev; it was composed in 1915 and revised in 1920 and was first performed by Serge Diaghilev's Ballets Russes (Paris, 1921). Prokofiev arranged an orchestral suite from the score (1920).

'Christmas' Concerto. Popular name for Corelli's Concerto Grosso in G minor op. 6 no. 8, for strings and continuo, published in Amsterdam in 1714; it was intended as a *concerto da chiesa* (for church use) and was inscribed 'fatto per la notte di Natale' ('made for Christmas night').

Christmas Eve (*Noch' pered rozhdestvom*). Opera in four acts by Rimsky-Korsakov to his own libretto after the story in Nikolay Gogol's *Evenings on a Farm near Dikanka* (ii, 1832) (St Petersburg, 1895).

Christmas Oratorio (*Weinachts-Oratorium*). Oratorio by J. S. Bach to texts, possibly by Picander, relating the biblical story of the Nativity with a commentary; it comprises six cantatas designed for performance in Leipzig on the six feast-days between Christmas Day and Epiphany (1734–5) and includes music adapted from his secular cantatas. Schütz also wrote a *Christmas Oratorio* (1664).

Christ on the Mount of Olives. *See* CHRISTUS AM ÖLBERGE.

Christophe Colomb ('Christopher Columbus'). Opera in two parts by Milhaud to a libretto by Paul Claudel (Berlin, 1930; revised Graz, 1968); on an enormous scale, it is in 27 scenes and incorporates film. Ottoboni (1690), Morlacchi (1828), Franchetti (1892), and Egk (1933) also wrote operas on the subject.

Christus. 1. Oratorio (1862–7) by Liszt for soprano, alto, tenor, baritone, and bass soloists, chorus, organ, and orchestra, a setting of a biblical and liturgical text.
   2. Oratorio, op. 97, by Mendelssohn to a text by Chevalier Bunsen; it was begun in 1844 but was left unfinished at Mendelssohn's death.

Christus am Ölberge ('Christ on the Mount of Olives'). Oratorio, op. 85 (1803; revised 1804), by Beethoven for soprano, tenor, bass, chorus, and orchestra, a setting of a text by Franz Xaver Huber; the English version, called *Engedi*, changes the subject to the story of David.

Chromatic Fantasia and Fugue. Keyboard work by J. S. Bach, BWV903 (*c*.1720); the fantasia makes remarkable chromatic modulations and the fugue subject is highly chromatic.

Chronochromie ('Time Colouration'). Orchestral work (1960) by Messiaen; it is permeated by birdsong, and the sixth of its seven movements ('Épode') is for 18 solo strings, each playing a different birdsong.

Chute de la maison Usher, La ('The Fall of the House of Usher'). Unfinished opera by Debussy to his own libretto after the story by Edgar Allan Poe (New Haven, CT, 1977). *See also* FALL OF THE HOUSE OF USHER, THE.

Cid, Le. Opera in four acts by Massenet to a libretto by Adolphe d'Ennery, Édouard Blau, and Louis Gallet after the play by Pierre Corneille (1637) (Paris, 1885). Gasparini (1717), Piccinni (1766), Paisiello (1775), Aiblinger (1821), and Cornelius (1865) are among those who also wrote operas on the subject.

Cinderella. 1. *See* CENERENTOLA, LA; CENDRILLON.
  2. (*Zolushka*). Ballet in three acts by Prokofiev to a scenario by Nikolay Volkov, choreographed by Rostislav Zakharov (Moscow, 1945).

Cinesi, Le ('The Chinese Ladies'). Opera (*azione teatrale*) in one act by Gluck to a libretto by Pietro Metastasio (Vienna, 1754).

Cinq rechants. Five works (1949) by Messiaen for three sopranos, three altos, three tenors, and three basses, settings of his own texts; like *Harawi* and *Turangalîla-symphonie*, they were inspired by the legend of Tristan and Isolda.

Circles. Work (1960) by Berio for female voice, harp, and two percussionists, a setting of texts by e. e. cummings from his *Poems 1923–54*.

Circus Polka (for a young elephant). Piece by Stravinsky composed for the Barnum and Bailey Circus; it was first performed, danced by a troupe of young elephants, in New York in 1942, scored for wind band by David Raksin. Stravinsky made a version for symphony orchestra and a piano reduction.

City Life. Work (1995) by Reich for two flutes, two oboes, two clarinets, two pianos, two samplers, three (or four) percussion, string quartet, and bass; in five movements, it incorporates voices heard on the streets of New York, and such sounds as car horns, slamming doors, car alarms, sirens, and pile drivers.

Clair de lune ('Moonlight'). **1.** Third movement of Debussy's *Suite bergamasque* (1890) for piano; it was orchestrated by André Caplet and exists in several other arrangements, none by Debussy.
  2. Song (1891) by Debussy to a poem by Paul Verlaine, the third of his first set of *Fêtes galantes.
  3. Song, op. 46 no. 2 (1887), by Fauré to the same poem by Verlaine.

Clapping Music. Piece (1972) by Reich for two pairs of hands.

Clarissa. Opera in two acts by Robin Holloway to a libretto by the composer after Samuel Richardson's epistolary novel (1748) (London, 1996).

Classical Symphony. Prokofiev's Symphony no. 1 in D major op. 25 (1916–17), written in the style of Haydn.

Clavier-Büchlein (*Clavierbüchlein*; 'Little Keyboard Book'). Title given by J. S. Bach to three of his collections of keyboard music: the first (1720), for his son Wilhelm Friedemann, contains early versions of the inventions and sinfonias and some preludes from book 1 of the '48', as well as pieces that may be by Wilhelm Friedemann; the second (1722) and third (1725), for his second wife Anna Magdalena (the 'Anna Magdalena Books'), include the first five French Suites, and the third and sixth partitas, as well as other pieces by J. S. Bach, C. P. E. Bach, and other composers.

Clavier-Übung ('Keyboard Practice'). Title given by J. S. Bach to four volumes of keyboard music: the first (1731) contains six partitas, BWV825–30, for harpsichord; the second (1735), also for harpsichord, consists of the Italian Concerto BWV971 and the Ouverture in the French Style BWV831; the third (1739) is mainly of liturgical organ music, BWV552, 669–89, and 802–5 (a prelude and fugue, 21 chorale preludes, and four duets); and the fourth (1741) the 'Goldberg' Variations for harpsichord. Kuhnau, Bach's predecessor at Leipzig, had used the title for two volumes of keyboard music (1689, 1692).

Clemenza di Tito, La ('The Clemency of Titus'). *Opera seria* in two acts by Mozart to a libretto by Pietro Metastasio adapted by Caterino Mazzolà (Prague, 1791). Metastasio's libretto was set by some 20 other composers, including Gluck (1752).

'Clock' Symphony. Nickname of Haydn's Symphony no. 101 in D major (1794), so called because of the 'tick-tock' accompaniment to the first subject of the second movement.

Cockaigne (In London Town). Concert overture, op. 40 (1901), by Elgar; it is dedicated to his 'friends the members of British orchestras'. The title refers to the imaginary land of idleness and luxury from which the word 'cockney' is said to be derived.

Cockles and Mussels. Irish folksong, of which the tune is *Molly Malone* and the words 'In Dublin's fair city'.

Coffee Cantata (*Kaffeekantate*). Nickname of J. S. Bach's cantata no. 211, *Schweigt stille, plaudert nicht* ('Be silent, don't chatter'), to a text by Picander; it was probably composed in 1734 and refers to the growing passion for coffee in Leipzig at the time.

Colas Breugnon (*Kola Bryun'on: Master iz Klamsi*; 'Colas Breugnon: Master of Clamecy'). Opera in a prologue and three acts by Kabalevsky to a libretto by V. G. Bragin after Romain Rolland's novel (1918) (Leningrad, 1938, as *Master iz Klamsi*).

Colour Symphony, A. Orchestral work (1922) by Bliss; the movements are 'Purple', 'Red', 'Blue', and 'Green', the colours being interpreted through their heraldic associations.

Combattimento di Tancredi, e Clorinda ('The Combat of Tancred and Clorinda'). Dramatic cantata by Monteverdi to a text from Torquato Tasso's *Gerusalemme liberata* (1581); partly acted and partly narrated, it was first performed in Venice in 1624 and was published in *Madrigali guerrieri e amorosi* (1638).

Come Ye Sons of Art. Ode (1694) by Henry Purcell for soprano, two altos, and bass soloists, chorus, and orchestra, composed for the birthday of Queen Mary, wife of William III; it contains the duet 'Sound the trumpet'.

Compass Rose, The. Suite of eight pieces for small orchestra (1988–94) by Kagel.

Comte Ory, Le ('Count Ory'). Opera in two acts by Rossini to a libretto by Eugène Scribe and Charles-Gaspard Delestre-Poirson after their own play (1816) (Paris, 1828). It uses much music from Rossini's Il *viaggio a Reims*.

Comus. Masque in three acts by John Milton performed at Ludlow Castle in 1634 with music by Henry Lawes. Arne composed new music for John Dalton's adaptation of Milton's verse, a version first performed in London in 1738. In 1942 Constant Lambert arranged music by Henry Purcell for a ballet in which some of Milton's verse was spoken. Another ballet was produced in 1946 with music by Handel and Lawes, arranged by Ernest Irving.

Concerto funebre. Work (1939) by Karl Amadeus Hartmann for violin and strings.

Concierto de Aranjuez ('Aranjuez Concerto'). Concerto (1939) for guitar and orchestra by Rodrigo; he also arranged it for harp and orchestra.

Concord Sonata. Piano work (c.1916–19) by Ives (its full title being Second Piano Sonata 'Concord, Mass., 1840–60'); it was written in honour of the Concord group of writers, whom Ives admired, and its movements are entitled 'Emerson', 'Hawthorne', 'The Alcotts', and 'Thoreau' (with optional flute).

Confession of Isobel Gowdie, The. Orchestral work (1990) by James MacMillan.

Conquest of Mexico, The. *See* EROBERUNG VON MEXICO, DIE.

Consecration of the House, The. *See* WEIHE DES HAUSES, DIE.

Consolations. Six pieces for solo piano (1844–8) by Liszt; the best known is no. 3, for which Liszt later recommended the use of the (then newly invented) sostenuto pedal.

Construction (in Metal). Three works for percussion by Cage; the *First Construction* is for six players and was composed in 1939, and the other two are for four players and date from 1940 and 1941 respectively.

Consul, The. Musical drama in three acts by Menotti to his own libretto (Philadelphia, 1950).

Contes d'Hoffmann, Les ('The Tales of Hoffmann'). Opera (*opéra fantastique*) in a prologue, three acts, and an epilogue by Offenbach to a libretto by Jules Barbier after the play (1851) by Barbier and Michel Carré after E. T. A. Hoffmann's stories *Der Sandmann*, *Die Abenteuer der Sylvester-Nacht*, *Rat Crespel*, and others (Paris, 1881); Offenbach died during rehearsals and it was completed by Ernest Guiraud.

Contrasts. Work (1938) by Bartók for violin, clarinet, and piano, composed for the jazz clarinettist Benny Goodman; the violinist uses two instruments, the second in scordatura (i.e. unconventional) tuning.

Coppélia, ou La Fille aux yeux d'émail ('Coppélia, or The Girl with Enamel Eyes'). Ballet in two acts by Delibes to a scenario by Charles Nuitter and Arthur Saint-Léon after E. T. A. Hoffmann's story *Der Sandmann*; it was choreographed by Saint Léon (Paris, 1870). Delibes arranged a suite from the ballet, of which there are now many different choreographic versions.

Coptic Light. Orchestral work (1986) by Michael Finnissy.

Coq d'or, Le. *See* GOLDEN COCKEREL, THE.

Corelli, Fantasia Concertante on a Theme of. *See* FANTASIA CONCERTANTE ON A THEME OF CORELLI.

Corelli Variations. *See* VARIATIONS ON A THEME OF CORELLI.

Coriolan ('Coriolanus'). Overture, op. 62, by Beethoven, composed in 1807 for a revival in Vienna of Heinrich Joseph von Collin's play *Coriolan* (on the same subject as Shakespeare's).

Coronation Anthems. **1**. Four anthems for chorus and orchestra by Handel, composed for the coronation of George II in 1727: *Zadok the Priest*, *The King Shall Rejoice*, *My Heart is Inditing*, and *Let thy Hand be Strengthened*.
   2. An anthem, *My Heart is Inditing*, for chorus and orchestra by Purcell, composed for the coronation of James II in 1685.

'Coronation' Concerto. Nickname of Mozart's Piano Concerto no. 26 in D major κ537 (1788), so called because it was performed at the coronation of Leopold II (1790), but it had in fact been performed by Mozart in 1789.

'Coronation' Mass. Nickname of Mozart's Mass in C major κ317 (1779), so called because it is believed to have been composed for, or associated with, the annual crowning of a statue of the Virgin in a church near Salzburg. Haydn's *Nelsonmesse* is sometimes referred to as the Coronation Mass.

Coronation Ode. Choral work, op. 44, by Elgar, for four soloists, chorus, and orchestra, a setting of words by A. C. Benson. It was commissioned for the Covent Garden gala performance to celebrate Edward VII's coronation in June 1902; the gala was cancelled because of the king's illness and the work was given its premiere at the Sheffield Festival in October that year. The finale, 'Land of Hope and Glory', is to a melody adapted from the trio section of Elgar's first *Pomp and Circumstance* march.

Coronation of Poppaea, The. *See* INCORONAZIONE DI POPPEA, L'.

Corps glorieux, Les ('The Glorious Hosts'). Organ work (1939) by Messiaen, in seven movements.

Corregidor, Der ('The Magistrate'). Opera in four acts by Wolf to a libretto by Rosa Mayreder after Pedro Antonio de Alarcón's novel *El sombrero de tres picos* ('The Three-Cornered Hat', 1874) (Mannheim, 1896). Falla's ballet *El sombrero de tres picos* is based on the same story.

Corsaire, Le ('The Corsair'). Overture, op. 21, by Berlioz, based on Byron's poem (1814); it was composed in 1844 and revised some time before 1852. It was first performed with the title *La Tour de Nice*, then as *Le Corsaire rouge* (the French title for Fenimore Cooper's *The Red Rover*).

Corsaro, Il ('The Corsair'). *Opera buffa* in three acts by Verdi to a libretto by Francesco Maria Piave after Byron's poem (1814) (Trieste, 1848).

Così fan tutte (*Così fan tutte, ossia La scuola degli amanti*; 'All Women Do the Same, or The School for Lovers'). Opera in two acts by Mozart to a libretto by Lorenzo Da Ponte (Vienna, 1790).

Coucou, Le ('The Cuckoo'). Harpsichord piece (1735) by Daquin.

Couleurs de la cité céleste ('Colours of the Celestial City'). Work (1963) by Messiaen for piano, 13 wind instruments, xylophone, xylorimba, marimba, and four percussion players.

Count of Luxembourg, The. *See* GRAF VON LUXEMBURG, DER.

Country Gardens. English country-dance tune. It first appeared in print in *The Quaker's Opera* (1728) and became well known through Percy Grainger's arrangements (1908–18) for piano and two pianos, orchestrated (1918) by L. Artok.

Cox and Box (*Cox and Box; or, The Long-Lost Brothers*). Operetta in one act by Sullivan to a libretto by F. C. Burnand after J. Maddison Morton's farce *Box and Cox* (1847) (London, private performance, 1866).

Cradle Will Rock, The. 'Play in music' in ten scenes by Blitzstein to his own libretto (New York, 1937).

Creation, The (*Die Schöpfung*). Oratorio (1796–8) by Haydn, for soprano, tenor, and bass soloists, chorus, and orchestra, to a text by Gottfried van Swieten after a poem by an unknown English author ('Mr Lidley', possibly Thomas Linley (ii)) based on John Milton's *Paradise Lost*.

Création du monde, La ('The Creation of the World'). Ballet in one act by Milhaud to a scenario by Blaise Cendrars, choreographed by Jean Börlin (Paris, 1923).

'Creation' Mass (*Schöpfungsmesse*). Haydn's Mass no. 13 in B♭ major (1801), so called because there is a quotation from his oratorio *The Creation* in the 'Qui tollis'.

Creatures of Prometheus, The. *See* GESCHÖPFE DES PROMETHEUS, DIE.

Crisantemi ('Chrysanthemums'). Work (1890) by Puccini for string quartet.

Crociato in Egitto, Il ('The Crusader in Egypt'). Opera (*melodramma eroico*) in two acts by Meyerbeer to a libretto by Gaetano Rossi (Venice, 1824).

Cronaca del luogo ('Chronicle of the Place'). Opera in a prologue and five scenes by Berio to a libretto by Talia Pecker Berio (Salzburg, 1999).

Crown Imperial. March by Walton, composed for the coronation of George VI in 1937; the score is headed by a line from the poem *In Honour of the City* by William Dunbar (1465–1520): 'In beautie beryng the crone imperiall'. It has been arranged for military band, for piano, and for organ.

Crown of India, The. Imperial masque, op. 66, by Elgar to words by Henry Hamilton; it was written to celebrate the Delhi Durbar in 1912. Elgar made an orchestral suite from it the same year.

Crucible, The. Opera in four acts by Robert Ward to a libretto by Bernard Stambler after Arthur Miller's play (1952) (New York, 1961).

Crucifixion, The. Oratorio (1887) by Stainer to a text by W. J. Sparrow-Simpson with extracts from the Bible; it is for tenor and bass soloists, chorus, organ, and orchestra, and the congregation may join in five hymns (omitted in some performances).

Cry. Work (1976–9) for 28 amplified voices by Giles Swayne.

Cuckoo, The. *See COUCOU, LE*.

Cunning Little Vixen, The (*Příhody Lišky Bystroušky*; 'The Adventures of the Vixen Bystrouška'). Opera in three acts by Janáček to his own libretto after Rudolf Těsnohlídek's novel *Liška Bystrouška* (originally texts to go with drawings by Stanislav Lolek, published in the Brno newspaper *Lidové noviny* in 1920) (Brno, 1924).

Cupid and Death. Masque in five entries by James Shirley, performed in 1653 with music probably by Christopher Gibbons; it was revived in 1659 with music by Gibbons and Locke.

Curlew, The. Song cycle (1920–2) by Warlock for tenor, flute, cor anglais, and string quartet, a setting of four poems by W. B. Yeats.

Curlew River. Church parable by Britten to a libretto by William Plomer after the Japanese nō play *Sumidagawa* by Jūrō Motomasa (1395–1431) (Orford, Suffolk, 1964).

Cwm Rhondda ('Rhondda Valley'). Hymn tune by John Hughes (1873–1932) sung to the words 'Guide me, o thou great Redeemer [Jehovah]' by William Williams (1717–91); it is one of the most popular hymns in the Welsh tradition.

Cyrano de Bergerac. Opera (*commedia eroica*) in four acts by Alfano to a libretto by Henri Cain after Edmond Rostand's play (1897) (Rome, 1936, in Italian; Paris, 1936, in the original French).

D. Abbreviation for *Deutsch, used as a prefix to the numbers of Schubert's works as given in the standard thematic catalogue of O. E. Deutsch.

Dafne ('Daphne'). Opera in a prologue and six scenes by Peri to a libretto by Ottavio Rinuccini (Florence, 1597). *Dafne* is generally supposed to be the earliest opera but most of the music is now lost. It was first performed in Jacopo Corsi's house, and from one of the surviving manuscripts of fragments of the music it appears that Corsi collaborated with Peri. Gagliano (1608) and Schütz (1627) wrote operas on the same subject.

Dalibor. Opera in three acts by Smetana to a libretto by Josef Wenzig translated from German into Czech by Ervín Špindler (Prague, 1868).

Dame blanche, La ('The White Lady'). *Opéra comique* in three acts by Boieldieu to a libretto by Eugène Scribe after Walter Scott's novels *Guy Mannering* (1815), *The Monastery* (1820), and *The Abbot* (1820) (Paris, 1825).

Damnation de Faust, La ('The Damnation of Faust'). Cantata (*légende dramatique*) in four parts by Berlioz, for mezzo-soprano, tenor, baritone, and bass soloists, chorus, and orchestra, to a libretto by the composer and Almire Gandonnière after Gérard de Nerval's French translation of Johann Wolfgang von Goethe's *Faust*; it incorporates the earlier *Huit scènes de Faust* (1828–9) (Paris, 1846). It was adapted by Raoul Gunsbourg as a fully staged opera (Monte Carlo, 1893), the form in which it is now often seen. *See also* RÁKÓCZI MARCH.

Damoiselle élue, La ('The Blessed Damozel'). Cantata (1888) by Debussy for solo voice, chorus, and orchestra, a setting of Gabriel Sarrazin's French translation of Dante Gabriel Rossetti's poem (1850).

Dance before the Golden Calf (*Der Tanz um das goldene Kalb*). The central part of Act II of Schoenberg's opera *Moses und Aron.

Dance of Death (Fr.: *danse macabre*; Ger.: *Totentanz*). The idea of Death as a dancer or as a skeletal fiddler of dance tunes was particularly important during the Middle Ages, especially following the Black Death in the 14th century. In the 19th and 20th centuries it was an influential concept in art and literature and also inspired several composers. Liszt's *Totentanz* for piano and orchestra (1849) drew on a poem by Johann Wolfgang von Goethe, and Saint-Saëns's symphonic poem *Danse macabre* (op. 40, 1874) was based on poetry by Henri Cazalis; both these works use the *Dies irae*, the traditional plainchant of the Requiem Mass. The *Danse des morts* for solo voices, chorus, and orchestra (1938) by Honegger was inspired by Hans Holbein's famous series of woodcuts *Imagines mortis* (Lyon, 1538).

Dance of the Blessed Spirits. Slow dance episode in Act II of Gluck's *Orfeo ed Euridice* (1762) characterized by a lyrical flute solo; it is often performed as a concert item.

Dance of the Hours. A ballet in Act III of Ponchielli's *La *Gioconda*, often played as a separate orchestral piece; an entertainment staged by one of the characters for his guests, it symbolizes the conflict between darkness and light.

Dance of the Seven Veils. Popular name for Salome's dance before Herod in Richard Strauss's opera *Salome* (1905); for orchestra alone, it is often performed as a concert item.

Dance of the Sylphs. Orchestral episode in the second part of Berlioz's *La Damnation de Faust*; it is often played separately.

Dance Rhapsody. Title given by Delius to two orchestral works: no. 1 (1908); no. 2 (1916, first performed in 1923). It is also the title of an orchestral work (1908) by Bridge.

Dances of Galánta (*Galántai táncok*). Orchestral suite (1933) by Kodály; based on Gypsy tunes collected in the market town of Galánta, it was composed for the 80th anniversary of the Budapest Philharmonic Society.

Dance Suite (*Táncszvit*). Orchestral work (1923) by Bartók, composed to celebrate the 50th anniversary of the merging of Buda and Pest; Bartók also arranged it for piano (1925).

Daniel, The Play of. *See* PLAY OF DANIEL, THE.

Danse macabre ('Dance of Death'). Symphonic poem, op. 40 (1874), by Saint-Saëns, based on a poem by Henri Cazalis in which Death the Fiddler summons skeletons from their graves at midnight to dance; it includes the *Dies irae* (Saint-Saëns had already set the poem as a song). Liszt made a piano transcription of it. *See also* DANCE OF DEATH.

Dante Sonata. Piano work by Liszt, the first version (in two movements) dating from 1839; it was revised twice and became, in one movement, the final piece in book 2 of the *Années de pèlerinage*, the full title of this version being *Après une lecture du Dante, fantasia quasi sonata*.

Dante Symphony. Orchestral work (1855–6) by Liszt, based on Johann Wolfgang von Goethe's play, its full title being *Eine Symphonie zu Dantes Divina commedia* ('A Symphony to Dante's Divine Comedy'); it is in two movements, 'Inferno' and 'Purgatorio', the latter concluding with a choral *Magnificat*. Tchaikovsky's *Francesca da Rimini* was heavily influenced by its first movement.

Dantons Tod ('Danton's Death'). Opera in two parts (six scenes) by Einem to a libretto by Blacher and the composer after Georg Büchner's play (1835) (Salzburg, 1947).

Daphne. Opera (*bukolische Tragödie*) in one act by Richard Strauss to a libretto by Joseph Gregor (Dresden, 1938).

Daphnis et Chloé. Ballet (*symphonie chorégraphique*) in three movements by Ravel to a scenario by Mikhail Fokine, who choreographed it for Serge Diaghilev's Ballets Russes (Paris, 1912); the score includes a part for wordless chorus. Ravel made two orchestral suites from it (1911, 1913).

Dardanus. Opera (*tragédie en musique*) in a prologue and five acts by Rameau to a libretto by Charles-Antoine Le Clerc de La Bruère (Paris, 1739). Sacchini wrote an opera on the same subject (Versailles, 1784).

Daughter of the Regiment, The. *See* FILLE DU RÉGIMENT, LA.

Davidde penitente ('David the Penitent'). Oratorio by Mozart, K469 (1785), to a text probably by Lorenzo Da Ponte; it is for two sopranos and a tenor soloist, chorus, and orchestra and incorporates material from an unfinished Mass in C minor K427/417a (1782–3).

Davidsbündlertänze. Schumann's op. 6 (1837), a set of 18 character pieces for piano.

Dead Man Walking. Opera in two acts by Jake Heggie to a libretto by Terrence McNally after Sister Helen Prejean's book *Dead Man Walking: An Eyewitness Account of the Death Penalty in the US* (1993) (San Francisco, 2000).

Dead March in 'Saul'. Popular name for the funeral march from Handel's oratorio *Saul; it is used on state occasions such as the funeral of a sovereign.

Death and the Maiden. *See* TOD UND DAS MÄDCHEN, DER.

Death and Transfiguration. *See* TOD UND VERKLÄRUNG.

Death in Venice. Opera in two acts (17 scenes) by Britten to a libretto by Myfanwy Piper after Thomas Mann's novella *Der Tod in Venedig* (1911) (Snape, 1973).

Death of Klinghoffer, The. Opera in a prologue and two acts by John Adams to a libretto by Alice Goodman (Brussels, 1991).

Death of Light/Light of Death. Work (1998) for chamber ensemble by Jonathan Harvey after Mathias Grünewald's 'Crucifixion' in the Isenheim altarpiece.

Death of Moses, The. Choral work, op. 53 (1991–2), by Goehr, for soprano, contralto or male alto, tenor, baritone and bass soloists, chorus, children's chorus (or semi-chorus), and 13 instrumentalists, a setting of a text adapted and translated from traditional Jewish poetry by John Hollander.

Deborah. Oratorio (1733) by Handel to a biblical text compiled by Samuel Humphreys.

Decoration Day. Orchestral work by Ives (*c.*1915–20); it became the second movement of *Holidays.

Deidamia. Opera in three acts by Handel to a libretto by Paolo Antonio Rolli (London, 1741).

Density 21.5. Work (1936) by Varèse for solo flute.

Des canyons aux étoiles ('From the Canyons to the Stars'). Work (1970–4) by Messiaen for piano, horn, and orchestra; it was inspired by the American landscape.

Desert Music, The. Work (1982–4) by Reich for small, amplified chorus and large orchestra, a setting of poems by William Carlos Williams.

Déserts. Work by Varèse for 14 wind, piano, five percussion, and two-track tape; it was completed in 1954 and the tape was revised in 1960 and twice in 1961.

Des Knaben Wunderhorn ('The Boy's Magic Horn'). A collection of the texts of over 700 German folksongs, assembled between 1804 and 1807 by the poets Achim von Arnim (1781–1831) and Clemens Brentano (1778–1842) and published, with a dedication to Goethe, in three volumes between 1805 and 1808. Both writers made substantial adjustments to the original material, and their editorial work is now regarded as suspect and unscholarly. The collection, however, had a powerful impact on composers and writers and is one of the most important documents in the history of both German Romanticism and German nationalism. Schumann, Mendelssohn, Brahms, and Richard Strauss all set individual texts as lieder; the composer most closely associated with the work is Mahler, who set nine poems for voice and piano, and 13 for voice and orchestra. His Second (*'Resurrection'), Third, and Fourth symphonies rework thematic material from his *Wunderhorn* songs and draw on further texts for their vocal and choral sections.

Dettingen Te Deum and Anthem. Choral works by Handel composed to celebrate the British victory over the French at Dettingen, near Frankfurt, in 1743; the anthem is to the text 'The king shall rejoice'.

Deuteromelia ('Second Honey'). The second collection of English rounds and catches (31 numbers) published in 1609 by Thomas Ravenscroft. The first is called *Pammelia.

Deutsch. Abbreviation for the standard thematic catalogue of the works of Schubert drawn up by the Austrian biographer and bibliographer Otto Erich Deutsch (1883–1967) and published in London in 1951 (enlarged Ger. edn, 1978). Schubert's works, especially those without distinguishing title or opus number, are often referred to by Deutsch number (usually further abbreviated to D).

Deutsches Requiem, Ein. *See* GERMAN REQUIEM, A.

Deutschland über alles. *See* EINIGKEIT UND RECHT UND FREIHEIT.

Deux Journées, Les (*Les Deux Journées, ou Le Porteur d'eau*; 'The Two Days, or The Water Carrier'). Opera (*comédie lyrique*) in three acts by Cherubini to a libretto by Jean-Nicolas Bouilly (Paris, 1800); in England it is generally known as *The Water Carrier* and in Germany as *Der Wasserträger*.

Deux Pigeons, Les. Ballet in three acts by Messager to a scenario by Henry Régnier and Louis Mérante, choreographed by Mérante (Paris, 1886). Frederick Ashton choreographed a new version (London, 1961).

Devil and Daniel Webster, The. Folk opera in one act by Douglas S. Moore to a libretto by Stephen Vincent Benét after his own short story (New York, 1939).

Devil and Kate, The (*Čert a Káča*). Opera in three acts by Dvořák to a libretto by Adolf Wenig after a Czech folk tale (Prague, 1899).

Devils of Loudon, The. Opera in three acts by Penderecki to a libretto by the composer after John Whiting's dramatization (translated into German by Erich Fried) of Aldous Huxley's novel *The Devils of Loudon* (1952) (Hamburg, 1969).

'Devil's Trill' Sonata. Nickname of a violin sonata in G minor (*c.*1714) by Tartini, first published in J. B. Cartier's *L'Art du violon* (Paris, 1798), so called because of the long trill in the last of its four movements. Legend has it that Tartini dreamt he had made a deal with the Devil, to whom he gave his violin; the Devil played such a beautiful solo that when Tartini woke, he tried to play it himself. He failed, but composed the 'Devil's trill'. This legend is the subject of Cesare Pugni's ballet *Le Violon du diable* (1849).

Devin du village, Le ('The Village Soothsayer'). Opera (*intermède*) in one act by Jean-Jacques Rousseau to his own libretto (Fontainebleau, 1752). The libretto of Mozart's *Bastien und Bastienne* is based on a parody.

Diabelli Variations. Beethoven's *Variations on a Waltz by Diabelli* op. 120 (1819–23), for piano. The publisher Anton Diabelli commissioned 51 composers to write a variation on his waltz tune, as a means of creating an anthology of contemporary Austrian music. The collection, entitled *Vaterländischer Künstlerverein* ('Society of Artists of the Fatherland'), was published in two volumes, the first containing Beethoven's variations (he provided 33), the second those of the other 50 composers, including Schubert, Moscheles, Kalkbrenner, Czerny, and the 11-year-old Liszt.

Dialogues des Carmélites ('Dialogues of the Carmelites'). Opera in three acts by Poulenc to his own libretto after Georges Bernanos's play (Milan, 1957).

Diary of One who Disappeared (*Zápisník zmizelého*). Song cycle (1917–20) by Janáček for tenor, contralto (or mezzo-soprano), three women's voices, and piano, settings of 21 poems by Ozef Kalda.

Dichterliebe ('Poet's Love'). Song cycle, op. 48 (1840), by Schumann for voice and piano, settings of 16 poems by Heinrich Heine.

Dido and Aeneas. Opera in three acts by Henry Purcell to a libretto by Nahum Tate after his play *Brutus of Alba, or The Enchanted Lovers* (1678) and book 4 of Virgil's *Aeneid* (London, 1689).

Dido's Lament. The lament 'When I am laid in earth', in Act III of Henry Purcell's *Dido and Aeneas*, which Dido sings before she dies.

Dienstag aus Licht ('Tuesday from Light'). Opera in a greeting and two acts by Stockhausen to his own libretto (Leipzig, 1993), the 'fourth day' of **Licht*.

Dies natalis ('Birthday'). Cantata, op. 8 (1926–39), by Finzi for soprano or tenor and strings; it is in five movements, the first instrumental, the second a setting of a prose passage from *Centuries of Meditation* by Thomas Traherne (1638–74), and the last three being settings of Traherne poems.

Dieu parmi nous ('God Among Us'). The ninth piece of Messiaen's *La *Nativité du Seigneur.*

Different Trains. Work (1988) by Reich for string quartet and tape; the taped material consists of fragments of interviews linking the composer's memories of rail journeys made in his childhood to the trains that transported Holocaust victims to their death in concentration camps.

Dimitrij. Grand opera in four acts by Dvořák to a libretto by Marie Červinková-Riegrová (Prague, 1882; revised Prague, 1894).

Dinorah (*Le Pardon de Ploërmel*; 'The Pilgrimage of Plouermel'). *Opéra comique* in three acts by Meyerbeer to a libretto by Michel Carré and Jules Barbier after Carré's play *Les Chercheurs de trésor* (Paris, 1859).

Dioclesian (*The Prophetess, or The History of Dioclesian*). Semi-opera in five acts by Henry Purcell to a libretto by Thomas Betterton after the play by John Fletcher and Philip Massinger (London, 1690).

'Dissonance' Quartet (*Les Dissonances*; *Dissonanzen-Quartett*). Nickname of Mozart's String Quartet in C major K465 (1785); one of the *'Haydn' Quartets, it is so called for the remarkable use of dissonance in the introduction.

Distratto, Il ('The Distraught Man'). Nickname of Haydn's Symphony no. 60 in C major (1774), so called because it includes the incidental music Haydn wrote for the comedy *Der Zerstreute* (after J. F. Regnard's *Le Distrait*) (Eszterháza, 1774).

'Dives and Lazarus', Five Variants of. See FIVE VARIANTS OF 'DIVES AND LAZARUS'.

Divine Poem, The (*Bozhestvennaya poema*; *Le Divin Poème*). Skryabin's Symphony no. 3 in C minor op. 43 (1902–4); it illustrates the composer's theosophical ideas, the three movements being called 'Struggles', 'Delights', and 'Divine Play'.

Djamileh. *Opéra comique* in one act by Bizet to a libretto by Louis Gallet after Alfred de Musset's story *Namouna* (1833) (Paris, 1872).

Docteur Miracle, Le. *Opérette* in one act by Bizet to a libretto by Léon Battu and Ludovic Halévy (Paris, 1857).

Doctor of Myddfai, The. Opera in two acts by Maxwell Davies to a libretto by David Pountney after a Welsh legend (Llandudno, 1996).

Doctor Ox's Experiment. Opera in two acts by Gavin Bryars to a libretto by Blake Morrison after Jules Verne's fantasy (1874) (London, 1998).

Doktor Faust. Opera in eight scenes by Busoni to his own libretto after the 16th-century puppet plays; the final scene was completed by Philipp Jarnach (Dresden, 1925).

Dollarprinzessin, Die ('The Dollar Princess'). Operetta in three acts by Leo Fall to a libretto by A. M. Willner and Fritz Grünbaum after a comedy by Emerich Gatti and Wilhelm von Trotha (Vienna, 1907).

Dolly. Suite for piano duet, op. 56 (1894–7), by Fauré. *See also* THREE TALES.

Don Carlos. Opera in five acts by Verdi to a libretto (in French) by Joseph Méry and Camille Du Locle after Friedrich von Schiller's dramatic poem (1787) (Paris, 1867); Verdi revised it into four acts (dropping Act I of the French version), with a revised libretto by Du Locle translated into Italian (as *Don Carlo*) by Achille de Lauzières and Angelo Zanardini (Milan, 1884).

Don Giovanni (*Il dissoluto punito, ossia Il Don Giovanni*; 'The Libertine Punished, or Don Giovanni'). Opera in two acts by Mozart to a libretto by Lorenzo Da Ponte after Giovanni Bertati's libretto for Gazzaniga (1787) (Prague, 1787).

Don Juan. 1. Tone-poem, op. 20 (1887 or 1888–9), by Richard Strauss, based on a poem by Nikolaus Lenau.
  2. The legend of the libertine Don Juan has been the basis of many plays since that of Tirso di Molina, *El burlador de Sevilla y el convidado de piedra* (1630), and of many operas, the best known being Mozart's *Don Giovanni*. Other composers who have treated the subject include Alessandro Melani (1669), Gazzaniga (1787), Vincenzo Fabrizi (1787), Pacini (1832), Dargomïzhsky (*The* *Stone Guest*, 1872), Alfano (1914, revised 1941), and Goossens (1937).
  3. *Don Juan, ou Le Festin de pierre*. Ballet-pantomime in one act and three scenes by Gluck to a scenario by Gasparo Angiolini, who also choreographed it (Vienna, 1761).

Donna del lago, La ('The Lady of the Lake'). Opera (*melodramma*) in two acts by Rossini to a libretto by Andrea Leone Tottola after Walter Scott's poem *The Lady of the Lake* (1810) (Naples, 1819).

Donne di buon umore, Le. *See* GOOD-HUMOURED LADIES, THE.

Donnerstag aus Licht ('Thursday from Light'). Opera in a greeting, three acts, and a farewell, by Stockhausen to his own libretto (Milan, 1981), the 'first day' of *Licht*.

Don Pasquale. Opera (*dramma buffo*) in three acts by Donizetti to a libretto by Giovanni Ruffini and the composer after Angelo Anelli's libretto for Stefano Pavesi's *Ser Marcantonio* (1810) (Paris, 1843).

Don Quichotte. Opera (*comédie-héroïque*) in five acts by Massenet to a libretto by Henri Cain after Jacques Le Lorrain's play *Le Chevalier de la longue figure* (1904), itself based on Miguel de Cervantes's novel *Don Quixote* (1605, 1615) (Monte Carlo, 1910).

Don Quichotte à Dulcinée. Three songs by Ravel (1932–3) for voice and orchestra, settings of poems by Paul Morand; Ravel arranged them for voice and piano (1932–3). They were written for a film based on Miguel de Cervantes, starring Fyodor Chaliapin, and were Ravel's last works.

Don Quixote. 1. Tone-poem, op. 35 (1896–7), by Richard Strauss, subtitled 'Fantastische Variationen über ein Thema ritterlichen Charakters' ('Fantastic Variations on a Theme of Knightly Character'); it has an introduction, theme and ten variations, and finale, with solo parts for cello and viola.

2. Miguel de Cervantes's novel, published in two parts (1605, 1615), has inspired many works for the stage. Operas on the subject have been composed by, among many others, J. P. Förtsch, F. B. Conti, Boismortier, Paisiello, Piccinni, Salieri, Garcia, Mendelssohn, Mercadante, Donizetti, Macfarren, and Falla. Purcell wrote incidental music to a play by Thomas D'Urfey. Ballets include Marius Petipa's (1869), with music by Léon Minkus, and those with music by Petrassi, Ibert, and Gerhard.

Don Rodrigo. Opera in three acts by Ginastera to a libretto by Alejandro Casona after a historical legend (Buenos Aires, 1964).

'Dorian' Toccata and Fugue. Nickname of J. S. Bach's Toccata and Fugue in D minor for organ, ʙᴡᴠ538 (1708–17), so called because the original copy omitted a B♭ from the key signature, thus suggesting the Dorian mode.

Down by the Greenwood Side. Dramatic pastoral in one act by Birtwistle to a libretto by Michael Nyman after an English mummers' play and 'The Ballad of the Cruel Mother'; it is for soprano, mime, and speech, and chamber ensemble (Brighton, 1969).

Down in the Valley. Folk opera in one act by Weill to a libretto by Arnold Sundgaard (Bloomington, IN, 1948).

Dragon of Wantley, The. Burlesque opera in three acts by John Frederick Lampe to a libretto by Henry Carey (London, 1737).

Dream of Gerontius, The. Choral work, op. 38 (1900), by Elgar, for mezzo-soprano, tenor, bass, chorus, semi-chorus, and orchestra, a setting of Cardinal Newman's poem (1866). Although it is frequently described as an oratorio, the term does not appear on the score and Elgar did not approve of it being referred to as such.

Dreigroschenoper, Die ('The Threepenny Opera'). Play with music in a prologue and three acts by Weill to a libretto by Bertolt Brecht, translated by Elisabeth Hauptmann, after John Gay's The *Beggar's Opera*, with additional poems by François Villon and Rudyard Kipling (Berlin, 1928).

Drei Pintos, Die ('The Three Pintos'). Opera (*komische Oper*) in three acts by Weber to a libretto by Theodor Hell (Carl Gottfried Theodor Winkler) after Carl Seidel's story *Der Brautkampf*. Weber worked on it in 1820–1 but left it unfinished; his grandson Carl showed the sketches to Mahler, who completed the score (Leipzig, 1888).

Dresden Amen. A threefold setting made by J. G. Naumann for the royal chapel in Dresden which achieved celebrity after being quoted by Mendelssohn in his 'Reformation' Symphony (1832) and later by Wagner in *Parsifal* (1882). In both cases it symbolizes the solemnity of religious faith.

Drowned Out. Orchestral work (1992–3) by Mark-Anthony Turnage; its title derives from a passage in William Golding's novel *Pincher Martin* (1956) which describes a man drowning.

'Drum' Mass. *See* PAUKENMESSE.

Drumming. Work (1971) by Reich for two solo women's voices (wordless), piccolo, four pairs of tuned bongos, three marimbas, and three glockenspiels; a 90-minute work written in response to Reich's visit to Ghana, it was highly influential in the last quarter of the 20th century.

'Drumroll' Symphony (*Paukenwirbel-Symphonie*). Nickname of Haydn's Symphony no. 103 in E♭ major (1795), so called because it opens with a roll on the kettledrums.

Due Foscari, I. Opera (*tragedia lirica*) in three acts by Verdi to a libretto by Francesco Maria Piave after Byron's play *The Two Foscari* (1821) (Rome, 1844).

Duenna, The. 1. Opera (*The Duenna, or The Double Elopement*) in three acts by Thomas Linley (i) and Thomas Linley (ii) to a libretto by Richard Brinsley Sheridan (London, 1775).

2. Opera in three acts by Gerhard to his own libretto after Sheridan (broadcast 1949; first staged Madrid, 1992).

3. Opera by Prokofiev; *see* BETROTHAL IN A MONASTERY.

Duke Bluebeard's Castle. *See* BLUEBEARD'S CASTLE.

'Dumbarton Oaks' Concerto. Popular name for Stravinsky's Concerto in E♭ major for chamber orchestra; 'in the style of the Brandenburg Concertos', it was commissioned by Mr and Mrs R. W. Bliss and first performed in 1938 at Dumbarton Oaks, their house in Washington, DC.

'Dumky' Trio. Nickname of Dvořák's Piano Trio op. 90 (1890–1); it is so called because it consists of six *dumka* movements, each in a different key, a *dumka* being a kind of Slavonic folk ballad in which elegiac and fast tempos alternate. Dvořák's piano pieces opp. 35 (1876) and op. 12 no. 1 (1884) are both also called 'Dumka'.

Dwarf, The. *See* ZWERG, DER.

Early One Morning. An English folksong, of which the melody's origin is unknown.

Earth Dances. Orchestral work (1985–6) by Birtwistle.

Ebony Concerto. Concerto by Stravinsky for clarinet (an 'ebony stick' in jazz slang) and orchestra, composed for the jazz musician Woody Herman, who gave its first performance with his band (New York, 1946).

Écho et Narcisse. Opera (*drame lyrique*) in a prologue and three acts by Gluck to a libretto by Baron Ludwig Theodor von Tschudi after Ovid's *Metamorphoses* (Paris, 1779).

Éclat/multiples ('Fragment/Multiples'). Orchestral work by Boulez, expanded from his *Éclat* (1965) for 15 instruments; he made this second version in 1971 and it remained a 'work in progress'.

Ecuatorial. Work (1932–4) by Varèse for bass (solo or unison chorus), four trumpets, four trombones, piano, organ, two ondes martenot, and percussion (six players), a setting of a prayer from the *Popol Vuh* of the Maya Quiché, translated by Father Jimines.

Edgar. Opera (*dramma lirico*) in three (originally four) acts by Puccini to a libretto by Ferdinando Fontana after Alfred de Musset's dramatic poem *La Coupe et les lèvres* (1832) (Milan, 1889; four-act version, Buenos Aires, 1905).

Egdon Heath. Orchestral work, op. 47 (1927), by Holst; subtitled 'Homage to Hardy', it was inspired by a passage in Thomas Hardy's *The Return of the Native* (1878) describing the Dorset landscape.

Egisto ('Aegisthus'). Opera (*favola dramatica musicale*) in a prologue and three acts by Cavalli to a libretto by Giovanni Faustini (Venice, 1643).

Egmont. Overture and incidental music, op. 84 (1809–10), by Beethoven, composed for Johann Wolfgang von Goethe's play; the overture is often performed separately.

1812. Concert overture, op. 49 (1880), by Tchaikovsky; written for the Moscow Exhibition, it commemorates Napoleon's retreat from Moscow in 1812 and incorporates *La Marseillaise* and the Tsarist national anthem. The original idea was for it to be performed in a Moscow square with large orchestra, military band, cathedral bells, and cannon fire. It is sometimes still performed with a cannon (especially at the popular Tchaikovsky evenings in the Royal Albert Hall, London, and at summer concerts outdoors).

Eight Lines. Piece by Reich for two string quartets, two piccolos (doubling flute), two clarinets (doubling bass clarinet), and two pianos; it was composed in 1979 (as Octet) and revised in 1983.

Eight Songs for a Mad King. Music-theatre piece by Maxwell Davies to a libretto by Randolph Stow and King George III; in eight movements, it is for a male actor-singer and ensemble (including railway whistle, didjeridu, and chains) (London, 1969).

Eine kleine Nachtmusik. *See* KLEINE NACHTMUSIK, EINE.

Ein' feste Burg (ist unser Gott) ('A Safe Stronghold (is our God)'). Lutheran Reformation hymn, a setting of Psalm 46 to a tune adapted from a plainchant melody. Bach used it in his Cantata no. 80 and it has been quoted in several other works including Meyerbeer's *Les Huguenots*, Mendelssohn's 'Reformation' Symphony, and Wagner's *Kaisermarsch*.

Einigkeit und Recht und Freiheit ('Unity, Justice, and Freedom'). German national anthem. The words, from a poem of aspiration for the unity of the German peoples, written before the revolutions of 1848, are by August Heinrich Hoffmann von Fallersleben (1798–1874) from a poem by Walther von der Vogelweide. It is sung to the tune Haydn wrote for the Austrian national anthem (*see* EMPEROR'S HYMN). In 1922 it was adopted by Germany, Hoffmann von Fallersleben's poem beginning with the words 'Deutschland über alles', and from 1933 it was sung in conjunction with the Nazi party Horst Wessel Song. In 1950 the Federal Republic replaced the first verse with the third; the German Democratic Republic the previous year adopted its own anthem, *Auferstanden aus Ruinen*. *Einigkeit und Recht und Freiheit* is the anthem of the reunited Germany.

Einstein on the Beach. Opera in four acts and five 'knee plays' (intermezzos) by Philip Glass and Robert Wilson to a libretto by Christopher Knowles, Lucinda Childs, and Samuel M. Johnson (Avignon, 1976).

Eislermaterial. Music-theatre piece by Heiner Goebbels for male voice and ensemble, reworkings of Eisler's songs (mostly to texts by Bertolt Brecht) (Berlin, 1998).

Electrification of the Soviet Union, The. Opera in two acts by Nigel Osborne to a libretto by Craig Raine after Boris Pasternak's novel *The Last Summer* (1929) and his poem *Spectorsky* (1930) (Glyndebourne, 1987).

Elegy for Young Lovers. Opera in three acts by Henze to a libretto by W. H. Auden and Chester Kallman (Schwetzingen, 1961).

Elektra. Opera (*Tragödie*) in one act by Richard Strauss to a libretto by Hugo von Hofmannsthal after his play (1903), itself based on Sophocles' tragedy *Electra* (Dresden, 1909).

Elijah (*Elias*). Oratorio, op. 70 (1846), by Mendelssohn for soprano, contralto, tenor, bass, and treble soloists, boys' chorus, chorus, and orchestra, a setting of a text by Julius Schubring after 1 Kings 17–19.

Elisabetta, regina d'Inghilterra ('Elizabeth, Queen of England'). Opera (*dramma*) in two acts by Rossini to a libretto by Giovanni Schmidt after Carlo Federici's play (1814) based on Sophia Lee's novel *The Recess* (1783–5) (Naples, 1815).

Elisir d'amore, L' ('The Love Potion'). Opera (*melodramma giocoso*) in two acts by Donizetti to a libretto by Felice Romani after Eugène Scribe's libretto for Auber's *Le Philtre* (1831) (Milan, 1832).

El salón México. *See* SALÓN MÉXICO, EL.

Emerald Isle, The. Opera in two acts by Sullivan to a libretto by Basil Hood; it was unfinished when Sullivan died and was completed by Edward German (London, 1901).

Emilia di Liverpool (*L'eremitaggio di Liverpool*; 'The Hermitage of Liverpool'). Opera (*dramma semiseria*) in two acts by Donizetti to a libretto based on the anonymous one for Vittorio Trento's *Emilia di Laverpaut* after Stefano Scatizzi's play of that name (Naples, 1824; revised Naples, 1828).

'Emperor' Concerto. Nickname of Beethoven's Piano Concerto no. 5 in E♭ major op. 73 (1809); the title may have been added by the pianist and publisher J. B. Cramer.

'Emperor' Quartet (*Kaiserquartett*). Nickname of Haydn's String Quartet in C major op. 76 no. 3 (1797), so called because the slow movement is a set of variations on ***'Emperor's Hymn'.

Emperor's Hymn. Austrian national anthem from the time of its composition (1797) by Haydn to 1918, when the Austro-Hungarian Empire was replaced by the new Austrian Republic. A new anthem was chosen, *Deutsch-Österreich, du herrliches Land*, but it was never popular and Haydn's melody was reinstated with new words. As Germany had also selected Haydn's tune, which it still uses (*see* EINIGKEIT UND RECHT UND FREIHEIT), in 1947 Austria chose another anthem, *Land der Berge*. Haydn was originally commissioned to write the tune to words by Lorenz Leopold Haschka (1749–1827), 'Gott erhalte Franz den Kaiser', for the emperor's birthday; he subsequently used it as the basis of a set of variations in his String Quartet op. 76 no. 3 (1797), thereafter called the 'Emperor' Quartet or *Kaiserquartett*.

Emperor Waltz. *See* KAISER-WALZER.

Enchanted Lake, The (*Volshebnoye ozero*). Symphonic poem (1909) by Lyadov.

Enchantress, The (*Charodeyka*). Opera in four acts by Tchaikovsky to a libretto by Ippolit Vasil'yevich Shpazhinsky after his own tragedy of that title (1885) (St Petersburg, 1887).

Endless Parade. Work (1986–7) by Birtwistle for trumpet, vibraphone, and strings.

Enfance du Christ, L' ('The Childhood of Christ'). Oratorio, op. 25 (1850–4), by Berlioz for seven soloists, chorus, and orchestra, to his own text.

Enfant et les sortilèges, L' ('The Child and the Spells'). Opera (*fantaisie lyrique*) in one act by Ravel to a libretto by Colette (Monte Carlo, 1925).

Enfant prodigue, L' ('The Prodigal Son').

1. Cantata by Debussy for soprano, tenor, and baritone soloists, chorus, and orchestra, to a text by Ernest Guiraud. With it Debussy won the Prix de Rome in 1884; it was first performed in Paris that year with a two-piano accompaniment and was revised in 1906–8. It was staged as an opera in London in 1910.

2. Opera in five acts by Auber to a libretto by Eugène Scribe (Paris, 1850).

3. Ballet by Prokofiev; *see* PRODIGAL SON, THE.

English Cat, The. A story for singers and instrumentalists in two acts by Henze to a text by Edward Bond after Honoré de Balzac's *Peines de coeur d'une chatte anglaise* (1840) (Schwetzingen, 1983; in German translation).

English Suites. Six keyboard suites by J. S. Bach, BWV806–11 (*c*.1715); the source of the title is unknown but it may refer to an English dedicatee.

'Enigma' Variations. Popular name for Elgar's orchestral work, op. 36 (1899), the *Variations on an Original Theme* ('Enigma'). Dedicated 'to my friends pictured within', the work consists of 14 musical portraits, each headed with initials or a pseudonym from which the subjects' identities have been deduced; the last is a portrait of the composer himself. Elgar revised the finale for the third performance. Frederick Ashton choreographed a one-act ballet, *Enigma Variations* (1968), using the original finale.

En saga ('A Saga'). Symphonic poem, op. 9 (1892, revised 1902), by Sibelius.

Entführung aus dem Serail, Die ('The Abduction from the Seraglio'). *Singspiel* in three acts by Mozart to a libretto by Christoph Friedrich Bretzner (*Belmont und Constanze, oder Die Entführung aus dem Serail*), adapted and enlarged by Gottlieb Stephanie the younger (Vienna, 1782).

Éolides, Les ('The Breezes'). Symphonic poem (1875–6) by Franck; it is based on a poem of the same name by C. M. R. Leconte de Lisle describing the flight of the breezes, daughters of Aeolus, over the southern lands.

Eonta. Work (1963–4) by Xenakis for piano, two trumpets, and three trombones.

Epifanie. Work by Berio for soprano and orchestra, settings of texts by Bertolt Brecht, Marcel Proust, James Joyce, Antonio Machado, Edoardo Sanguineti, and Claude Simon; it was composed in 1961, revised in 1965, and revised further in 1992 as *Epiphanies*.

Épigraphes antiques, Six. *See* SIX ÉPIGRAPHES ANTIQUES.

Epitaffio per Federico García Lorca ('Epitaph for Federico García Lorca'). Work (1951–3) by Nono. It is in three parts: 'España en la corazón', for soprano, baritone, small chorus, and instruments; 'Y su sangre ya viene cantando', for flute and chamber orchestra; and 'Memento: romance de la guardia civil española', for female speaker, speaking chorus, chorus, and orchestra.

Ercole amante ('Hercules in Love'). Opera in a prologue and five acts by Cavalli to a libretto by Francesco Buti after Ovid's *Metamorphoses* (book 9) (Paris, 1662).

Erlkönig ('The Erl-King'). Song (1814) by Schubert to a poem from Johann Wolfgang von Goethe's ballad opera *Die Fischerin* (1782). Several composers set the poem, including Reichardt, Zelter, and Loewe, and Beethoven left sketches of a setting.

Ermione ('Hermione'). Opera (*azione tragica*) in two acts by Rossini to a libretto by Andrea Leone Tottola after Jean Racine's *Andromaque* (1667) (Naples, 1819).

Ernani. Opera (*dramma lirico*) in four parts by Verdi to a libretto by Francesco Maria Piave after Victor Hugo's play *Hernani* (1830) (Venice, 1844).

Ernste Gesänge, Vier. *See* VIER ERNSTE GESÄNGE.

Eroberung von Mexico, Die ('The Conquest of Mexico'). Music-theatre piece in four acts by Wolfgang Rihm to a libretto by the composer after Anton Artaud's scenario *La Conquête du Mexique* (1933) and essay *Le Théâtre de Séraphin* (1936), Octavio Paz's cycle of poems *Raiz del hombre* (1937), and three anonymous native American poems (16th century) (Hamburg, 1992).

'Eroica' Symphony. Beethoven's Symphony no. 3 in E♭ major (1803–4); he composed it in honour of Napoleon and planned to call it *Bonaparte*, but when he heard that Napoleon had declared himself emperor, in 1804, he changed the title to *Sinfonia eroica, composta per festiggiare il sovvenire di un grand uomo* ('Heroic Symphony, Composed to Celebrate the Memory of a Great Man') and dedicated it to Prince Franz Joseph von Lobkowitz. The finale is a set of variations on a theme Beethoven had used in earlier works, notably *Die *Geschöpfe des Prometheus* (1801) and the *'Eroica' Variations.

'Eroica' Variations. Beethoven's Piano Variations in E♭ major op. 35 (1802), so called because he used the theme in the finale of the *'Eroica' Symphony. Beethoven had used the theme in the seventh of his *Contredanses* for orchestra (1802) and in *Die *Geschöpfe des Prometheus* (1800–1); the work is therefore also known as the *Prometheus Variations*.

Erste Walpurgisnacht, Die ('The First Walpurgis Night'). Cantata, op. 60 (1832, revised 1843), by Mendelssohn, a setting for chorus and orchestra of Johann Wolfgang von Goethe's ballad. Walpurgis Night is the spring festival when witches ride to the Brocken in the Harz Mountains.

Erwartung ('Expectation'). Monodrama (composed in 1909) in one act by Schoenberg for soprano and orchestra, to a libretto by Marie Pappenheim (Prague, 1924).

Esclarmonde. Opera (*opéra romanesque*) in four acts by Massenet to a libretto by Alfred Blau and Louis de Gramont after *Parthenopoeus de Blois*, a medieval *chanson de geste* (Paris, 1889).

Esmeralda. Opera in four acts by Dargomïzhsky to a libretto by the composer and two assistants after Victor Hugo's libretto *Esmeralda*, on his own novel *Notre-Dame de Paris* (1831) (Moscow, 1847).

Espaces du sommeil, Les ('The Space of Sleep'). Work (1975) by Lutosławski for baritone and orchestra, a setting of a poem by Robert Desnos (1900–45).

España ('Spain'). Rhapsody (1883) by Chabrier for orchestra.

Espansiva, Sinfonia. *See* SINFONIA ESPANSIVA.

Estampes ('Engravings'). Three piano pieces by Debussy (1903): *Pagodes* ('Pagodas'), *La Soirée dans Grenade* ('Evenings in Granada'), and *Jardins sous la pluie* ('Gardens in the Rain'); the first was orchestrated by André Caplet, and the second by Henri Busser.

Esther. Oratorio (1732) by Handel to a text after Jean Racine; in its first version it was a masque (?Cannons, ?1718); Handel revised and expanded it into an oratorio, with additions to the text by Samuel Humphreys.

Estro armonico, L' ('The Harmonious Inspiration'). Vivaldi's op. 3 (Amsterdam, 1711 and 1712), 12 concertos for different solo combinations of violin, two violins, four violins, and cello, with orchestra and continuo. Six of them were transcribed by J. S. Bach.

Eternal Father, Strong to Save. Hymn of which the words were written by William Whiting (1825–78) in 1860; it was published in the *Anglican Hymn Book* (1868) in its original version, with words beginning 'O thou who bidd'st the ocean deep'. Revised versions appeared in *Hymns Ancient and Modern* (1861) and the appendix to *Psalms and Hymns* (1869). It has become known as the Royal Navy's hymn.

Et exspecto resurrectionem mortuorum ('And I look forward to the resurrection of the dead'). Work (1964) by Messiaen for 18 woodwind, 16 brass, and three percussionists (scoring which makes it suitable for vast spaces); each of its five movements is headed with a biblical quotation.

Étoile, L' ('The Star'). *Opéra bouffe* in three acts by Chabrier to a libretto by Eugène Leterrier and Albert Vanloo (Paris, 1877).

Étoile du nord, L' ('The North Star'). *Opéra comique* in three acts by Meyerbeer to a libretto by Eugène Scribe (Paris, 1854).

Études d'exécution transcendante d'après Paganini ('Transcendental Studies after Paganini'). Work for solo piano by Liszt, transcriptions of six of Paganini's violin caprices, including *La campanella*; they were composed in 1838–9 and revised in 1851 as *Grandes études de Paganini*. Liszt also composed a set of 12 *Études d'exécution transcendante* ('Transcendental Studies') in 1851.

Études symphoniques (*Symphonische Etüden*; 'Symphonic Studies'). Schumann's op. 13 (1834–7), for solo piano; it was originally called *Etüden im Orchestercharakter für Pianoforte von Florestan und Eusebius* and was revised in 1852 as *Études en formes de variations* as a theme, 12 variations, and a finale. Five variations that were originally suppressed were published posthumously in 1873.

Eugene Onegin (*Yevgeny Onegin*). Opera in three acts by Tchaikovsky to a libretto by the composer and Konstantin Stepanovich Shilovsky after Aleksandr Pushkin's novel in verse (1833) (Moscow, 1879 (privately); Moscow, 1881).

Eulenspiegels lustige Streiche, Till. See TILL EULENSPIEGELS LUSTIGE STREICHE.

Euridice. 1. Opera in five scenes by Peri, with some arias and choruses by Caccini, to a libretto by Ottavio Rinuccini after Ovid's *Metamorphoses* (Florence, 1600). It is the first opera of which the music is extant. **2.** Opera in a prologue and five scenes by Caccini, to a libretto by Rinuccini (Florence, 1602).

Europeras 1–5. A series of 'operas' by Cage: *Europeras 1 and 2*, in one act, are for ten and nine singers, respectively, who perform random extracts from over 60 operas (Frankfurt, 1987); *Europeras 3 and 4* also consist of fragments from the opera repertory, *Europera 3* being for six singers, 12 record-players playing 78s, and two singers, and *Europera 4* for two singers, a wind-up gramophone, and a pianist (London, 1990); *Europera 5* is for two singers performing extracts from arias, a wind-up gramophone playing old opera recordings, a pianist playing opera transcriptions, and a local radio station (Buffalo, NY, 1991).

Euryanthe. Opera (*grosse heroisch-romantische Oper*) in three acts by Weber to a libretto by Helmina von Chézy after the early French romance *L'Histoire du très-noble et chevalereux prince Gérard, comte de Nevers, et de la très-virtueuse et très chaste princesse Euriant de Savoye, sa mye* (Vienna, 1823).

Éventail de Jeanne, L' ('Jeanne's Fan'). Ballet in ten numbers choreographed by Yvonne Franck and Alice Bourgat (Paris, 1928). Madame Jeanne Dubost gave the ten leaves of her fan to ten composers, asking each to compose one dance number for the students of her ballet school; they were Ravel, Pierre-Octave Ferroud, Ibert, Roland-Manuel, Marcel Delannoy, Roussel, Milhaud, Poulenc, Schmitt, and an unknown tenth.

Évocations. Three symphonic poems (1910–12) by Roussel; they are *Les Dieux dans l'ombre des cavernes*, *La Ville rose*, and *Aux bords du fleuve sacré*.

Excursions of Mr Brouček, The (*Výlety páně Broučkovy*). Opera in two parts by Janáček to his own libretto, with contributions from František Gellner, Viktor Dyk, and F. S. Procházka after Svatopluk Čech's *Brouček* novels (1888, 1889) (Prague, 1920).

Exody (23.59.59). Orchestral work (1996–7) by Birtwistle.

'...explosante-fixe...'. Work by Boulez for electronic flute and chamber orchestra, composed between 1971 and 1993.

Exsultate, jubilate ('Rejoice, be Glad'). Motet by Mozart, κ165/158*a* (1773), for soprano, organ, and orchestra; the second part is the famous setting of the 'Alleluia'. It was written for the castrato Venanzio Rauzzini.

Fabbrica illuminata, La ('The Illuminated Factory'). Work (1964) by Nono for mezzo-soprano and pre-recorded tape, to texts by Giovanni Scabia and Cesare Pavese.

Façade. 'Entertainment' (1921–2) by Walton for reciter and ensemble (flute doubling piccolo, clarinet doubling bass clarinet, saxophone, trumpet, percussion, and cello); the speaker, or speakers, declaim in notated rhythm poems by Edith Sitwell. It has undergone several revisions, the last in 1942; the final published version (*Façade I*) comprises 21 items. Eight unpublished numbers were performed in 1977 under the title *Façade Revived*, three of them having been rejected before publication and three others (nos. 4, 6, and 7) having been substituted by the composer; this version was revised, and was performed in 1979 as *Façade II*. Walton arranged the work without the poems as two orchestral suites (1926 and 1938). The score has been used by several choreographers (including Frederick Ashton) and many numbers from it have been arranged by different composers for a variety of instruments.

Facing Goya. Opera in two acts by Michael Nyman to a libretto by Victoria Hardie (Santiago de Compostela, 2000).

Fair Maid of Perth, The. *See* JOLIE FILLE DE PERTH, LA.

Fairy Queen, The. Semi-opera in five acts by Henry Purcell to a libretto anonymously adapted from Shakespeare's *A Midsummer Night's Dream* (1595–6) (London, 1692). The score was lost by 1700 but was found in the library of the Royal Academy of Music in 1901.

Fairy's Kiss, The. *See* BAISER DE LA FÉE, LE.

Fall and Resurrection. Work (1999) by Tavener, to biblical texts, for chorus and orchestra.

Fall of the House of Usher, The. Chamber opera in a prologue and two acts by Philip Glass to a libretto by Arthur Yorinks after Edgar Allan Poe's short story (1839) (Cambridge, MA, 1988). Larry Sitsky wrote an opera on the same subject (Sydney, 1973) and Debussy made some sketches (1908–17) towards a projected *La Chute de la maison Usher*.

Falstaff. 1. Opera (*commedia lirica*) in three acts by Verdi to a libretto by Arrigo Boito after Shakespeare's *The Merry Wives of Windsor* (1600–1) and *Henry IV*, parts 1 and 2 (1597–8) (Milan, 1893). Among composers who have written operas on the same subject are Salieri (1799), Balfe (1838), Holst (**At the Boar's Head*), and Vaughan Williams (**Sir John in Love*). *See also* LUSTIGEN WEIBER VON WINDSOR, DIE.

    2. Symphonic study, op. 68 (1902–13), by Elgar.

Fanciulla del West, La ('The Girl of the Golden West'). Opera in three acts by Puccini to a libretto by Guelfo Civinini and Carlo Zangarini after David Belasco's play *The Girl of the Golden West* (1905) (New York, 1910).

Fanfare for the Common Man. Work (1942) by Copland for brass and percussion, one of a series of wartime fanfares commissioned by Eugene Goossens.

Fantaisies symphoniques. The subtitle of Martinů's Symphony no. 6 (1951–3).

Fantasia Concertante on a Theme of Corelli. Work (1953) by Tippett for strings; the theme is from Corelli's Concerto Grosso op. 6 no. 2 and the work quotes Bach's Fugue on themes of Corelli. It was composed in the tercentenary year of Corelli's birth.

Fantasia contrappuntistica. Work (1910) by Busoni for solo piano; a second version was composed also in 1910, a third in 1912, and a fourth (for two pianos) in 1922. It is subtitled 'Preludio al corale "Gloria al Signori nei Cieli" e fuga a quattro soggetti obbligati sopra un fragmento di Bach'. Busoni based it on the Contrapunctus XVIII from *The Art of Fugue* in a desire to complete Bach's unfinished fugue; he created a fourth subject (Bach composed only three) and added a fifth. Wilhelm Middelschulte, the work's dedicatee, adapted it for organ.

Fantasia on a Theme by Thomas Tallis. Work by Vaughan Williams for double string orchestra and string quartet; it was composed in 1910 and later revised, the last revision being in 1919. The theme is the third (*Why Fumeth in Fight*) of nine psalm tunes Tallis composed in 1567 for Archbishop Parker's psalter. *See also* TALLIS'S CANON.

Fantasia on British Sea Songs. Henry Wood's orchestral arrangement of traditional and other songs, made in 1905 to celebrate the centenary of Nelson's victory at Trafalgar. Malcolm Sargent added a solo contralto to the last of the nine songs, 'Rule, Britannia!', when they were first performed at the Promenade Concerts in London, and they became the traditional finale to the last night of the Proms.

Fantasia on 'Greensleeves'. Ralph Greaves's arrangement (1934) for one or two flutes, harp, and strings of an interlude from Vaughan Williams's opera *Sir John in Love*, the middle section being based on the folksong *Lovely Joan*. There are several other arrangements, none by Vaughan Williams.

Fantasiestücke. *See* PHANTASIESTÜCKE.

Fantastic Symphony. *See* SYMPHONIE FANTASTIQUE.

'Farewell' Symphony (*Abschiedsymphonie*). Nickname of Haydn's Symphony no. 45 in F♯ minor (1772); in the extra (Adagio) finale, the orchestra is gradually reduced until only two violins are left. Haydn composed it to persuade Prince Nicolaus, his employer, not to prolong the court musicians' stay at the prince's summer residence at Eszterháza but to allow them to return to their families at Eisenstadt. At the symphony's first performance the players left as their music finished, leaving only Haydn and the violinist Luigi Tomasini.

Faschingsschwank aus Wien ('Viennese Carnival Prank'). Schumann's op. 26 (1939–40), for solo piano; subtitled 'Fantasiebilder', it is in five movements.

Fate. *See* OSUD.

Faust. 1. Opera (*romantische Oper*) in two acts by Spohr to a libretto by Joseph Carl Bernard after the Faust legend (not J. W. von Goethe) (Prague, 1816; revised London, 1852).

2. Opera in five acts by Gounod to a libretto by Charles-François Barbier and Michel Carré after Carré's *Faust et Marguerite* and Johann Wolfgang von Goethe's *Faust* part 1 (in the French translation by Gérard de Nerval) (Paris, 1859).

See also DAMNATION DE FAUST, LA; DOKTOR FAUST; HISTORIA VON D. JOHANN FAUSTEN; MEFISTOFELE; VOTRE FAUST; and the works immediately following this entry.

Faust Overture, A (*Eine Faust-Ouvertüre*). Concert overture (1840) by Wagner, originally intended as the first movement of a Faust symphony.

'Faust', Scenes from Goethe's. Overture and six movements (1844–53) by Schumann, for soloists, chorus, and orchestra, settings of texts by Johann Wolfgang von Goethe.

Faust Symphony, A (*Eine Faust-Symphonie*). Symphony (1854–7) by Liszt, based on Johann Wolfgang von Goethe's play. It is subtitled 'in drei Charakterbildern' ('in three character studies'), the movements being 'Faust', 'Gretchen', and 'Mephistopheles'; the last has alternative endings, one purely orchestral, the other a setting for tenor, men's chorus, and orchestra of the final words of Goethe's play.

Favola d'Orfeo, La. *See* ORFEO, L'.

Favorite, La (*La favorita*; 'The Favoured One'). Opera in four acts by Donizetti to a libretto by Alphonse Royer and Gustave Vaëz with additions by Eugène Scribe, partly after *L'Ange de Nisada* (derived from Baculard d'Arnaud's *Le Comte de Comminges*) onto which the story of Eleonora di Guzman is grafted (Paris, 1840).

Fearful Symmetries. Orchestral work (1988) by John Adams.

Fedeltà premiata, La ('Fidelity Rewarded'). Opera (*dramma giocoso*) in three acts by Haydn to a libretto by Giambattista Lorenzi (Eszterháza, 1781).

Fedora. Opera in three acts by Giordano to a libretto by Arturo Colautti after Victorien Sardou's play (1882) (Milan, 1898).

Feen, Die ('The Fairies'). Opera (*grosse romantische Oper*) in three acts by Wagner (his first) to his own libretto after Carlo Gozzi's *La donna serpente* (1762) (Munich, 1888).

Felix namque (Lat., 'For thou art happy'). The title of a large number of 15th- and 16th-century English keyboard pieces (by Redford, Tallis, Blitheman, and Tomkins among others) that set the plainchant *Felix namque es*, an offertory for certain Marian Masses.

Fennimore and Gerda. Opera in 11 pictures (scenes) by Delius to his own libretto after Jens Peter Jacobsen's novel *Niels Lyhne* (1880) (Frankfurt, 1919). The intermezzo performed as a concert item is based on material in the last scene.

Feria. Orchestral work (1997) by Magnus Lindberg.

Fernand Cortez, ou La Conquête du Mexique ('Hernán Cortez, or The Conquest of Mexico'). Opera in three acts by Spontini to a libretto by Étienne de Jouy and Joseph Alphonse d'Esmenard (Paris, 1809).

Ferne Klang, Der ('The Distant Sound'). Opera in three acts by Schreker to his own libretto (Frankfurt, 1912).

Feste romane ('Roman Festivals'). Symphonic poem (1928) by Respighi.

Festgesang ('Festive Hymn'). Work (1840) by Mendelssohn for male voices to words by A. E. Prölss; it was composed for the festival in Leipzig to celebrate the 400th anniversary of the invention of the Gutenberg printing press (**Lobgesang* was composed for the same occasion). The second number of *Festgesang* was adapted by W. H. Cummings to the words of the hymn *Hark, the Herald Angels Sing*.

Festin de l'araignée, Le ('The Spider's Banquet'). Ballet-pantomime by Roussel to a scenario by Gilbert de Voisins, choreographed by Léo Staats (Paris, 1913); Roussel made an orchestral suite (1912) from it.

Festivo ('Festive'). Orchestral work by Sibelius, the third of his *Scènes historiques*, op. 25 (1899, revised 1911).

Fêtes galantes. Two sets of three songs (1891, 1904) by Debussy to poems by Paul Verlaine; the second of the second set was orchestrated by Roland-Manuel (1923) and the third by Louis Beydts (1929).

Feuersnot ('Fire Famine'). Opera (*Singgedicht*, 'sung poem' or 'lyrical epigram') in one act by Richard Strauss to a libretto by Ernst von Wolzogen after a Dutch legend (Dresden, 1901).

Feux d'artifice ('Fireworks'). Piano piece by Debussy, no. 12 of his *Préludes* book 2.

'Fiddle' Fugue. Nickname of J. S. Bach's Fugue in D minor for organ, BWV539:2 (1720), so called because it is an arrangement of the second movement of the Sonata in G minor for solo violin (1720).

Fidelio (*Leonore, oder Der Triumph der ehelichen Liebe*; 'Leonore, or The Triumph of Married Love'). Opera in two (originally three) acts by Beethoven to a libretto by Joseph von Sonnleithner (1805), with revisions by Stephan von Breuning (1806) and Georg Friedrich Treitschke (1814), after Jean-Nicolas Bouilly's French libretto *Léonore, ou L'Amour conjugal*; the first version was given its premiere in Vienna in 1805, the second version in 1806, and the final version in 1814. Beethoven wrote four overtures for the opera: the first three are known as the *Leonore overtures; the fourth, the Fidelio overture (the one now usually played), was composed for the final version.

Fierrabras (Fierabras). Opera (heroisch-romantische Oper) in three acts by Schubert to a libretto by Josef Kupelwieser after J. G. G. Büsching and F. H. von der Hagen's story in Buch der Liebe (1809) and Friedrich de la Motte Fouqué's Eginhard und Emma (1811); commissioned in 1823, it was not performed until after Schubert's death, in a revised form (Karlsruhe, 1897).

Fiery Angel, The (Ognennïy angel; 'The Flaming Angel'). Opera in five acts by Prokofiev to his own libretto after the novel by Valery Bryusov (1907); it was composed between 1919 and 1923 and revised in 1926–7 (Paris, 1955). It was given in concert in Paris in 1954 as L'Ange de feu. Prokofiev used material from the opera in his Symphony no. 3 in C minor (1928).

'Fifths' Quartet. Nickname of Haydn's String Quartet in D minor op. 76 no. 2 (1797), so called because the opening theme begins with melodic leaps of a 5th.

Fille aux cheveux de lin, La ('The Girl with the Flaxen Hair'). Piano piece (1910) by Debussy, no. 8 of his Préludes book 1; it was suggested by a poem by C. M. R. Leconte de Lisle.

Fille du régiment, La (La figlia del reggimento; 'The Daughter of the Regiment'). Opéra comique in two acts by Donizetti to a libretto by Jules-Henri Vernoy de Saint-Georges and Jean-François-Alfred Bayard (Paris, 1840). It was later revised to an Italian translation by Calisto Bassi (Milan, 1840).

Fille mal gardée, La ('The Unchaperoned Girl'). Ballet in two acts to a scenario and with choreography by Jean Bercher Dauberval, originally to a potpourri of French songs and airs (Bordeaux, 1789). Hérold created a new score, using some of the earlier music, extracts from Donizetti and Rossini, and his own contributions (Paris, 1828). Peter Ludwig Hertel provided music for a new version (Berlin, 1864). The ballet was recreated with a new score by John Lanchbery, based on Hérold but with Hertel's 'Clog Dance', choreographed by Frederick Ashton (London, 1960).

Fingal's Cave. See HEBRIDES, THE.

Finlandia. Orchestral work, op. 26 (1899, revised 1900), by Sibelius; it was written as the final tableau of a nationalist pageant to raise money for a press pension fund in Helsinki. Its patriotic fervour (though no folksong material was used) has led to its adoption as a symbol of Finnish nationalist aspirations.

Finta giardiniera, La ('The Feigned Gardener's Girl'). Opera buffa in three acts by Mozart to a libretto of unknown authorship which had been set by Anfossi (1774) (Munich, 1775).

Finta semplice, La ('The Feigned Simpleton'). Opera buffa in three acts by Mozart to a libretto by Carlo Goldoni with alterations by Marco Coltellini (Salzburg, 1769).

Firebird, The (*Zhar'-ptitsa*). Ballet in two scenes by Stravinsky to a scenario by Mikhail Fokine, who also choreographed it for Serge Diaghilev's Ballets Russes (Paris, 1910). The original score was in 19 sections but Stravinsky wrote a five-movement suite from the ballet in 1911 and revised it in 1919; he composed a ten-movement version in 1945.

Fireworks. Orchestral fantasy, op. 4 (1908), by Stravinsky.

Fireworks Music (*Music for the Royal Fireworks*). Instrumental suite (1749) by Handel written for and played at the fireworks display at Green Park, London, to mark the Peace of Aix-la-Chapelle; Handel composed it for wind band but later added string parts. It has become well known in modern orchestrations by Hamilton Harty and Charles Mackerras.

Fitzwilliam Virginal Book (Cambridge, Fitzwilliam Museum, 32.g29, Mus. MS 168). A manuscript volume left to Cambridge University in 1816 by Viscount Fitzwilliam as part of a valuable collection of books, music, and paintings. It was once called 'Queen Elizabeth's Virginal Book', but it is now known not to have belonged to her. The manuscript constitutes the largest single collection of Jacobean keyboard music (not only for the virginals), containing nearly 300 pieces. At one time it was thought to have been compiled by Francis Tregian, a Catholic recusant, between 1609 and 1619, but the nature of its connection with his family is now unclear. Although most of the major keyboard composers of the time are represented (e.g. Byrd, Bull, and Farnaby), there are some surprising omissions, for example Orlando Gibbons. A modern edition was published in 1894–9 (revised 1979–80).

Five Mystical Songs. Choral work (1911) by Vaughan Williams, settings for baritone, chorus, and orchestra of poems by George Herbert.

Five Tudor Portraits. Choral suite (1935) by Vaughan Williams, settings for alto or mezzo-soprano, baritone, chorus, and orchestra of poems by John Skelton (?1460–1529).

Five Variants of 'Dives and Lazarus'. Work by Vaughan Williams for strings and harp (or harps), composed in 1939 for the New York World Fair. 'Dives and Lazarus' is an English folksong.

Flavio (*Flavio, re di Longobardi*; 'Flavio, King of the Lombards'). Opera in three acts by Handel to a libretto by Nicola Francesco Haym adapted from Matteo Noris's *Il Flavio Cuniberto* (1682, revised 1696) (London, 1723).

Fledermaus, Die ('The Bat'). Operetta (*komische Operette*) in three acts by Johann Strauss (ii) to a libretto by Carl Haffner and Richard Genée after Henri Meilhac and Ludovic Halévy's vaudeville *Le Réveillon* (1872) (Vienna, 1874).

Fliegende Holländer, Der ('The Flying Dutchman'). Opera (*romantische Oper*) in one act, later three acts, by Wagner to his own libretto after Heinrich Heine's *Aus den Memoiren des Herren von Schnabelewopski* (1831) (Dresden, 1843).

Flight. Opera in three acts by Jonathan Dove to a libretto by April de Angelis (Glyndebourne, 1998).

Flight of the Bumble Bee, The. Orchestral interlude in Rimsky-Korsakov's opera *The Tale of Tsar Saltan* (1899–1900) in which a prince becomes a bee and stings his villainous relatives. Many (often spurious) arrangements have been made for a variety of solo instruments.

Flock Descends into the Pentagonal Garden, A. Orchestral work (1977) by Takemitsu.

Flood, The. Musical play by Stravinsky to a libretto arranged by Robert Craft from the book of Genesis and the York and Chester mystery plays; for three speakers, tenor and two basses, chorus, orchestra, and actors, it was performed on television in 1962 and staged in Hamburg in 1963.

Florentinische Tragödie, Eine ('A Florentine Tragedy'). Opera in one act by Zemlinsky to his own libretto after Oscar Wilde's play fragment *A Florentine Tragedy* (1908) (Stuttgart, 1917).

Flos campi ('Flower of the Field'). Suite (1925) by Vaughan Williams for solo viola, (wordless) chorus, and small orchestra; each of the six movements is prefaced by a Latin quotation from the Song of Solomon.

Floss der 'Medusa', Das ('The Raft of the *Medusa*'). 'Popular and military oratorio' (or cantata) by Henze, to a text by Ernst Schnabel, for narrator, soprano and baritone soloists, boys' chorus, chorus, and orchestra, a requiem for Che Guevara. It is based on the same story as J.-L.-A.-Théodore Géricault's painting: when the French frigate *Medusa* ran aground (1816), the officers escaped in the boats, leaving the crew to their fate on an improvised raft. The premiere (Hamburg, 1968) was aborted because of a clash between students and police; the first performance was in Vienna in 1971.

Flowers o' the Forest. Scottish lament of which the original words are lost, but many lines were incorporated into an 18th-century version by Jane Elliott; the forest is a district of Selkirk and Peebles and the flowers are young men killed in battle. The tune is played by pipers at the Remembrance Day ceremony at the Cenotaph, London.

Flying Dutchman, The. *See* FLIEGENDE HOLLÄNDER, DER.

Fontane di Roma ('Fountains of Rome'). Symphonic poem (1914–16) by Respighi; its four sections depict the sensations of the composer when he was contemplating four of the city's most famous fountains—Valle Giulia at dawn, Tritone in mid-morning, Trevi at noon, and Villa Medici at sunset.

Force of Destiny, The. *See* FORZA DEL DESTINO, LA.

Forelle, Die ('The Trout'). Song (1817) for voice and piano by Schubert to words by C. F. D. Schubart; it exists in five versions that differ only slightly, the last version (1821) having a five-bar piano prelude. Schubert used the theme for variations in his Piano Quintet in A major D667, known as the **'Trout' Quintet.

Forgotten Rite, The. Orchestral work ('prelude') by John Ireland (1913); the unspecified rite is associated with the Channel Islands.

Formazione. Orchestral work (1988) by Berio.

'Forty-Eight, The'. Popular title of Bach's collection of 48 preludes and fugues The *Well-Tempered Clavier*.

Forty-part motet. *See* SPEM IN ALIUM NUNQUAM HABUI.

Forza del destino, La ('The Force of Destiny'). Opera in four acts by Verdi to a libretto by Francesco Maria Piave after Angel de Saavedra, Duke of Rivas's play *Don Alvaro, o La fuerza del sino* (1835), with a scene from Friedrich von Schiller's play *Wallensteins Lager* (1799), translated by Andrea Maffei (St Petersburg, 1862); Verdi revised it, with additional text by Antonio Ghislanzoni (Milan, 1869).

Fountains of Rome. *See* FONTANE DI ROMA.

Four Last Songs. 1. *See* VIER LETZTE LIEDER.
    2. Songs (1954–8) for voice and piano by Vaughan Williams to words by Ursula Vaughan Williams.

4′ 33″. Piece (1952) by Cage consisting of four minutes and 33 seconds of silence for any instrument or instruments.

Four Sacred Pieces. *See* QUATTRO PEZZI SACRI.

Four Saints in Three Acts. 'An opera to be sung' in a prologue and four acts by Virgil Thomson to a libretto by Gertrude Stein with a scenario by Maurice Grosser (Hartford, CT, 1934).

Four Sea Interludes. Orchestral work, op. 33*a* (1945), by Britten, consisting of the descriptive orchestral interludes from his opera **Peter Grimes* ('Dawn', 'Sunday Morning', 'Moonlight', and 'Storm'); the Passacaglia (op. 33*b*) from the opera is often performed with the interludes.

Four Seasons, The (*Le quattro stagioni*). Four violin concertos by Vivaldi, the first four of his *Il cimento dell'armonia e dell'inventione* op. 8, a set of 12 violin concertos published in two volumes (Amsterdam, 1725); they are 'Spring' in E major, 'Summer' in G minor, 'Autumn' in F major, and 'Winter' in F minor.

Four Serious Songs. *See* VIER ERNSTE GESÄNGE.

Four Temperaments, The. 1. Subtitle (*De fire Temperamenter*) of Nielsen's Symphony no. 2, op. 16 (1901–2); it was inspired by a painting of that name, each movement being descriptive of one of the medieval 'temperaments' of human character: choleric, phlegmatic, melancholic, and sanguine.
    2. Subtitle of Hindemith's Theme and Variations for piano and strings (1940), the four variations denoting the melancholic, sanguine, phlegmatic, and choleric.

Fra Diavolo (*Fra Diavolo, ou L'Hôtellerie de Terracine*; 'Brother Devil, or The Inn of Terracina'). *Opéra comique* in three acts by Auber to a libretto by Eugène Scribe (Paris, 1830).

Fragmente; Stille, an Diotima ('Silence, for Diotima'). Work (1980) by Nono for string quartet.

Francesca da Rimini. The story of the adulterous lovers Paolo and Francesca in canto V of Dante Alighieri's *Inferno* (*c.*1307–21) has been the basis of several compositions, the best known being the following.
   1. Symphonic fantasia by Tchaikovsky, op. 32 (1876), based on an illustration by Gustave Doré.
   2. Opera in a prologue, two scenes, and an epilogue by Rakhmaninov to a libretto by Modest Tchaikovsky (Moscow, 1906).
   3. Opera in four acts by Zandonai to a libretto by Tito Ricordi (ii) from the play by Gabriele D'Annunzio (Turin, 1914).

Francs-juges, Les ('The Judges of the Secret Court'). Overture, op. 3 (1826), by Berlioz, composed for an opera he later abandoned.

Frankenstein!! 'Pan-Demonium' (1978) by H. K. Gruber for baritone and orchestra to a text by H. C. Artmann.

Fratres. Work (1977) by Pärt for chamber ensemble, later arranged for several smaller-scale instrumental combinations.

Frauenliebe und -leben ('Woman's Love and Life'). Song cycle, op. 42 (1840), by Schumann for female voice and piano, settings of eight poems by Adalbert von Chamisso.

Frau ohne Schatten, Die ('The Woman without a Shadow'). Opera in three acts by Richard Strauss to a libretto by Hugo von Hofmannsthal after his own story (1919) (Vienna, 1919).

Freischütz, Der ('The Freeshooter'). Opera (*romantische Oper*) in three acts by Weber to a libretto by Johann Friedrich Kind after Johann August Apel and Friedrich Laun's *Gespensterbuch* (1811) (Berlin, 1821).

Freitag aus Licht ('Friday from Light'). Opera in a greeting, two acts, and a farewell by Stockhausen to his own libretto (Leipzig, 1996), the 'first day' of *Licht*.

French Suites. Six keyboard suites, bwv812–17 (1722–5), by J. S. Bach; first drafts for several of them are in the first *Clavier-Büchlein* (1722) for Anna Magdalena Bach. The title does not appear in any source traceable to Bach and the suites are not in the style of Bach's French contemporaries.

Frescoes of Piero della Francesca. A group of three orchestral works (1953) by Martinů.

Friedenstag ('Day of Peace'). Opera in one act by Richard Strauss to a libretto by Joseph Gregor (Munich, 1938).

'Frog' Quartet (*Froschquartett*). Nickname of Haydn's String Quartet in D major op. 50 no. 6 (1787), which has a 'croaking' theme in the finale.

Froissart. Concert overture, op. 19 (1890), by Elgar; the title refers to a passage in Walter Scott's *Old Mortality* in which Claverhouse speaks of his enthusiasm for the historical romances and *Chronicles* of the French writer

Jean Froissart (1337–1410), and the score is headed by a quotation from John Keats: 'When chivalry lifted up her lance on high'.

From Bohemia's Woods and Fields (*Z Českých luhů a hájů*). Symphonic poem (1875) by Smetana, the fourth of his cycle *Má vlast and often played separately.

From My Life (*Z mého života*). Smetana's String Quartet no. 1 in E minor (1876); although he gave the same title to his other string quartet, no. 2 in D minor (1882–3), a similarly autobiographical work, it is now used only for the first, which culminates in a sustained high E in the finale, representing the whistling in Smetana's ear that heralded his deafness.

From Stone to Thorn. Work by Maxwell Davies (1971) for mezzo-soprano, basset clarinet, guitar, harpsichord, and percussion, a setting of a text by George Mackay Brown.

From the Diary of Virginia Woolf. Song cycle (1974) by Dominick Argento, for medium voice and piano, settings of eight songs by Virginia Woolf.

From the House of the Dead (*Z mrtvého domu*). Opera in three acts by Janáček to his own libretto after Fyodor Dostoyevsky's *Zapiski iz myortvogo doma* ('Memoirs from the House of the Dead', 1862) (Brno, 1930).

From the New World. *See* NEW WORLD, FROM THE.

Froschquartett. *See* 'FROG' QUARTET.

Frühlingsrauschen. *See* RUSTLE OF SPRING.

Frühlingssonate. *See* 'SPRING' SONATA.

Funeral Music. Orchestral work (1954–8) by Lutosławski, composed as a homage to Bartók.

Funeral Music for Queen Mary. Music by Henry Purcell, composed in 1694 for the funeral of Queen Mary II. It is a setting of two sentences from the Burial Service, the anthem *Thou Know'st, Lord, the Secrets of our Hearts*, two canzonas for slide trumpets and trombones, and a march originally written as incidental music for a scene in Thomas Shadwell's play *The Libertine* (1692). Some of the music was played at Purcell's own funeral in Westminster Abbey in 1695.

Funiculì, funiculà. Song (1880) by Luigi Denza composed in honour of the opening of the Naples funicular railway. It was quoted in *Aus Italien* (1886) by Richard Strauss, who apparently thought it was a genuine folksong.

Für Elise ('For Elise'). Beethoven's Bagatelle in A minor for piano (1808–10), of which the autograph score is inscribed 'Für Elise am 27. April zur Erinnerung von L. v. Bthvn'.

Gambler, The (*Igrok*). Opera in four acts by Prokofiev to his own libretto after Fyodor Dostoyevsky's short story (1866) (Brussels, 1929). Prokofiev arranged *Four Portraits* for orchestra from the score (1931).

Gamblers, The (*Igroki*). Opera by Shostakovich after Nikolay Gogol's play (1832); it was begun in 1941 but was left unfinished. It was performed in concert (Leningrad, 1978) after the composer's death. Krzysztof Meyer completed it in three acts (Wuppertal, 1983).

Game of Cards. *See* JEU DE CARTES.

Garden of Fand, The. Symphonic poem (1913) by Bax; Fand is a heroine of Irish legend whose garden was the sea.

Garland for the Queen, A. A collection of songs for unaccompanied mixed chorus by ten British composers to texts by ten contemporary poets, written to celebrate the coronation of Elizabeth II in 1953 (to emulate *The *Triumphes of Oriana* of Elizabeth I's reign). They are Bliss's *Aubade for Coronation Morning* (Henry Reed), Bax's *What is it Like to be Young and Fair?* (C. Bax), Tippett's *Dance, Clarion Air* (Christopher Fry), Vaughan Williams's *Silence and Music* (Ursula Wood), Lennox Berkeley's *Spring at this Hour* (Paul Dehn), Ireland's *The Hills* (James Kirkup); Howells's *Inheritance* (Walter De la Mare), Finzi's *White Flowering Days* (Edmund Blunden), Rawsthorne's *Canzonet* (Louis MacNeice), and Rubbra's *Salutation* (Christopher Hassall).

Gaspard de la nuit. Three piano pieces (1908) by Ravel: *Ondine*, *Le Gibet*, and *Scarbo*; the title of the set is from Aloysius Bertrand's *Histoires vermoulous et poudreuses du Moyen Age* (1842).

'Gastein' Symphony. A supposedly lost symphony in C major by Schubert, of which nothing survives, said to have been composed in 1825 in Gastein, in Tyrol; it is now thought to have been the *'Great' Symphony in C major.

Gawain. Opera in two acts by Birtwistle to a libretto by David Harsent after the anonymous Middle English poem *Sir Gawain and the Green Knight* (London, 1991; revised and shortened, London, 1994).

Gayané (*Gayaneh*). Ballet in four acts by Khachaturian to a scenario by Konstantin Derzhavin, choreographed by Nina Anisimova (Molotov-Perm, 1942); it was revised in 1945 (Leningrad). In 1943 Khachaturian made three suites from the score, which includes the famous Sabre Dance.

Gazza ladra, La ('The Thieving Magpie'). Opera (*melodramma*) in two acts by Rossini to a libretto by Giovanni Gherardini after the comedy *La Pie voleuse* (1815) by J. M. T. Badouin d'Aubigny and Louis-Charles Caigniez (Milan,

1817). Although the opera was not revived until the mid-20th century, the overture, in Rossini's most brilliant style, always remained very popular.

Geistertrio. *See* 'GHOST' TRIO.

General William Booth Enters into Heaven. Song (1914) by Ives for voice and piano, a setting of lines from a poem by Vachel Lindsay; it also exists in a version for bass soloist, chorus, and chamber orchestra.

Genoveva. Opera in four acts by Schumann to his own libretto after Ludwig Tieck's *Leben und Tod der heiligen Genoveva* (1799) and Friedrich Hebbel's *Genoveva* (1843) (Leipzig, 1850).

German Requiem, A (*Ein deutsches Requiem*). Choral work, op. 45 (1865–8), by Brahms for soprano and baritone soloists, chorus, and orchestra; it is so called because the text is not that of the Roman Catholic liturgy but passages selected by Brahms from Martin Luther's translation of the Bible.

Gesang der Jünglinge ('Song of the Young Boys'). Electronic work (1955–6) by Stockhausen in which a boy's voice, speaking and singing the *Benedicite*, is transformed, multiplied, and combined with electronic sounds; it is played by five spatially separated loudspeaker groups.

Geschöpfe des Prometheus, Die ('The Creatures of Prometheus'). Ballet in an overture, introduction, and 16 numbers by Beethoven, choreographed by Salvatore Viganò (Vienna, 1801). Beethoven used two themes from the finale in other works: one, in G major, is no. 11 of his *12 contredanses* for orchestra (1802); another, in E♭ major, is used in no. 7 of the *Contredanses*, as the theme of the 'Eroica' Variations, and in the finale of the 'Eroica' Symphony. The overture is often performed as a concert item.

Ghosts of Versailles, The. *Opera buffa* in two acts by John Corigliano to a libretto by William M. Hoffman after Beaumarchais's play *La Mère coupable* (1792) (New York, 1991).

'Ghost' Trio (*Geistertrio*). Nickname of Beethoven's Piano Trio in D major op. 70 no. 1 (1808), so called because of the atmosphere of the slow movement, which includes 'mysterious' chromatic chords and tremolos.

Gianni Schicchi. Opera in one act by Puccini to a libretto by Giovacchino Forzano after a passage from Dante Alighieri's *Inferno* (*c*.1307–21), the third part of Puccini's *Il* *trittico (New York, 1918).

'Giant' Fugue. Nickname of J. S. Bach's organ chorale *Wir glauben all an einen Gott* BWV680, from part 3 of the *Clavier-Übung*, so called because of the giant strides of the bass figure played on the pedals.

Gioconda, La ('The Joyful Girl'). Opera (*dramma lirico*) in four acts by Ponchielli to a libretto by 'Tobia Gorrio' (Arrigo Boito) after Victor Hugo's play *Angélo, tyran de Padoue* (1835) (Milan, 1876); the third act includes the *Dance of the Hours.

Gioielli della Madonna, I (*Der Schmuck der Madonna*; 'The Jewels of the Madonna'). Opera in three acts by Wolf-Ferrari to a libretto by Carlo Zangarini and Enrico Golisciani (Berlin, 1911); the text was revised in 1933.

Giorno di regno, Un ('King for a Day'; *Il finto Stanislao*, 'The False Stanislaus'). Opera (*melodramma giocoso*) in two acts by Verdi to a libretto by Felice Romani (probably revised by Temistocle Solera) from his libretto for Gyrowetz's *Il finto Stanislao* (1818) after Alexandre Vincent Pineu-Duval's play *Le Faux Stanislas* (1808) (Milan, 1840).

Giovanna d'Arco ('Joan of Arc'). Opera (*dramma lirico*) in a prologue and three acts by Verdi to a libretto by Temistocle Solera partly after Friedrich von Schiller's play *Die Jungfrau von Orleans* (1801) (Milan, 1845).

Gipsy Baron, The. *See* ZIGEUNERBARON, DER.

Girl I Left Behind Me, The. Song traditionally associated with the British army, played on occasions of departure. The (anonymous) tune, sometimes known as *Brighton Camp*, can be traced back to the end of the 18th century (Brighton Camp was held in 1793–5), as can the (anonymous) words.

Girl of the Golden West, The. *See* FANCIULLA DEL WEST, LA.

Giselle, ou Les Wilis ('Giselle, or The Wilis'). Ballet in two acts by Adam to a scenario by Jules-Henri Vernoy de Saint-Georges and Théophile Gautier after a story by Heinrich Heine, choreographed by Jean Coralli and Jules Perrot (Paris, 1841); modern productions are based on Marius Petipa's last St Petersburg production of 1884. The Wilis are the ghosts of girls who die before their intended marriages.

Giulio Cesare (*Giulio Cesare in Egitto*; 'Julius Caesar in Egypt'). Opera in three acts by Handel to a libretto by Nicola Francesco Haym adapted from Giacomo Francesco Bussani's *Giulio Cesare in Egitto* (1677) and a later version of the same libretto (1685) (London, 1724).

Giustino ('Justin'). Opera (*dramma per musica*) in three acts by Handel to a libretto adapted anonymously from Pietro Pariati's *Giustino* (1711) as revised for Vivaldi (1724), after Nicolò Beregan's *Il Giustino* (1683) (London, 1737).

Glagolitic Mass (*Glagolská mše*; *Mša glagolskaja*). Cantata (1926) by Janáček for soprano, alto, tenor, and bass soloists, chorus, orchestra, and organ, a setting of an old Slavonic church text adapted by Miloš Weingart.

Gloriana. Opera in three acts by Britten to a libretto by William Plomer after Lytton Strachey's *Elizabeth and Essex*; it was commissioned by Covent Garden for the coronation of Elizabeth II, who attended its first performance on 8 June 1953.

'Gloria tibi Trinitas', Missa. Mass for six voices by Taverner that uses the antiphon *Gloria tibi Trinitas* as a cantus firmus.

Glückliche Hand, Die ('The Fortunate Hand'; 'The Knack'). Drama with music in one act by Schoenberg to his own libretto (Vienna, 1924); it contains mimed parts for a man and a woman, and the use of coloured lights is of fundamental importance.

Gnarly Buttons. Work (1996) for clarinet and chamber ensemble by John Adams.

Gnossiennes. Three piano pieces (1890) by Satie; their 'oriental' flavour was influenced by a visit to the Paris Exposition in 1889.

God Save the King [Queen]. British national anthem. Its origins are obscure but the tune seems first to have appeared in print in 1744 and is the first national anthem. The earliest recorded performances of it were in an arrangement by Thomas Arne in 1745 at the Theatre Royal, Drury Lane, London, following Sir John Cope's defeat at Prestonpans. In the 19th century the tune was used as the national anthem of many other countries, including Denmark, Sweden, Switzerland, Russia, and the USA, with many different texts. It has been incorporated into works by several composers including Beethoven, Weber, Paganini, Marschner, Brahms, and Debussy; Ives used it as the theme for his *Variations on 'America' for organ (1891–2). Several composers have made choral arrangements of it, notably Elgar (1902) and Britten (1961).

God's Liar. Opera in two acts by John Casken to a libretto by Emma Warner after Leo Tolstoy's novella *Father Sergius* (1898) (London, 2001).

'Goldberg' Variations. Work for harpsichord by J. S. Bach, BWV988, 30 variations on an original theme, published in part 4 of the *Clavier-Übung* (1741–2); Bach gave a copy of them to Johann Gottlieb Goldberg (1727–56), harpsichordist to Count Keyserlingk, but it is unlikely that they were commissioned by him.

Golden Age, The (*Zolotoy vek*). Ballet in three acts by Shostakovich to a scenario by Aleksandr Ivanovsky, choreographed by Emanuel Kaplan and Vasily Vainonen (Leningrad, 1930); Shostakovich made an orchestral suite (op. 22a) from the score.

Golden Cockerel, The (*Zolotoy petushok*; *Le Coq d'or*). Opera ('dramatized fable') in a prologue, three acts, and an epilogue by Rimsky-Korsakov to a libretto by Vladimir Bel'sky after Pushkin's poem (1834), itself based on 'The House of the Weathercock' and 'Legend of the Arabian Astrologer' from Washington Irving's *The Alhambra* (Moscow, 1909); it was completed in 1907 but its performance was banned during the composer's lifetime because of its satire on autocracy. The habit of referring to it as *Le Coq d'or* arose from Serge Diaghilev's production, choreographed by Mikhail Fokine, in which the roles were enacted by dancers while singers sat at the side of the stage (Paris and London, 1914).

Golden Legend, The. Cantata (1886) by Sullivan, for soloists, chorus, and orchestra, to a text based on H. W. Longfellow's poem.

'Golden' Sonata. Nickname of Henry Purcell's Trio Sonata in F major for two violins and continuo, the ninth of *Ten Sonata's in Four Parts* published posthumously in 1697.

Gold und Silber ('Gold and Silver'). Waltz by Lehár composed for a gold and silver ball given by Prince Metternich in 1902.

Golem. Opera in two parts ('Prelude' and 'Legend') by John Casken to a libretto by the composer with Pierre Audi (London, 1989). Several composers have written operas on the legend, notably Larry Sitsky (1993).

Golliwogg's Cake-Walk. The sixth piece of Debussy's piano suite *Children's Corner*.

Gondoliers, The (*The Gondoliers; or, The King of Barataria*). Operetta in two acts by Sullivan to a libretto by W. S. Gilbert (London, 1889).

Good Friday Music (*Karfreitagzauber*). The music in Act III of Wagner's *Parsifal* heard as Parsifal is anointed in preparation for his entry into the castle of the Grail; it is sometimes performed as a separate concert piece.

Good-Humoured Ladies, The (*Le donne di buon umore*). Choreographic comedy in one act by Vincenzo Tommasini based on harpsichord sonatas by Domenico Scarlatti to a scenario after Carlo Goldoni; it was choreographed by Leonid Massine (Rome, 1917). Tommasini arranged a suite for orchestra from the score.

Gothic Symphony. Havergal Brian's first symphony (1919–27); the last of its four movements is a setting of the *Te Deum* for soprano, alto, tenor, and bass soloists, quadruple chorus, children's chorus, four brass bands, and large orchestra.

Götterdämmerung ('The Twilight of the Gods'). Opera in three acts by Wagner to his own libretto, the 'third day' of Der *Ring des Nibelungen*.

Goyescas ('Pieces in the Style of Goya'; *Los majos enamorados*; 'Youth in Love').
   1. Suite for piano (1911) by Granados, six pieces in two sets, inspired by the paintings of Francisco Goya; it is usually performed with the addition of *El pelele* ('The Worthless Man').
   2. Opera in one act (three scenes) by Granados to a libretto by Fernando Periquet (New York, 1916); it was expanded and scored from the above piano pieces.

Gradualia. Latin motets by Byrd: the first book (1605) contains 32 for five voices, 20 for four voices, and 11 for three voices; the second (1607) contains 9 for six voices, 17 for five voices, and 19 for four voices.

Gradus ad Parnassum ('Steps to Parnassus'). A title, referring to the mountain sacred to Apollo and the Muses, given from the early 18th century onwards to dictionaries of Latin prosody. It was also given to two musical publications, each designed to lead to a form of musical perfection: Fux's treatise on counterpoint (Vienna, 1725, rev. 1842) and Clementi's three-volume collection of piano studies op. 44 (Leipzig and Paris, 1817, 1819, 1826). The first piece in Debussy's *Children's Corner* (1906–8) for piano is called *Doctor Gradus ad Parnassum* and is a parody of a child's attempt to play a Clementi study.

Graf von Luxemburg, Der ('The Count of Luxembourg'). Operetta in three acts by Lehár to a libretto by A. M. Willner and Robert Bodanzky (Vienna, 1909).

Grand Duo. Subtitle given by the publisher (in 1838) to Schubert's Sonata in C major for piano duet, D812 (1824); it was once thought to be a piano version of a 'lost' symphony but that theory has been discredited. There are orchestral versions of the work by Joseph Joachim and Anthony Collins.

Grande-Duchesse de Gérolstein, La ('The Grand-Duchess of Gerol-stein'). *Opéra bouffe* in three acts by Offenbach to a libretto by Henri Meilhac and Ludovic Halévy (Paris, 1867).

Grande Messe des morts ('High Mass for the Dead'). French title of Berlioz's Requiem op. 5 (1837), for tenor solo, boys' chorus, chorus, and orchestra; it was revised in 1852 and 1867.

Grand Macabre, Le ('The Grand Macabre'). Opera in two acts by Ligeti to a libretto by the composer and Michael Meschke after Michel de Ghelder-ode's play *La Balade du Grand Macabre* (1934) (Stockholm, 1978).

Great Gatsby, The. Opera in two acts by John Harbison to a libretto by the composer after F. Scott Fitzgerald's novel (1925) (New York, 1999).

Great Learning Paragraphs 1 and 2, The. Work (1972) by Cornelius Cardew for chorus, percussion, organ, and banners, a setting of a text by Confucius translated by the composer.

'Great' Symphony Name by which Schubert's Symphony no. 9 in C major (1825–8) is known.

Greek. Opera in two acts by Mark-Anthony Turnage to a libretto by the composer and Jonathan Moore after Steven Berkoff's play *Greek* (1980) (Munich, 1988).

Greek Passion, The (*Řecké pašije*). Opera in four acts by Martinů to his own libretto with Nikos Kazantzakis after Jonathan Griffin's translation (1954) of Kazantzakis's novel *Christ Recrucified* (1948) (Zürich, 1961).

Greensleeves. Old English tune. It was twice mentioned by Shakespeare in *The Merry Wives of Windsor* (1600–1) and by other writers of this and later periods. The first known reference to it occurs in 1580 in the Registers of the Stationers' Company, where it is called 'a new Northern Dittye'. There are ballads to the tune, which was also adopted for sacred use (e.g. 'Green Sleeves moralised to the Scriptures', 1580). During the 17th-century Civil War it was adopted by the Cavaliers, who set many political ballads to it. From this period the tune was sometimes known as *The Blacksmith*; Pepys alluded to it under that name in his diary (23 April 1660). In the 20th century it was used by Vaughan Williams in his opera *Sir John in Love*, by Holst in his *St Paul's Suite* and Suite no. 2 for military band, and by Busoni in *Turandot*.

Gretchen am Spinnrade ('Gretchen at the Spinning-Wheel'). Song (1814) for voice and piano by Schubert (D118) to words from Johann Wolfgang von Goethe's *Faust*.

Grisélidis. Opera (*conte lyrique*) in a prologue and three acts by Massenet to a libretto by Armand Sylvestre and Eugène Morand after their dramatization (1891) of the medieval French story (Paris, 1901).

Grosse Fuge ('Great Fugue'). Beethoven's fugue for string quartet in Bb major op. 133 (1825–6), composed as the last movement of his String Quartet op. 130; Beethoven wrote another finale for op. 130 in 1826 and published the *Grosse Fuge* separately in 1827.

Grosse Orgelmesse ('Great Organ Mass'). Haydn's Mass no. 4 in Eb major (1768 or 1769), so called because of its prominent organ part; its full title is *Missa in honorem Beatae Mariae Virginis* or *Missa Sancti Josephi*. See also KLEINE ORGELMESSE.

Gruppen ('Groups'). Work (1955–7) by Stockhausen for three orchestras; they are placed in different parts of the hall and each plays different music.

Guarany, Il (*O Guarani*; 'The Guaraní'). Opera (*opera-ballo*) in four acts by Carlos Gomes to a libretto by Antonio Scalvini and Carlo D'Ormeville after José de Alencar's novel (1857) (Milan, 1870).

Guide me, o thou great Redeemer. See CWM RHONDDA.

Guide to Strange Places, A. Orchestral work (2001) by John Adams.

Guillaume Tell (*Guglielmo Tell*; 'William Tell'). Opera in four acts by Rossini to a libretto by Étienne de Jouy and Hippolyte-Louis-Florent Bis, assisted by Armand Marrast and Adolphe Crémieux, after Friedrich von Schiller's play *Wilhelm Tell* (1804) (Paris, 1829); the opera's four-movement overture is a popular concert item. Grétry (1791) wrote an opera on the same subject.

Guntram. Opera in three acts by Richard Strauss to his own libretto (Weimar, 1894).

Gurrelieder ('Songs of Gurra'). Work (1900–11) by Schoenberg for solo voices, choruses, and orchestra to a text translated into German by R. F. Arnold from Jens Peter Jacobsen's poems; it is scored for a huge orchestra (including ten horns, four Wagner tubas, six timpani, and iron chains). Gurra is the castle where the 14th-century heroine Tove lived. Schoenberg arranged the *Lied der Waldtaube* ('Song of the Wood Dove') from *Gurrelieder* for voice and chamber orchestra in 1922.

Gwendoline. Opera in three acts by Chabrier to a libretto by Catulle Mendès (Brussels, 1886).

Gymnopédies. Three piano pieces by Satie (1888); the first and third were orchestrated by Debussy in 1896, and the second by Roland-Manuel and Herbert Murrill. The title is said to refer to the ancient Greek annual festival in Sparta in honour of Apollo.

Gypsy Baron, The. See ZIGEUNERBARON, DER.

'Haffner' Serenade. Nickname of Mozart's Serenade in D major K250/248b (1776), so called because it was composed for a marriage in the Haffner family of Salzburg.

'Haffner' Symphony. Nickname of Mozart's Symphony no. 35 in D major K385 (1782); it was originally intended as a serenade (but not the 'Haffner' Serenade, K250/248b) and was written for the Haffner family.

Hail to the Chief. A march played at formal American events to announce the arrival of the President, first used at the inauguration of Martin Van Buren in 1837. The tune (c.1812) is by James Sanderson (1769–?1841), an Englishman, and the words are from Walter Scott's *The Lady of the Lake* (1810).

Halka. Opera in four (originally two) acts by Moniuszko to a libretto by Włodzimierz Wolski after a story from Kazimierz Wójcicki's *Stary gawędy i obrazy* ('Legends and Pictures') (concert performance, Vilnius, 1848; staged Vilnius, 1854); it was revised into its standard version (Warsaw, 1858).

Hallelujah Chorus. Popular name for the chorus that closes part 2 of Handel's *Messiah* in which the word 'Hallelujah' is repeated many times.

Hamlet. Shakespeare's play *Hamlet, Prince of Denmark* (c.1602) has inspired several operas and other works, including the following.

    1. Opera in five acts by Ambroise Thomas to a libretto by Michel Carré and Jules Barbier (Paris, 1868).

    2. Opera in three acts by Humphrey Searle to his own libretto (Hamburg, 1968).

    3. Symphonic poem (1858) by Liszt, composed as a prelude to Shakespeare's play.

    4. Fantasy overture (1888) and incidental music to the play (1891) by Tchaikovsky.

    There are other operas on the subject by Gasparini (1706), Mercadante (1822), Faccio (1865), and Hignard (1888). Ballets on the subject have used music by Tchaikovsky, Liszt, Blacher, Shostakovich, and Copland.

Hamletmaschine, Die ('The Hamlet Machine'). Music-theatre piece in five parts by Wolfgang Rihm to a libretto by the composer after Heiner Müller's play (1977) (Mannheim, 1987).

'Hammerklavier' Sonata. Beethoven's Piano Sonata no. 29 in B♭ major op. 106 (1817–18). Beethoven used the word 'Hammerklavier' (Ger., 'pianoforte') in the subtitle of other piano sonatas, but this is the only one commonly referred to by this appropriate title.

Handel in the Strand. A 'clog dance' by Percy Grainger; it exists in many different arrangements, by the composer and others, including Grainger's own for two pianos and those for orchestra by Henry Wood and Leopold Stokowski.

Handel Variations. *See* VARIATIONS AND FUGUE ON A THEME BY HANDEL.

Handmaid's Tale, The. Opera in two acts by Poul Ruders to a libretto by Paul Bentley after Margaret Atwood's novel (1985) (Copenhagen, 2000).

Hänsel und Gretel. Opera (*Märschenspiel*) in three acts ('Bilder') by Humperdinck to a libretto by Adelheid Wette after a fairy tale (1812–14) by Jacob Ludwig and Wilhelm Carl Grimm (Weimar, 1893).

Hans Heiling. Opera (*grosse romantische Oper*) in a prelude and three acts by Marschner to a libretto by Eduard Devrient after legends about the Hans Heiling Cliffs in Bohemia (Berlin, 1833).

Happy Birthday to You. Song composed by Clayton F. Summy, head of a Chicago music publishing firm at the end of the 19th century. Without knowing it was Summy's copyright, Stravinsky used it as the basis for his short *Greeting Prelude*, composed for Pierre Monteux's 80th birthday in 1955.

Happy End. Comedy with music in three acts by Weill to a book by Dorothy Lane (Elisabeth Hauptmann) and with lyrics by Bertolt Brecht (Berlin, 1929).

Harawi, chant d'amour et de mort ('Harawi, Song of Love and Death'). Song cycle (1945) by Messiaen for soprano and piano, settings of 12 of his own texts; like *Cinq rechants* and the *Turangalîla-symphonie*, they were inspired by the legend of Tristan and Isolda, as well as by Peruvian mythology.

Hark, the Herald Angels Sing. Hymn originally written by Charles Wesley in 1743; it appeared in various hymn publications between 1760 and 1782. W. H. Cummings, organist of Waltham Abbey, set the words to the melody of the second number of Mendelssohn's *Festgesang* and published it in 1856; it soon became very popular.

Harmonie der Welt, Die ('The Harmony of the World'). Opera in five acts by Hindemith to his own libretto based on the life of the 17th-century astronomer Johannes Kepler, author of *De harmonia mundi* (Munich, 1957). Hindemith had previously written a three-movement symphony with the same title (1951).

Harmonielehre. Orchestral piece (1984–5) by John Adams.

Harmoniemesse ('Wind-Band Mass'). Haydn's Mass no. 14 in B♭ major (1802), so called because it makes fuller (though not exclusive) use of wind instruments than do Haydn's other masses.

Harmonious Blacksmith, The. Nickname for the air and variations in Handel's Harpsichord Suite no. 5 in E major from the first set of eight suites (1720); the title was first used after Handel's death and has no connection with the circumstances of the work's composition.

Harmonium. Work (1981) for chorus and orchestra by John Adams, a setting of texts by John Donne and Emily Dickinson.

Harold en Italie ('Harold in Italy'). Symphony, op. 16 (1834), by Berlioz for viola and orchestra, inspired by Byron's *Childe Harold*; it was composed at Paganini's request for a work in which he could display his newly acquired Stradivari viola, but Paganini rejected it because the viola part gave him little opportunity for displays of virtuosity.

'Harp' Quartet. Nickname of Beethoven's String Quartet in E♭ major op. 74 (1809), so called because of the harp-like pizzicato arpeggios in the first movement.

Háry János (*Háry János kalandozásai Nagyabonytul a Burgváráig*; 'János Háry: His Adventures from Nagyabony to the Vienna Burg'). *Singspiel* in a prologue, four adventures (five at the first three performances), and an epilogue by Kodály to a libretto by Béla Paulini and Zsolt Harsányi after János Garay's comic epic *Az obsitos* ('The Veteran') (Budapest, 1926). Kodály arranged a suite (1927) from the opera's orchestral music.

Hashirigaki. Music-theatre piece by Heiner Goebbels to texts by Gertrude Stein, reworkings of songs by the Beach Boys (Lausanne, 2000).

Haunted Manor, The (*Straszny dwór*). Opera in four acts by Moniuszko to a libretto by Jan Chęciński after a story from Kazimierz Wójcicki's *Stary gawędy i obrazy* ('Legends and Pictures') (Warsaw, 1865).

'Haydn' Quartets. Name given to six string quartets by Mozart: no. 14 in G major к387 (1782); no. 15 in D minor к421/417b (1783); no. 16 in E♭ major к428/421b (1783); no. 17 in B♭ major к458, the *'Hunt' Quartet (1784); no. 18 in A major к464 (1785); and no. 19 in C major к465, the *'Dissonance' Quartet (1785). They are so called because he dedicated them to Haydn, who played the first violin in performances in Mozart's house (Mozart played the viola).

Haydn Variations. *See* VARIATIONS ON A THEME BY HAYDN.

Hear My Prayer. Hymn (1844) by Mendelssohn for soprano solo, choir, and organ, composed for Bartholomew's concerts in Crosby Hall, London, where it was first performed in 1845.

Heart of Oak. Patriotic song from the pantomime *Harlequin's Invasion* (1759) by David Garrick, with music by Boyce; it is a topical song alluding to 'this wonderful year' (the victories of Minden, Quiberon Bay, and Quebec). The title is sometimes incorrectly given as 'Hearts of Oak'.

Hebrides, The (*Die Hebriden*; *Fingals Höhle*, 'Fingal's Cave'). Overture, op. 26 (1830), by Mendelssohn; it was based on an earlier version (1829) called *Die einsame Insel* ('The Lonely Island') and was revised in 1832. It is said that Mendelssohn conceived the principal theme while on a visit to the Hebrides and the Isle of Staffa in 1829, but he had in fact jotted it down before that visit.

Heidenröslein ('Little Rose on the Heath'). Song (1815) for voice and piano by Schubert (D257) to words by Johann Wolfgang von Goethe.

Heiligmesse ('Holy Mass'). Nickname of Haydn's Mass no. 10 in B♭ major (1796), so called because of the special treatment of the words 'Holy, Holy' in the Sanctus; its full title is *Missa Sancti Bernardi von Offida*.

Heldenleben, Ein ('A Hero's Life'). Tone-poem, op. 40 (1897–8), by Richard Strauss; the 'hero' is Strauss himself, and one of the work's six sections contains several self-quotations.

Helicopter String Quartet. Work (1993) by Stockhausen for string quartet, four helicopters, and television and audio relay equipment, scene 3 of his *Mittwoch aus Licht*.

Hen, The. *See* POULE, LA.

Herma. Work (1960–1) for piano by Xenakis.

Hérodiade ('Herodias'). Opera in four acts by Massenet to a libretto by Paul Milliet and Henri Grémont (Georges Hartmann) after the story by Gustave Flaubert (1877) (Brussels, 1881; revised Paris, 1884).

Heterophonie. Work (1959–61) by Kagel for 42 solo instruments.

Heure espagnole, L' ('The Spanish Hour'). Opera (*comédie musicale*) in one act by Ravel after the play by Franc-Nohain (Paris, 1911).

Hexaméron. Six variations for piano on a march from Bellini's *I Puritani*; they are by Liszt, Thalberg, Pixis, Herz, Czerny, and Chopin, Liszt also contributing an introduction and a finale. They were composed for a Paris charity concert in 1837 but were not finished in time; Liszt played them on his concert tours of the 1840s.

Hiawatha. Cantata in three parts by Coleridge-Taylor to a text from H. W. Longfellow's poem; the three parts are *Hiawatha's Wedding Feast* (1898), *The Death of Minnehaha* (1899), and *Hiawatha's Departure* (1900).

Hidden Variables. Work (1989) for 15 players by Colin Matthews; he revised it for orchestra in 1991.

Higglety Pigglety Pop! Fantasy opera in one act by Oliver Knussen to a libretto by Maurice Sendak after his children's book (1967) (incomplete version, Glyndebourne, 1984; preliminary version, Glyndebourne, 1985; definitive version, Los Angeles, 1990); it was conceived as a companion-piece to *Where the Wild Things Are*.

Hindenburg. *See* THREE TALES.

Hin und zurück ('There and Back'). Opera ('sketch with music') in one act by Hindemith to a libretto by Marcellus Schiffer (Baden-Baden, 1927); the plot and, in part, the music go into reverse at the halfway point.

Hippolyte et Aricie ('Hippolytus and Aricia'). Opera (*tragédie en musique*) in a prologue and five acts by Rameau to a libretto by Simon-Joseph Pellegrin after Jean Racine's *Phèdre* (1677), Euripides' *Hippolytos*, and Seneca's *Phaedra* (Paris, 1733).

Hirt auf dem Felsen, Der ('The Shepherd on the Rock'). Song (1828) by Schubert, D965, for soprano and piano, with clarinet obbligato, to words by Wilhelm Müller and possibly Helmina von Chézy.

Histoire du soldat ('The Soldier's Tale'). Work in two parts by Stravinsky, 'to be read, played and danced', to a French text by Charles-Ferdinand Ramuz based on a Russian tale; it is for three actors, female dancer, clarinet, bassoon, cornet, trombone, percussion, violin, and double bass (Lausanne, 1918). Stravinsky arranged a five-movement suite from it for violin, clarinet, and piano (1919) and an eight-movement one for the original instrumental ensemble (1920).

Histoires naturelles ('Natural Histories'). Song cycle by Ravel (1906), settings for voice and piano of five poems by Jules Renard. Manuel Rosenthal made a version for voice and orchestra.

Historia von D. Johann Fausten ('History of Dr Johann Faustus'). Opera in three acts and an epilogue by Schnittke to a libretto by Jörg Morgener and the composer after the Spiess chapbook (1587) (Hamburg, 1995).

HMS Pinafore (*HMS Pinafore; or, The Lass that Loved a Sailor*). Operetta in two acts by Sullivan to a libretto by W. S. Gilbert (London, 1878).

Hoboken. Abbreviation for the standard thematic catalogue of the works of Haydn drawn up by the Dutch collector and bibliographer Anthony van Hoboken (1887–1983) and published in Mainz, 1957–78. Haydn's works, especially those without distinguishing title or opus number, are often referred to by Hoboken number, as in the form 'Hob. XVII: 6' (the so-called Variations in F minor for piano).

Hochzeitsmarsch (Ger.). 'Wedding march'. Celebrated examples were composed by Mendelssohn (in his incidental music to *A Midsummer Night's Dream*) and Wagner (in *Lohengrin*).

Hodie (This Day). Christmas cantata (1954) by Vaughan Williams, for soprano, tenor, and baritone soloists, boys' choir, chorus, and orchestra; it is a setting of words from the Bible, John Milton, George Herbert, Thomas Hardy, William Drummond, Miles Coverdale, and Ursula Vaughan Williams.

Holberg Suite (*Fra Holbergs tid*; *Aus Holbergs Zeit*; 'From Holberg's Time'). Piano suite, op. 40 (1884), by Grieg, orchestrated for strings the same year and for full orchestra in 1885; in five movements, it was written to celebrate the bicentenary of the birth of the Norwegian dramatist Ludvig Holberg (1684–1754).

Holidays (*New England Holidays*). Orchestral work by Ives assembled c.1917–19 from four pieces previously published separately; they are *Washington's Birthday* (c.1915–17), *Decoration Day* (c.1915–20), *The Fourth of July* (c.1914–18), and *Thanksgiving and Forefathers' Day* (c.1911–16).

Home, Sweet Home. Melody (1821) by Henry R. Bishop composed for an album of national airs described as 'Sicilian'; with words by J. H. Payne

(1791–1852) it was incorporated in 1823 into Bishop's opera *Clari*. The tune occurs in an altered version in Donizetti's *Anna Bolena*.

Homme armé, L' ('The Armed Man'). A 15th-century melody which was used extensively as the tenor cantus firmus of polyphonic masses between about 1450 and 1600 by such composers as Dufay, Busnois, Ockeghem, Obrecht, Tinctoris, Josquin, La Rue, Senfl, Morales, and Palestrina. Carissimi composed an example in the 17th century. There are also several polyphonic chanson settings, by Robert Morton and Josquin among others. The origin of the melody is uncertain; it has been suggested that it first appeared in a French chanson composed by Morton, an English member of the Burgundian chapel, 1457–75, but it has also been attributed to Busnois; research has revealed that it may have been named after a popular tavern. Maxwell Davies used the tune as the basis of a dramatic chamber piece (1968), later revised (1971) for speaker and ensemble.

Horizon chimérique, L' ('The Fanciful Horizon'). Song cycle, op. 118 (1921), by Fauré, to poems by J. de la Ville de Mirmont.

Horn Signal. Nickname of Haydn's Symphony no. 31 in D major (1765), so called because the slow movement includes calls for four horns.

Housatonic at Stockbridge, The. Third movement of Ives's First Orchestral Set *Three Places in New England*; it was composed *c.*1912–17 and is sometimes performed separately.

House of the Dead, From the. *See* FROM THE HOUSE OF THE DEAD.

Hugh the Drover (*Hugh the Drover, or Love in the Stocks*). Ballad opera in two acts by Vaughan Williams to a libretto by Harold Child (London, 1924).

Huguenots, Les ('The Huguenots'). Grand opera in five acts by Meyerbeer to a libretto by Eugène Scribe and Émile Deschamps (Paris, 1836).

Hungarian Dances (*Ungarische Tänze*). Piano duets by Brahms, published in four volumes between 1852 and 1869; he orchestrated three of the 21 (nos. 1, 3, and 10; 1873) and arranged some for piano solo.

Hungarian Rhapsodies. A group of works for solo piano by Liszt, nos. 1–15 composed between 1846 and 1853, nos. 16–19 composed about 30 years later; they are based on an earlier set (1839–47) of 21 pieces (some also called *Hungarian Rhapsodies*, others *Magyar dallok*) that draw on Hungarian Gypsy music. Several were orchestrated by Franz Döppler with advice from Liszt. The *Hungarian Fantasy* (1853) for piano and orchestra is based on no. 14.

Hungarian Rock. Chaconne (1978) for harpsichord by Ligeti.

Hunnenschlacht ('Battle of the Huns'). Symphonic poem (1856–7) by Liszt; it was inspired by Wilhelm von Kaulbach's painting depicting the combat in the air between the ghosts of the slain Huns and the Christian armies of Emperor Theodoric after the battle of the Catalanian Fields in AD 451.

Hunting: Gathering. Volans's String Quartet no. 2 (1987).

'Hunt' Quartet. Nickname of Mozart's String Quartet no. 17 in B♭ major к458 (1784); one of the *'Haydn' Quartets, it is so called because of the hunting motifs which introduce the first movement.

'Hunt' Symphony. *See* CHASSE, LA.

Hunyadi László. Opera in four acts by Ferenc Erkel to a libretto by Béni Egressy after Lórinc Tóth's play *Hunyadi László* (1841) (Pest, 1844).

Hymnen ('Anthems'). Work (1966–7) by Stockhausen for four-track tape, composed using national anthems. Stockhausen also made a version with solo instruments (1966–7) and a shortened version with orchestra (1969).

Hymn of Jesus, The. Choral work, op. 37 (1917), by Holst for two choruses, female semi-chorus, and orchestra, to a text he translated from the apocryphal Acts of St John.

Hymns from the Rig Veda. Settings (1907–12) by Holst of his translations of words from the Sanskrit; there are 23, in five sets, for different combinations of voices and instruments.

Hymn to St Cecilia. Choral work, op. 27 (1942), by Britten, a setting of a text by W. H. Auden.

Hymn to St Magnus. Work (1972) by Maxwell Davies for soprano and chamber ensemble, a setting of a Latin text after the 12th-century Orcadian hymn.

Hymnus paradisi ('Hymn of Paradise'). Requiem (1938) by Herbert Howells to texts from the Latin Mass for the Dead, Psalm 23, Psalm 121, the Burial Service, and the Salisbury Diurnal (translated by G. H. Palmer); composed in memory of Howells's son, it was not released for performance until 1950.

Hyperprism. Work (1922–3) by Varèse for nine wind and seven percussion players (all using 'noise' instruments).

Iberia. Suite of 12 piano pieces by Albéniz, published in four sets of three (1906–8), with titles evoking Spanish scenes or places; Albéniz orchestrated two of them but the five orchestrated by his friend Enrique Arbós are better known.

Ibéria. Orchestral work (1905–8) by Debussy, the second of his *Images*; its three sections are 'Par les rues et par les chemins' ('By highways and byways'), 'Les parfums de la nuit ('Night Scents'), and 'Le matin d'un jour de fête' ('Feast-Day Morning').

Ice Break, The. Opera in three acts by Tippett to his own libretto (London, 1977).

Idomeneo, re di Creta ('Idomeneus, King of Crete'). Opera (*dramma per musica*) in three acts by Mozart to a libretto by Giovanni Battista Varesco after Antoine Danchet's *Idomenée* (1712) (Munich, 1781); Danchet's libretto was set by André Campra (Paris, 1712).

Illuminations, Les ('The Illuminations'). Song cycle, op. 18 (1940), by Britten for soprano or tenor solo and orchestra, settings of nine prose poems (1872–3) by Arthur Rimbaud.

Images ('Pictures'). **1.** Orchestral work by Debussy consisting of *Gigues* (1909–12), *Ibéria* (1905–8), and *Rondes de printemps* (1905–9).

2. Six piano pieces by Debussy in two sets of three: the first (1905)—*Reflets dans l'eau* ('Reflections in the Water'), *Hommage à Rameau*, and *Mouvement*; the second (1907)—*Cloches à travers les feuilles* ('Bells through the Leaves'), *Et la lune descend sur le temple qui fut* ('And the moon descends on the temple that used to be'), and *Poissons d'or* ('Goldfish').

Imaginary Landscape. The title of five pieces by Cage (1939, 1942, 1942, 1951, 1952) for different forces, including turntables and other electrical equipment; the fourth is for 12 radios with two players at each, one operating the volume and the other the wavelength, and the fifth is for tape.

Imeneo ('Hymen'). Opera in three acts by Handel to a libretto adapted anonymously from Silvio Stampiglia's *Imeneo* (1723) (London, 1740).

Immortal Hour, The. Music drama in two acts by Rutland Boughton to his own libretto after plays and poems by 'Fiona Macleod' (the pseudonym of William Sharp) (Glastonbury, 1914).

Imperial, The (*L'Impériale*). Nickname of Haydn's Symphony no. 53 in D major (1778 or 1779); the name was first used, for an unknown reason, in a 19th-century Paris catalogue of Haydn's symphonies.

Imperial Mass. *See* NELSONMESSE.

Impresario, The. *See* SCHAUSPIELDIREKTOR, DER.

In a Summer Garden. Rhapsody for orchestra (1908) by Delius; the garden was Delius's own, at Grez-sur-Loing.

In C. Work (1963) by Terry Riley for an unspecified number of instruments; it consists of 53 simple melodic phrases each repeated as many times as desired, at a mutually agreed pace. It was the work that defined minimalism and brought it to a wide audience.

In Central Asia. *See* IN THE STEPPES OF CENTRAL ASIA.

Incontro improvviso, L' ('The Unexpected Meeting'). Opera (*dramma giocoso*) in three acts by Haydn to a libretto by Carl Friberth after L. H. Dancourt's *La Rencontre imprévue* (set by Gluck, 1764) (Eszterháza, 1775).

Incoronazione di Poppea, L' ('The Coronation of Poppaea'). Opera (*dramma musicale*) in a prologue and three acts by Monteverdi to a libretto by Giovanni Francesco Busenello mainly after Tacitus' *Annals* (books 13–16), but also after Suetonius' *The Twelve Caesars* (book 6), Dio Cassius' *Roman History* (books 61–2), and pseudo-Seneca's *Octavia* (Venice, 1643).

Indes galantes, Les ('The Amorous Indies'). *Opéra-ballet* in a prologue and four *entrées* by Rameau to a libretto by Louis Fuzelier (Paris, 1735); it was first performed with three *entrées*, the fourth being added in 1736.

Indian Queen, The. Semi-opera in a prologue and five acts by Henry Purcell adapted from the play by John Dryden and Robert Howard, with a final masque by Daniel Purcell (London, 1695).

In dulci jubilo ('In Sweet Joy'). German 14th-century macaronic carol; the English version dates from *c*.1540.

Inés de Castro. Opera in two acts by James MacMillan to a libretto by John Clifford after his own play (1989) (Edinburgh, 1996). Niccolò Antonio Zingarelli (1798) and Giuseppe Persiani (1835) wrote operas on the same subject.

Inextinguishable, The (*Det Uudslukkelige*). Nielsen's Symphony no. 4 op. 29 (1914–16).

Infedeltà delusa, L' ('Deceit Outwitted'). Opera (*burletta per musica*) in two acts by Haydn to a libretto by Marco Coltellini, possibly revised by Carl Friberth (Eszterháza, 1773).

Inganno felice, L' ('The Happy Deception'). Opera (*farsa*) in one act by Rossini to a libretto by Giuseppe Maria Foppa (Venice, 1812).

In Nature's Realm. *See* NATURE, LIFE, AND LOVE.

Inner Light. Three pieces by Jonathan Harvey: *Inner Light I* (1973) is for seven players and tape; *Inner Light II* (1977) is for two sopranos, alto, tenor, and bass soloists, 12 players, and tape, settings of texts by William Blake, T. S. Eliot, Rudyard Kipling, Rudolf Steiner, and the Bible (St John); *Inner Light III* (1975) is for large orchestra and tape.

Inori (*Adorations*). Work (1973–4) by Stockhausen for mime, dancer, and orchestra.

Inquest of Love. Opera in two acts by Jonathan Harvey to a text by the composer and David Rudkin (London, 1993).

In Sleep, in Thunder. Song cycle (1981) by Elliott Carter, settings for tenor and 14 players of poems by Robert Lowell.

Intégrales. Work (1924–5) by Varèse for 11 wind instruments and percussion.

Intelligence Park, The. Opera in three acts by Gerald Barry to a libretto by Vincent Deane (London, 1990).

Intermezzo. Opera (*bürgerliche Komödie mit sinfonischen Zwischenspielen*) in two acts by Richard Strauss to his own libretto (Dresden, 1924).

Internationale. A socialist song by Pierre Degeyter (1848–1932), composed in 1870 to words by Eugène Pottier (a Lille woodworker) and first sung in 1888; it was the official anthem of Communist Russia until 1 January 1944. (It is not the same as *The Red Flag*.)

In the Faery Hills (*An Sluagh Sidhe*). Tone-poem (1909) by Bax, the second in a series of three called *Eire*; the Faery Hills are in County Kerry.

In the Mist (*V mlhách*). A group of four piano pieces (1912) by Janáček; they were revised in 1949 by Bohumir Štědroň.

In the South (*Alassio*). Concert overture, op. 50 (1903–4), by Elgar; it was sketched at Alassio and is a symphonic impression of Italy, its landscape, and its imperial past.

In the Steppes of Central Asia (*V sredney Azii*, 'In Central Asia'). 'Orchestral picture' by Borodin, composed in 1880 to accompany a *tableau vivant* at an exhibition marking Alexander II's silver jubilee; it represents the approach and passing of a caravan.

Intimate Letters (*Listy důvěrné*). Subtitle of Janáček's String Quartet no. 2, composed in 28 days in 1928; it is autobiographical, the letters concerned being those he wrote to Kamila Stösslová between 1917 and 1928.

Intolleranza 1960 ('Intolerance 1960'). Opera (*azione scenica*) in two parts by Nono, after an idea by Angelo Maria Ripellino, to texts by Ripellino, Henri Alleg, Bertolt Brecht, Aimé Césaire, Paul Éluard, Vladimir Mayakovsky, Julius Fucik, and Jean-Paul Sartre, assembled by the composer (Venice, 1961); because of its use of contemporary references, Nono revised it for a performance in 1974, changing its name to *Intolleranza 1970*.

Introduction and Allegro. Elgar's op. 47 (1905) for string quartet and string orchestra.

Invisible City of Kitezh and the Maiden Fevroniya, The Legend of the. *See* LEGEND OF THE INVISIBLE CITY OF KITEZH AND THE MAIDEN FEVRONIYA, THE.

Invitation to the Dance. *See* AUFFORDERUNG ZUM TANZ.

Iolanta ('Iolanthe'). Lyric opera in one act by Tchaikovsky after Henrik Hertz's play *Kong Renés Datter* ('King René's Daughter', 1864), translated from the Danish by Fyodor Miller, adapted for Moscow by Vladimir Rafailovich Zotov (St Petersburg, 1892).

Iolanthe (*Iolanthe; or, The Peer and the Peri*). Operetta in two acts by Sullivan to a libretto by W. S. Gilbert (London, 1882).

Ion. Opera in two acts by Param Vir to a libretto by David Lan after Euripides (London, 2003).

Ionisation ('Ionization'). Work (1929–31) by Varèse for 13 percussion instruments.

Io Passion, The. Music-theatre piece by Birtwistle in a continuous series of nine cycles ('fits') to a text by Stephen Plaice incorporating elements of the Greek myth of Io (Aldeburgh, 2004).

Iphigénie en Aulide ('Iphigenia in Aulis'). Opera (*tragédie*) in three acts by Gluck to a libretto by Marie François Louis Gand Leblanc Roullet after Jean Racine's *Iphigénie en Aulide* (1674), itself based on Euripides (Paris, 1774).

Iphigénie en Tauride ('Iphigenia in Tauris'). Opera (*tragédie*) in four acts by Gluck to a libretto by Nicolas-François Guillard after Claude Guymond de la Touche's *Iphigénie en Tauride* (1757), itself based on Euripides (Paris, 1779). Piccinni wrote an opera on the same subject (Paris, 1781).

Iris. Opera (*melodramma*) in three acts by Mascagni to a libretto by Luigi Illica (Rome, 1898).

Irish Symphony. Sullivan's Symphony in E major (1864). It is also the subtitle of Stanford's Symphony no. 3 in F minor (1887) and the title of a symphony by Hamilton Harty (1904).

Irmelin. Opera in three acts by Delius to his own libretto (Oxford, 1953).

Islamey. 'Oriental fantasy' for piano by Balakirev, composed in 1870 and revised in 1902. Lyapunov made an orchestral version of it.

Isle joyeuse, L' ('The Island of Joy'). Piano piece (1904) by Debussy, inspired by *L'Embarquement pour Cythère*, a painting by Antoine Watteau depicting a party about to embark for the island sacred to Venus.

Isle of the Dead, The (*Ostrov myortvïkh*). Symphonic poem, op. 29 (1909), by Rakhmaninov, inspired by *Insel der Toten*, a painting by Arnold Böcklin (1827–1901).

Isola disabitata, L' ('The Deserted Island'). Opera (*azione teatrale*) in two acts by Haydn to a libretto by Pietro Metastasio (Eszterháza, 1779).

Israel. Work (1912–16) by Bloch for two sopranos, two contraltos, bass, and orchestra, using a text drawn from the Song of Songs.

Israel in Egypt. Oratorio (1739) by Handel to a text probably compiled by the composer.

Istar. Symphonic variations, op. 42 (1896), by d'Indy, based on the sixth canto of the Assyrian epic poem of Izdubar. They depict the voyage of self-discovery and denudation of Istar, daughter of Sin, the variations being progressively stripped of their ornamentation to reveal their theme.

Italiana in Algeri, L' ('The Italian Girl in Algiers'). Opera (*dramma giocoso*) in two acts by Rossini to a libretto substantially derived from Angelo Anelli's libretto for Luigi Mosca's *L'italiana in Algeri* (1808) (Venice, 1813).

Italian Capriccio. Orchestral work, op. 45 (1880), by Tchaikovsky, often known as the *Capriccio italien*.

Italian Concerto. Work for harpsichord, BWV971, by J. S. Bach, published with the Ouverture in the French Style BWV831 to form the second part of the *Clavier-Übung* (1735). Bach intended to highlight the contrast between the two national styles: the concerto is in three movements like the Italian concerto grosso and imitates tutti–solo contrasts and colourful orchestral effects.

Italian Girl in Algiers, The. *See* ITALIANA IN ALGERI, L'.

Italian Symphony. Mendelssohn's Symphony no. 4 in A major, which he began during a trip to Italy in 1830–1 and completed in 1833, subsequently revising it several times; it contains allusions to Italian folk music, notably in the finale, a 'Saltarello'.

Italienische Serenade ('Italian Serenade'). Work for string quartet (1887) by Wolf; it was arranged for orchestra in 1892 and by Reger for piano duet.

Italienisches Liederbuch ('Italian Songbook'). Collection of 46 songs for voice and piano by Wolf, settings of German translations by Paul Heyse of anonymous Italian poems; they were published in two volumes (1892, 1896). Some were later orchestrated by Wolf, others by Reger.

Ivanhoe. Opera in three acts by Sullivan to a libretto by Julian Sturgis after Walter Scott's novel (1819) (London, 1891): Sullivan's only 'serious' opera.

Ivan IV. Opera in five acts by Bizet to a libretto by François-Hippolyte Leroy and Henri Trianon (Württemberg, 1946).

Ivan Susanin. *See* LIFE FOR THE TSAR, A.

I Vow to Thee, My Country. Hymn with words (1918) by Cecil A. Spring-Rice, sung to Holst's tune *Thaxted* (1921), which is quoted in 'Jupiter, the Bringer of Jollity' in Holst's The **Planets*.

I Was Glad. Anthem (1902) by Parry, with processional music, composed for the coronation of Edward VII.

I Was Looking at the Ceiling and Then I Saw the Sky. 'Songplay' in two parts by John Adams to texts by June Jordan (Berkeley, CA, 1995).

Jacobin, The (*Jakobín*). Opera in three acts by Dvořák to a libretto by Marie Červinková-Riegrová (Prague, 1889; revised Prague, 1898).

Jagden und Formen ('Hunts and Forms'). Orchestral work (1995–9) by Wolfgang Rihm.

Jahreszeiten, Die. *See* SEASONS, THE.

Jakob Lenz. Chamber opera in one act by Wolfgang Rihm to a libretto by Michael Fröhling after Georg Büchner's novella *Lenz* (1836) (Hamburg, 1979).

Jakobsleiter, Die ('Jacob's Ladder'). Unfinished oratorio by Schoenberg, a setting of his own text for solo voices, chorus, and orchestra; he worked on it between 1917 and 1922 and the scoring was completed posthumously by Winifred Zillig. The first part was first performed in Hamburg in 1958 and the work was given complete in Vienna in 1961.

Jamaican Rumba. Piece for two pianos (1938) by Arthur Benjamin; it has been arranged for many other combinations, particularly small orchestra.

Jane Eyre. Opera in two acts by Michael Berkeley to a libretto by David Malouf (Cheltenham, 2000).

Jeanie Deans. Grand opera in four acts by Hamish MacCunn to a libretto by Joseph Bennett after Walter Scott's novel *The Heart of Midlothian* (1818) (Edinburgh, 1894).

Jeanne d'Arc au bûcher ('Joan of Arc at the Stake'). **1.** Dramatic oratorio (1934–5) by Honegger, for four speakers, three sopranos, contralto, tenor, bass, ondes martenot, chorus, and orchestra, a setting of a text by Paul Claudel.
  2. Scena (1845) by Liszt for mezzo-soprano and piano, a setting of a text by Alexandre Dumas; Liszt later arranged it for voice and orchestra.

'Jena' Symphony. Name given to a symphony by Friedrich Witt (1770–1836) found in 1909 in Jena, Germany, and long attributed to Beethoven.

Jenůfa (*Její pastorkyňa*; 'Her Stepdaughter', 'Her Foster Daughter'). Opera in three acts by Janáček to his own libretto after Gabriela Preissová's play (1890) (Brno, 1904).

Jephtha. Oratorio (1752) by Handel to a biblical text by Thomas Morell.

Jeremiah Symphony. Bernstein's Symphony no. 1 (1944); in the last movement a mezzo-soprano sings words from the book of Jeremiah.

Jerusalem. Choral song for unison voices (1916) by Hubert Parry to William Blake's short poem beginning 'And did those feet...' (not his long poem *Jerusalem*); Elgar orchestrated it for the 1922 Leeds Festival.

Jérusalem. Opera in four acts by Verdi to a libretto by Alphonse Royer and Gustave Vaëz from Temistocle Solera's libretto for Verdi's I **Lombardi alla prima crociata* (1843) (Paris, 1847).

Jessonda. Opera (*grosse Oper*) in three acts by Spohr to a libretto by Eduard Gehe after Antoine-Marin Lemièrre's play *La Veuve de Malabar* (Kassel, 1823).

Jesu, Joy of Man's Desiring. Title of a piano transcription by Myra Hess of J. S. Bach's chorale 'Wohl mir, dass ich Jesum habe' which ends each part of his cantata no. 147, *Herz und Mund und Tat und Leben*; the hymn text, from which the English title derives, is Martin Jahn's *Jesu, meine Seelen Wonne*. Hess's transcription was published in 1926 and for piano duet in 1934; it has since been arranged in various ways. In spite of its bright original scoring—for trumpet, oboes, strings, and continuo—arrangements are often played slowly and solemnly.

Jesu, meine Freude ('Jesus, my Joy'). Motet (BWV227) by Bach, of unknown date, for five voices, a setting of a text from Romans 8 and Johann Franck's hymn *Jesu, meine Freude*.

Jeu de cartes ('Game of Cards'). Ballet 'in three deals' by Stravinsky to a scenario by the composer and M. Melaïeff, choreographed by George Balanchine (New York, 1937).

Jeu de Robin et de Marion, Le ('The Play of Robin and Marion'). Pastoral play with music, written by Adam de la Halle during the period 1283–5, while he was in the service of the French court at Naples; it is a blend of rustic spoken comedy and simple songs.

Jeux ('Games'). Ballet (*poème dansé*) by Debussy to a scenario by Vaslav Nijinsky; it was choreographed by Nijinsky, with designs by Léon Bakst, and performed by Serge Diaghilev's Ballets Russes (Paris, 1913).

Jeux d'eau ('Fountains'). Piano piece (1901) by Ravel.

Jeux d'enfants ('Children's Games'). Suite of 12 pieces (1871) by Bizet for piano duet. Nos. 2, 3, 6, 11, and 12 were orchestrated (1873) by Bizet as *Petite suite d'orchestre*. Five (nos. 6, 3, 4, 11, and 12) were orchestrated by Sigfrid Karg-Elert and five (nos. 6, 3, 2, 11, and 12) were arranged by Herman Finck.

Jeux vénitiens. *See* VENETIAN GAMES.

Jewels of the Madonna, The. *See* GIOIELLI DELLA MADONNA, I.

Job. 1. 'Masque for dancing' in nine scenes and an epilogue by Vaughan Williams to a scenario by Geoffrey Keynes and Gwen Raverat after Blake's *Illustrations of the Book of Job*; it was performed first as an orchestral work (Norwich, 1930) and was staged the following year in London.

2. Oratorio by Hubert Parry (Gloucester, 1892).

3. Opera (*sacra rappresentazione*) by Dallapiccola to his own libretto after the book of Job (Rome, 1950).

John Brown's Body. American popular song; the tune is that of a well-known 19th-century camp-meeting and revival hymn written by a Philadelphia musician and still sung to the words 'Mine eyes have seen the glory of the coming of the Lord', a poem (1862) by Julia Ward Howe (the 'Battle Hymn of the Republic').

'Joke' Quartet. Nickname of Haydn's String Quartet in E♭ major op. 33 no. 2 (1781), so called because at the end of the finale Haydn teases the listener's expectations with rests and repeated phrases.

Jolie Fille de Perth, La ('The Fair Maid of Perth'). Opera in four acts by Bizet to a libretto by Jules-Henri Vernoy de Saint-Georges and Jules Adenis after Walter Scott's novel *The Fair Maid of Perth* (1823) (Paris, 1867).

Jongleur de Notre-Dame, Le ('The Juggler of Notre Dame').
   1. Opera (*miracle*) in three acts by Massenet to a libretto by Maurice Léna after the medieval legend recounted by Anatole France in his *L'Étui de nacre* (1892) (Monte Carlo, 1902).
   2. Masque in one act by Maxwell Davies to his own libretto (Kirkwall, 1978).

Jonny spielt auf ('Jonny Strikes Up'). Opera in two parts (11 scenes) by Krenek to his own libretto (Leipzig, 1927).

Joseph. 1. (*Joseph and his Brethren*). Oratorio (1744) by Handel to a biblical text by James Miller.
   2. Opera (*drame mêlé de chants*) in three acts by Méhul to a libretto by Alexandre Duval after Genesis 37–46 (Paris, 1807).

Josephslegende ('The Legend of Joseph'). Ballet in one act by Richard Strauss to a scenario by Harry Graf Kessler and Hugo von Hofmannsthal; it was choreographed by Mikhail Fokine for Serge Diaghilev's Ballets Russes (Paris, 1914).

Joshua. Oratorio (1748) by Handel to a text probably by Thomas Morell.

Judas Maccabaeus. Oratorio (1747) by Handel to a text by Thomas Morell based on biblical incidents; composed to celebrate the English victory at Culloden and the return to London of the victorious general, the Duke of Cumberland, it contains the chorus 'See, the conquering hero comes'.

Judgment of Paris, The. Pastoral masque in one act, set by John Eccles, Gottfried Finger, Daniel Purcell, and John Weldon to a libretto by William Congreve (London, 1701).

Judith. 1. Oratorio (1888) by Hubert Parry to a biblical text.
   2. Biblical opera in three acts by Honegger to a libretto by René Morax (Monte Carlo, 1926).
   3. Oratorio (1761) by Arne to a text by Isaac Bickerstaff.

Juditha triumphans. Oratorio (1716) by Vivaldi to a text by Giacomo Cassetti.

Juive, La ('The Jewish Woman'). Opera in five acts by Halévy to a libretto by Eugène Scribe (Paris, 1835).

Julietta (*Snář*, 'The Dream-Book'). Opera in three acts by Martinů to his own libretto after Georges Neveux's play *Juliette, ou La Clé des songes* (1930) (Prague, 1938).

Julius Caesar. *See* GIULIO CESARE.

Jumping Frog of Calaveras County, The. Comic opera in one act by Lukas Foss to a libretto by Jean Karsavina after Mark Twain's story *The Celebrated Jumping Frog of Calaveras County* (1867) (Bloomington, IN, 1950).

Junge Lord, Der ('The Young Lord'). Opera (*komische Oper*) in two acts by Henze to a libretto by Ingeborg Bachmann after Wilhelm Hauff's story 'Der Affe als Mensch' from *Der Scheik von Alexandria und seine Sklaven* (1826) (Berlin, 1965).

'Jupiter' Symphony. Nickname of Mozart's Symphony no. 41 in C major K551 (1788). It is not known why or when the name originated but it was possibly first used in a programme for a Philharmonic Society of London concert, conducted by Henry R. Bishop, on 26 March 1821; according to Mozart's son F. X. Mozart, the nickname was coined by J. P. Salomon.

K. Abbreviation for *Köchel and *Kirkpatrick, used as a prefix to the numbers of Mozart's works and Domenico Scarlatti's keyboard sonatas respectively, as given in the standard thematic catalogues of Ludwig Köchel and Ralph Kirkpatrick.

Kaffeekantate. *See* COFFEE CANTATA.

Kai. Work (1989–90) for cello and ensemble by Mark-Anthony Turnage; it was written in memory of the cellist Kai Scheffler.

Kaisermarsch ('Emperor March'). Work (1871) by Wagner for unison male voices and orchestra, composed to celebrate the German victory in the Franco-Prussian War (1870) and the election of Wilhelm I as emperor.

Kaiserquartett. *See* 'EMPEROR' QUARTET.

Kaiser von Atlantis, Der (*Der Kaiser von Atlantis, oder Der Tod dankt ab*; 'The Emperor of Atlantis, or Death Abdicates'). Opera ('legend') in four scenes by Viktor Ullmann to a libretto by Petr Kien, composed in 1943 at Terezín (Amsterdam, 1975).

Kaiser-Walzer ('Emperor Waltz'). Waltz, op. 437 (1888), by Johann Strauss (ii), composed in honour of Emperor Franz Joseph. Schoenberg arranged it for chamber ensemble (1925).

Kakadu Variations. Beethoven's variations for piano trio, op. 121*a* (1803), on Wenzel Müller's song 'Ich bin der Schneider Kakadu' ('I am the tailor Kakadu') from the musical play *Die Schwestern von Prag* ('The Sisters from Prague', 1794).

Kalevala. Finnish epic songs from the Kalevala region, transmitted orally for several centuries. In 1835 Elias Lönnrot published an edition of 12,000 verses, and in 1949 he brought out a second edition of 23,000, in trochaic verse, unrhymed, divided into 50 cantos or runes; it has been translated into Swedish, German, English, and French. Several Finnish composers have based works on parts of this epic, notably Sibelius, in his *Kullervo, *Pohjola's Daughter, *Tapiola, and the *Lemminkäinen Suite.

Kamarinskaya. Orchestral piece (1848) by Glinka, arranged for piano duet in 1856.

Kammermusik ('Chamber Music'). Title given by Hindemith to seven instrumental works (1922–7): no. 1 (1922) is for small orchestra; no. 2 (1924) is a piano concerto; no. 3 (1925) is a cello concerto; no. 4 (1925) is a violin concerto; no. 5 (1927) is a viola concerto; no. 6 (1927) is a viola d'amore concerto; and no. 7 (1927) is an organ concerto.

Kantrimiusik ('Country Music'). A 'pastorale for voices and instruments' (seven players and at least three singers) with tape (1973–5) by Kagel.

Karelia. Overture and suite for orchestra, opp. 10 and 11 (1893), by Sibelius. Karelia is a province in southern Finland.

Kát'a Kabanová. Opera in three acts by Janáček to his own libretto after Alexander Ostrovsky's play *Groza* ('The Storm', 1859) (Brno, 1921).

Kate and the Devil. *See* DEVIL AND KATE, THE.

Katerina Izmaylova. A revision of Shostakovich's *The *Lady Macbeth of the Mtsensk District*.

Keel Row. English north-country song. Its origin is unknown but it first appeared in print in *A Collection of Favourite Scots Tunes* (Edinburgh, 1770); it is, however, principally associated with the Tyneside district (where 'keel' means boat in the local dialect). Debussy quoted it in *Gigues*, the first of his *Images* for orchestra.

'Kettledrum' Mass. *See* PAUKENMESSE.

Khamma. Ballet-pantomime (*légende dansée*) in three scenes by Debussy to a scenario by W. L. Courtney and Maud Allan. Debussy composed it in 1911–12 with piano accompaniment; he orchestrated the prelude and Koechlin orchestrated the rest under the composer's supervision (Paris, 1947).

Khovanshchina ('The Khovansky Affair'). Opera ('national music drama') in six scenes, usually given in five acts, by Musorgsky to his own libretto compiled with Vladimir Stasov from historical sources. It was left unfinished at the composer's death and was completed and orchestrated by Rimsky-Korsakov (St Petersburg, 1886); there is a version by Ravel and Stravinsky (Paris, 1913) and one by Shostakovich (Leningrad, 1960).

Khovorod. Work (1994) by Julian Anderson for 15 instrumentalists.

Kinderszenen ('Scenes from Childhood'). Schumann's op. 15 (1838), for piano, a set of 13 pieces (for adults); the seventh piece is *Träumerei.

Kindertotenlieder ('Songs on the Death of Children'). Song cycle (1901–4) by Mahler for baritone or contralto and orchestra, settings of five poems by Friedrich Rückert.

King Arthur (*King Arthur, or The British Worthy*). Semi-opera in five acts by Henry Purcell and John Dryden (London, 1691).

Kingdom, The. Oratorio, op. 51 (1906), by Elgar, for four soloists, chorus, and orchestra, to a biblical text compiled by the composer; Elgar composed it as a sequel to *The *Apostles*.

King Goes Forth to France, The (*Kuningas lähtee Ranskaan*). Opera in three acts by Sallinen to a libretto by Paavo Haavikko (Savonlinna, 1984).

King Lear. Shakespeare's play (1604–5) has inspired several musical works, principally the following.
   1. Overture (*Le Roi Lear*), op. 4 (1831), by Berlioz.

2. Opera (*Kuningas Lear*) in two acts by Sallinen to a libretto by the composer after Matti Rotti's Finnish translation of Shakespeare's play (Helsinki, 2000).

3. Overture and incidental music by Balakirev (1858–61, revised 1902–5).

4. Incidental music (two movements) by Debussy (1904).

5. Music by Shostakovich (1970) for a Russian film of the play in Boris Pasternak's translation.

Verdi and Britten planned but abandoned operas on the subject. *See also* LEAR.

'King of Prussia' Quartets. *See* 'PRUSSIAN' QUARTETS.

King Priam. Opera in three acts by Tippett to his own libretto after Homer's *Iliad* (Coventry, 1962).

King Roger (*Król Roger*; *Pasterz*, 'The Shepherd'). Opera in three acts by Szymanowski to a libretto by Jarosław Iwaszkiewicz and the composer, loosely based on Euripides' *Bacchae* (Warsaw, 1926).

King Stag. *See* KÖNIG HIRSCH.

Kirkpatrick. Abbreviation for the standard thematic catalogue of the keyboard sonatas of Domenico Scarlatti drawn up by the American keyboard player and scholar Ralph Kirkpatrick (1911–84) and published in his study of the composer (Princeton, NJ, 1953, 3/1968). The sonatas are often referred to by Kirkpatrick number, usually further abbreviated to K or Kk.

Kiss, The (*Hubička*). Opera in two acts by Smetana to a libretto by Eliška Krásnohorská after the story by Karolina Světlá (1871) (Prague, 1876).

Klagende Lied, Das ('The Song of Sorrow'). Cantata (1880) by Mahler, a setting of his own text for soprano, alto, and tenor soloists, chorus, and orchestra; he composed it in three parts—*Waldmärchen* ('Forest Legend'), *Der Spielmann* ('The Minstrel'), and *Hochzeitsstück* ('Wedding Piece')—but revised it in 1892–3 and 1898–9 omitting *Waldmärchen*.

Klavierbüchlein. *See* CLAVIER-BÜCHLEIN.

Klavierübung. *See* CLAVIER-ÜBUNG.

Kleine Nachtmusik, Eine ('A Little Night Music'). Mozart's title for his Nocturne in G major K525 (1787); it is scored for string quartet and double bass and was originally in five movements but the second, a minuet, is lost. It is now often performed with orchestra.

Kleine Orgelmesse ('Little Organ Mass'). Haydn's Mass no. 7 in B♭ major (c.1775); its full title is *Missa brevis Sancti Joannis de Deo*. *See also* GROSSE ORGELMESSE.

Knaben Wunderhorn, Des. *See* DES KNABEN WUNDERHORN.

Knot Garden, The. Opera in three acts by Tippett to his own libretto (London, 1970).

Knoxville: Summer of 1915. Scena (1947) for soprano and orchestra by Samuel Barber, a setting of a text by James Agee; Barber arranged it for soprano and chamber orchestra (1950).

Koanga. Lyric drama in a prologue, three acts, and an epilogue by Delius to a libretto by the composer and Charles F. Keary after George W. Cable's novel *The Grandissimes* (1880) (Elberfeld, 1904).

Köchel. Abbreviation for the standard thematic catalogue of the works of Mozart drawn up by the Austrian music historian Ludwig Köchel (1800–77) and published in Leipzig in 1862. The catalogue has been revised several times, notably by Alfred Einstein for the third edition (1937, often referred to as 'k-e') and by Franz Giegling, Alexander Weinmann, and Gerd Sievers for the sixth (1964, often referred to as 'k6'). A further revision, *Der neue Köchel* ('nk'), was begun in the closing years of the 20th century under the editorship of Neal Zaslaw. Mozart's works, especially those without distinguishing title, are nearly always referred to by Köchel number, usually further abbreviated to k.

Kol Nidrei (*Kol Nidre*; 'All Vows').

1. Bruch's op. 47 (1881), for cello and orchestra, an Adagio on Hebrew melodies which was also arranged for cello and piano.

2. Schoenberg's op. 39 (1938), for speaker, chorus, and orchestra, a setting of the *Kol Nidre*, the opening prayer of the Jewish service on the evening of the Day of Atonement (Yom Kippur), which has tragic associations with the Spanish persecution of Jews in the 17th century.

König Hirsch ('King Stag'). Opera in three acts by Henze to a libretto by Heinz von Cramer after the fable by Carlo Gozzi (1762) (cut version, Berlin, 1956); Henze revised it as *Il re cervo, oder Die Irrfahrten der Wahrheit* ('King Stag, or The Meanderings of Truth') (Kassel, 1963) (complete performance, Stuttgart, 1985).

Königin von Saba, Die ('The Queen of Sheba'). Opera in four acts by Karl Goldmark to a libretto by Salomon Hermann Mosenthal after 1 Kings 10 (Vienna, 1875).

Königskinder ('The King's Children'). Opera (*Märchenoper*) in three acts by Humperdinck to a libretto by Ernst Rosmer (pseudonym of Else Bernstein-Porges) after her play (1897) of the same name (New York, 1910).

Kontakte ('Contacts'). Work (1959–60) by Stockhausen for four-track tape alone and, in another version, with piano and percussion; the tape was used in the music-theatre piece *Originale* (1961).

Kontra-Punkte ('Counterpoints'). Work (1952, revised 1953) by Stockhausen for ten instruments; it is a revision of the orchestral work *Punkte* (1952), itself revised in 1962, 1964, and 1966.

Kopernikus. Chamber opera ('ritual opera of death') in two acts by Claude Vivier to a libretto by the composer (Montreal, 1980).

Kossuth. Symphonic poem (1903) in ten tableaux by Bartók, based on the life of Lajos Kossuth (1802–94), leader of the unsuccessful uprising against Austria in 1848–9; it includes a distorted arrangement of the Austrian national hymn.

Koteletten Walzer. *See* CHOPSTICKS.

Kraanerg. Ballet by Xenakis for orchestra and tape (Ottawa, 1969).

Kraft. Work (1985) by Magnus Lindberg for clarinet, percussion, piano, cello, electronics, and orchestra.

Kreisleriana. Schumann's op. 16 (1838, revised 1850), for piano, consisting of eight fantasies; it is dedicated to Chopin. The title refers to Kreisler, a character in E. T. A. Hoffmann's stories.

'Kreutzer' Sonata. 1. Popular name for Beethoven's Violin Sonata in A major op. 47 (1802–3), dedicated to the violinist Rodolphe Kreutzer, who is believed never to have played it.

2. Subtitle of Janáček's String Quartet no. 1 (1923); it incorporates part of a scrapped piano trio of 1908–9 and on the score the composer wrote 'Inspired by L. N. Tolstoy's *Kreutzer-sonata*', a novel published in 1890.

Kullervo. 1. Symphonic poem, op. 7 (1892), by Sibelius, for soprano, baritone, male chorus, and orchestra, based on the *Kalevala; it was withdrawn after its first performance and not played again until 1958.

2. Opera in two acts by Sallinen to his own libretto after a play by Aleksis Kivi (1864) (Los Angeles, 1992).

Kunst der Fuge, Die. *See* ART OF FUGUE, THE.

KV. Abbreviation for *Köchel-Verzeichnis, sometimes used as a prefix to the numbers of Mozart's works as given in the standard thematic catalogue of Ludwig Köchel.

Lac des cygnes, Le. *See* SWAN LAKE.

Lachrimae, or Seaven Teares. A collection (1604) of 21 pieces for five viols and lute by Dowland; the 'teares' are seven 'passionate' pavans, each a set of variations on Dowland's song *Flow my Teares*, and the other 14 pieces are dances. They were transcribed for keyboard by several composers, notably Byrd.

Lady Macbeth of the Mtsensk District, The (*Ledi Makbet Mtsenskogo uyezda*). Opera in four acts by Shostakovich to a libretto by the composer and Aleksandr Preys after the short story by Nikolay Leskov (1865) (Leningrad, 1934). Shostakovich revised it as *Katerina Izmaylova* (Moscow, 1963) but for reasons of political compromise; the original version is regarded as definitive.

Lady Nevell's Book. *See* MY LADYE NEVELLS BOOKE.

Lakmé. Opera in three acts by Delibes to a libretto by Edmond Gondinet and Philippe Gille after Pierre Loti's novel *Rarahu* (1882) (Paris, 1883).

'Lamentation' Symphony. Nickname of Haydn's Symphony no. 26 in D minor (late 1760s), so called because some of its themes resemble the plainchant melodies sung in Roman Catholic churches in the week before Easter. It is also sometimes referred to as *Weihnachtssymphonie* ('Christmas Symphony'), but that title has no apparent relevance.

Lamento d'Arianna. The only surviving music from Monteverdi's opera *L'Arianna* (1608); Monteverdi arranged it as a five-part madrigal, *Lasciatemi morire* ('Leave me to Die'), published in 1623.

Lamento della ninfa ('The Nymph's Lament'). Vocal work by Monteverdi for soprano over an ostinato bass, published in his **Madrigali guerrieri ed amorosi*.

Land der Berge. *See* EMPEROR'S HYMN.

Land des Lächelns, Das ('The Land of Smiles'). Operetta (*romantische Operette*) in three acts by Lehár to a libretto by Ludwig Herzer and Fritz Löhner (Berlin, 1929).

Land of Hope and Glory. The title of the finale of Elgar's *Coronation Ode, for alto, chorus, and orchestra, a setting of words by A. C. Benson to a melody adapted from the trio section of Elgar's first **Pomp and Circumstance* march. It was also published as a separate song, for alto and orchestra, with words different from those in the *Coronation Ode*; this is the version sung generally and communally.

Land of my Fathers (*Hen Wlad fy Nhadau*). Welsh national anthem. The music (1856) is by James James (1832–1902) and the words are by Evan James (1809–93); it first appeared in print in John Owain's *Gems of Welsh Melody* (1860).

Land of Smiles, The. *See* LAND DES LÄCHELNS, DAS.

Land of the Mountain and the Flood, The. Overture (1887) by Hamish MacCunn.

Lark Ascending, The. Romance (1914) by Vaughan Williams for violin and orchestra, inspired by the poem of that name by George Meredith; it was revised in 1920.

'Lark' Quartet (*Lerchenquartett*). Nickname of Haydn's String Quartet in D major op. 64 no. 5 (1790), so called because of the soaring violin theme of its opening; the rhythm of the last movement has given rise to another, less frequently used nickname, the 'Hornpipe' Quartet.

'La sol fa re mi', Missa. Mass for four voices by Josquin des Prez based entirely on a five-note solmization.

Lass of Richmond Hill, The. Song by James Hook to words by Leonard McNally; it is a reference to Richmond, Yorkshire, not Surrey.

Last Post. British army bugle call. The First Post, at 9.30 p.m., calls all men back to their barracks; the Last Post ends the day. By a natural and poetical association, it has become the custom to sound the Last Post at military funerals.

Last Rose of Summer, The. Irish air, originally *Castle Hyde*, which became R. A. Millikin's *The Groves of Blarney* (c.1790). Thomas Moore included it, with his own, new words, in his *Irish Melodies* (1813). Beethoven set it, Mendelssohn wrote a piano fantasia on it, and it is used extensively by Flotow in his opera *Martha* (1847).

Last Sleep of the Virgin, The (*Le Dernier Sommeil de la Vierge*). Orchestral interlude from Massenet's oratorio *La Vierge* (1880), much favoured as an encore by Thomas Beecham.

Last Supper, The. Opera (dramatic tableaux) by Birtwistle to a libretto by Robin Blaser (Berlin, 2000).

Laudon Symphony (Loudon Symphony). Haydn's Symphony no. 69 in C major (mid-1770s), so called because it is dedicated to the Austrian field marshal Ernst Gideon Freiherr von Loudon (1716–90).

Lead, Kindly Light. Hymn of which the words were written by John Henry Newman (1801–90) after he had been ill in Sicily. The tune, *Lux benigna*, is by John Bacchus Dykes; it was first published under the name *St Oswald* in *Psalms and Hymns for the Church, School and Home* (1867, edited by D. T. Barry) and in an appendix (1868) to *Hymns Ancient and Modern*.

Lear. Opera in two parts by Aribert Reimann to a libretto by Claus H. Henneberg after Shakespeare's *King Lear* (1604–5) (Munich, 1978).

Lebewohl, Das ('The Farewell'). Beethoven's title for his Piano Sonata no. 26 in E♭ major op. 81*a*, usually known as *Les *Adieux*.

Legende von der heiligen Elisabeth, Die ('The Legend of St Elizabeth'). Oratorio (1857–62) by Liszt, for soprano, alto, three baritones, bass, chorus, organ, and orchestra, to a text by Otto Roquette.

Legend of the Invisible City of Kitezh and the Maiden Fevroniya, The (*Skazaniye o nevidimom grade Kitezhe i deve Fevronii*). Opera in four acts by Rimsky-Korsakov to a libretto by Vladimir Bel'sky drawn from E. S. Meledin's 'Kitezh Chronicle', Pavel Mel'nikov's novel *V lesakh* ('In the Woods'), and songs, epics, and traditional tales (St Petersburg, 1907).

Legend of Tsar Saltan, The. *See* TALE OF TSAR SALTAN, THE.

Leggende di Sakùntala, La. *See* SAKUNTALA.

Lélio, ou Le Retour à la vie ('Lélio, or The Return to Life'). Monodrama, op. 14*bis* (1830–2), by Berlioz to his own text but with one number by Albert DuBoys after Johann Wolfgang von Goethe; for soloists, chorus, and orchestra, it was composed as a sequel to the *Symphonie fantastique*.

Lemminkäinen Suite (*Lemminkäis-sarja*). Four symphonic poems, op. 22, by Sibelius on legends in the *Kalevala* of the warrior Lemminkäinen; they are *Lemminkäinen and the Maidens of the Island* (1895; revised 1897, 1939), *Lemminkäinen in Tuonela* (1895; revised 1897, 1939), *The Swan of Tuonela* (1893; revised 1897, 1900), and *Lemminkäinen's Return* (1895; revised 1897, 1900).

Leningrad Symphony. The subtitle of Shostakovich's Symphony no. 7 in C major op. 61 (1941), composed during the German siege of Leningrad and dedicated to the city.

Leonore. The original title of Beethoven's opera *Fidelio*. Beethoven wrote three overtures with this title: no. 2 for the first production (1805), no. 3 (a revision of no. 2) for the 1806 revival, and no. 1 (1806–7) for a proposed production in Prague that never took place. He composed the *Fidelio* overture for the final version (1814).

Lerchenquartett. *See* 'LARK' QUARTET.

Les Adieux. *See* ADIEUX, LES.

Let's Make an Opera. 'An entertainment for young people' by Britten to a libretto by Eric Crozier (Aldeburgh, 1949); it incorporates as its third act the opera *The *Little Sweep*. Britten composed it to involve local young people and adult amateurs, who, in the first two acts, plan the opera of the third act and rehearse four songs with the audience.

L'Homme armé. *See* HOMME ARMÉ, L'.

Libuše. 'Festival' opera in three acts by Smetana to a libretto by Josef Wenzig (Prague, 1881).

Licht: Die sieben Tage der Woche ('Light: The Seven Days of the Week'). A cycle of seven operas by Stockhausen to his own librettos, begun in 1977; their order of performance is *Donnerstag aus Licht*, *Samstag aus Licht*, *Montag aus Licht*, *Dienstag aus Licht*, *Freitag aus Licht*, *Mittwoch aus Licht*, *Sonntag aus Licht*.

Liebe der Danae, Die ('The Love of Danae'). Opera (*heitere Mythologie*, 'cheerful mythology') in three acts by Richard Strauss to a libretto by Joseph Gregor (Salzburg, 1952); there was a public dress rehearsal in Salzburg in 1944 but the opening performance was cancelled.

Liebesliederwalzer ('Love-Song Waltzes'). 18 waltzes, op. 52 (1868–9), by Brahms, for two pianos, with soprano, alto, tenor, and bass soloists, settings of texts from Georg Friedrich Daumer's *Polydora*; a version was published (op. 52*a*) without the vocal parts. In 1874 Brahms composed 15 more, *Neue Liebesliederwalzer* (op. 65), for the same forces (op. 65*a* without voices).

Liebesmahl der Apostel, Das ('The Love Feast of the Apostles'). 'Biblical scene' (1843) for male chorus and orchestra by Wagner to his own text.

Liebestod ('Love-Death'). Isolde's final aria at the end of Act III of Wagner's *Tristan und Isolde* (or the orchestral arrangement of it, often played as a concert item with the Prelude to Act I); Wagner applied the term to the love duet in Act II.

Liebesträume ('Dreams of Love'). Three nocturnes for solo piano by Liszt, composed *c*.1850; they are transcriptions of his songs *Hohe Liebe*, *Gestorben war ich*, and *O Lieb, so lang du lieben kannst*, the third (in A♭ major) being one of the best-known Romantic melodies.

Liebesverbot, Das (*Das Liebesverbot, oder Die Novize von Palermo*; 'The Ban on Love, or The Novice of Palermo'). Opera (*grosse komische Oper*) in two acts by Wagner to his own libretto after Shakespeare's *Measure for Measure* (1604) (Magdeburg, 1836).

Lieder eines fahrenden Gesellen ('Songs of a Wayfarer'). Cycle of four songs (1883–5) by Mahler for baritone or mezzo-soprano and orchestra (or piano), settings of his own poems based on, or imitative of, *Des Knaben Wunderhorn*; he revised them (1891–6), and orchestrated them (1891–3). The second and fourth songs are linked thematically with the first and slow movements of his First Symphony.

Liederkreis. The German term for 'song cycle', first used by Beethoven to describe his *An die ferne Geliebte*. Schumann used it for two song cycles for voice and piano: op. 24, settings of nine poems by Heinrich Heine, and op. 39, settings of 12 poems by Joseph von Eichendorff, both composed in 1840.

Lieder ohne Worte ('Songs without Words'; *Romances sans paroles*). 48 piano pieces by Mendelssohn, in which a songlike melody progresses against an accompaniment, published in eight books of six each: 1, op. 19 (1830); 2, op. 30 (1835); 3, op. 38 (1837); 4, op. 53 (1841); 5, op. 62 (1844); 6, op. 67 (1845); 7, op. 85 (1850); 8, op. 102 (*c*.1845). Most of the individual titles were not Mendelssohn's, the exceptions being the three *Auf einer Gondel* (nos. 6, 12, and 29), the *Duetto* (no. 18), and *Volkslied* (no. 23). He also wrote a *Lied ohne Worte*, op. 109 (*c*.1845), for cello and piano.

Lied von der Erde, Das ('The Song of the Earth'). Cycle of six songs (1908–9) by Mahler for tenor and alto or baritone soloists and orchestra, settings of poems from Hans Bethge's *Die chinesische Flöte*, German translations of 8th- and 9th-century Chinese poems; Mahler called it a 'symphony'.

Lieutenant Kijé (*Poruchik Kizhe*). Orchestral suite, op. 60 (1934), by Prokofiev; it is derived from the music he wrote for the film of the same name and has an optional baritone part.

Life for the Tsar, A. (*Zhizn' za tsarya*; *Ivan Susanin*). 'Patriotic heroic-tragic opera' in five acts (or four acts and an epilogue) by Glinka to a libretto by Yegor Fyodorovich Rozen, Vladimir Sollogub, Nestor Vasil'yevich Kukol'nik, and Vasily Andreyevich Zhukovsky (who suggested the subject) (St Petersburg, 1836). In the Soviet era Sergey Gorodetsky rewrote the libretto, refocusing interest on the leaders of the uprising against the Poles rather than on the Romanov dynasty, and it was given as *Ivan Susanin* (Moscow, 1939). Catterino Cavos wrote an opera on the same plot (1815).

Life with an Idiot (*Zhizn' s idiotom*). Opera in two acts by Schnittke to a libretto by Viktor Yerofeyev after his own short story (1908) (Amsterdam, 1992).

Light Cavalry (*Leichte Cavallerie*). Operetta in two acts by Suppé to a libretto by Carl Costa (Vienna, 1866); its overture is popular as a concert item.

Lighthouse, The. Chamber opera in a prologue and one act by Maxwell Davies to his own libretto (Edinburgh, 1980).

Lighthouses of England and Wales. Orchestral work (1988) by Benedict Mason.

Lilliburlero. Tune of unknown origin which first appeared in print in 1686 in a book of 'lessons' for the recorder or flute, where it is styled 'Quickstep'. The following year it achieved popularity when sung to satirical verses, with the mock Irish word 'Lilliburlero' as a refrain. It has remained a song of the Orange party, set to different words as 'Protestant Boys'. In Henry Purcell's *Musick's Hand-Maid* (1687) it appears under the title 'A New Irish Tune' for harpsichord; Purcell also used it as a ground bass in his incidental music for the play *The Gordian Knot Unty'd* (1691).

Lily of Killarney, The. Grand romantic opera in three acts by Julius Benedict to a libretto by John Oxenford and Dion Boucicault after Boucicault's play *The Colleen Bawn, or The Brides of Garryowen* (1860) (London, 1862).

Lincoln Portrait, A. Work (1942) for speaker and orchestra by Copland, with words taken from Abraham Lincoln's speeches and letters; it was proposed for performance at Dwight Eisenhower's inauguration as president (1953) but was rejected because of Copland's alleged Communist sympathies. In performance it has attracted a wide range of speakers including Copland himself, Adlai Stevenson, Eleanor Roosevelt, Henry Fonda, John Gielgud, Katharine Hepburn, Margaret Thatcher, and Norman Schwarzkopf.

Lincolnshire Posy. A suite of British folksongs assembled by Percy Grainger: 'Lisbon (Dublin Bay)', 'Horkstow Grange', 'Rufford Park Poachers', 'The Brisk Young Sailor', 'Lord Melbourne', and 'The Lost Lady Found'; it exists in many different arrangements, by the composer and others, including Grainger's own for two pianos and several for wind ensembles.

Linda di Chamounix ('Linda of Chamonix'). Opera (*melodramma semiserio*) in three acts by Donizetti to a libretto by Gaetano Rossi after Adolphe-Philippe d'Ennery and Gustave Lemoine's play *La Grâce de Dieu* (1841) (Vienna, 1842).

'Linz' Symphony. Nickname of Mozart's Symphony no. 36 in C major к425 (1783), so called because it was composed and first performed in Linz.

'Little Russian' Symphony. Nickname of Tchaikovsky's Symphony no. 2 in C major op. 17 (1872), so called because it uses folksongs from Ukraine ('Little Russia'). It is sometimes called the 'Ukrainian' Symphony.

Little Sweep, The. 'An entertainment for young people' by Britten to a libretto by Eric Crozier, the third act of *Let's Make an Opera* (Aldeburgh, 1949).

Liturgy of St John Chrysostom. Choral work, op. 31 (1910), by Rakhmaninov for large unaccompanied mixed choir. Tchaikovsky made an unaccompanied setting (1878) of the same text.

Lobgesang ('Hymn of Praise'). Symphony-cantata by Mendelssohn, his Symphony no. 2 (1840), with solo voices, chorus, and organ in the last movement. It was composed for the same occasion as *Festgesang*.

Lodoïska. Opera (*comédie-héroïque*) in three acts by Cherubini to a libretto by Claude-François Fillette-Loraux after an episode from Jean-Baptiste Louvet de Couvrai's novel *Les Amours du chevalier de Faublas* (Paris, 1791). Rodolphe Kreutzer (1791), Storace (1794), and Simon Mayr (1796) wrote operas on the same subject.

Lohengrin. Opera (*romantische Oper*) in three acts by Wagner to his own libretto after the anonymous German epic (Weimar, 1850). Salvatore Sciarrino wrote an opera (*azione invisibile*) on the same subject (1983).

Lombardi alla prima crociata, I ('The Lombards at the First Crusade'). Opera (*dramma lirico*) in four acts by Verdi to a libretto by Temistocle Solera after Tommaso Grossi's poem (1826) (Milan, 1843); Verdi revised it as *Jérusalem* (1847).

Londonderry Air. Irish folk tune first published in the Petrie collection (1855). Several sets of words have been fitted to it: 'Would I were Erin's apple blossom' and 'Emer's Farewell', both by Alfred Perceval Graves, and 'Danny Boy' by F. E. Weatherly. Stanford used it in his *Irish Rhapsody* no. 1 and Percy Grainger made several arrangements of it (as *Irish Tune from County Derry*).

London Overture, A. Orchestral work (1936) by John Ireland; it was originally written for brass band (1934) under the title *Comedy Overture*, and one of its principal themes is said to have been inspired by a bus conductor's call of 'Piccadilly'.

'London' Symphonies ('Salomon' Symphonies). Haydn's last 12 symphonies, nos. 93–104 (1791–5), composed for the impresario J. P. Salomon and first performed during Haydn's visits in 1791–2 and 1794–5. They include the *'Miracle' (no. 96), the *'Surprise' (no. 94), the *'Military' (no. 100), the *'Clock' (no. 101), and the *'Drumroll' (no. 103); the last, no. 104 in D major (1795), is known as the 'London' Symphony, or the 'Salomon' Symphony.

London Symphony, A. Vaughan Williams's second symphony; it was composed in 1912–13, revised substantially in 1920, and revised finally in 1933. It is not a programmatic work but it includes evocations of London life, such as Westminster chimes, a lavender-seller's cry, the jingle of hansom cabs, and the sounds of street musicians.

Lontano. Orchestral work (1967) by Ligeti.

Lorelei [*Loreley*]. The legendary figure who sings on a mountain by the Rhine, luring sailors to their death on the rocks below, has been the subject of several operas, including an unfinished one by Mendelssohn (1847) to a libretto by Emanuel Geibel (the 'Ave Maria' is sometimes given in the concert hall); among others are those by Vincent Wallace (1860), Bruch (1863), and Catalani (1890). Liszt wrote a song (1841) for voice and piano to Heinrich Heine's poem; he arranged it with orchestra and transcribed it for solo piano.

Lost Chord, The. Song (1877) by Sullivan, a setting of a poem by Adelaide Anne Procter; composed in sorrow at his brother's death, it is regarded as the archetypal Victorian drawing-room ballad.

Loudon Symphony. *See* LAUDON SYMPHONY.

Louise. Opera (*roman musical*) in four acts by Gustave Charpentier to a libretto by the composer with assistance from Saint-Pol-Roux (Paris, 1900).

Love for Three Oranges, The (*Lyubov' k tryom apel'sinam*). Opera in a prologue and four acts by Prokofiev to his own libretto after Carlo Gozzi's play *L'amore delle tre melarance* (1761) adapted by Vsevolod Meyerhold, Vladimir Solov'yov, and Konstantin Vogak (Chicago, 1921, as *L'Amour des trois oranges*). Prokofiev arranged an orchestral suite from the score (1919, revised 1924).

Love in a Village. Comic opera in three acts by Arne to a libretto by Isaac Bickerstaff after Charles Johnson's *The Village Opera* (1729); it is a pasticcio of 42 items, of which Arne composed five, borrowed 13 from his earlier works and arranged the rest from several composers including C. F. Abel, Geminiani, and Galuppi (London, 1762).

Love Potion, The. *See* ELISIR D'AMORE, L'.

Lover and the Nightingale, The. *See* MAJA Y EL RUISENOR, LA.

Love-Song Waltzes. *See* LIEBESLIEDERWALZER.

Love, the Magician. *See* AMOR BRUJO, EL.

Luce mie traditrici ('Treacherous Eyes'). Opera in two acts by Salvatore Sciarrino to a libretto by the composer after Giacinto Andrea Cicognini's play *Il tradimento per l'onore* (1664), with an elegy by Claude Le Jeune (1608) (Schwetzingen, 1998).

Lucia di Lammermoor ('Lucy of Lammermoor'). Opera (*dramma tragico*) in three acts by Donizetti to a libretto by Salvadore Cammarano after Walter Scott's novel *The Bride of Lammermoor* (1819) (Naples, 1835).

Lucio Silla ('Lucius Sulla'). Opera (*dramma per musica*) in three acts by Mozart to a libretto by Giovanni De Gamerra (Milan, 1772). Pasquale Anfossi (1774) and J. C. Bach (1775) also wrote operas on the subject.

Lucrezia Borgia. Opera (*melodramma*) in a prologue and two acts by Donizetti to a libretto by Felice Romani after Victor Hugo's play *Lucrèce Borgia* (1833) (Milan, 1833).

Ludus tonalis ('The Play of Notes'). Piano studies (1942) by Hindemith; consisting of a prelude, 12 fugues with 11 interludes, and a postlude (an inverted version of the prelude), they are studies in counterpoint, tonal organization, and piano technique.

Ludwig van. A film (1969–70) by Kagel for which he wrote the music, processing works by Beethoven.

Luisa Miller. Opera (*melodramma tragico*) in three acts by Verdi to a libretto by Salvadore Cammarano after Friedrich von Schiller's play *Kabale und Liebe* (1784) (Naples, 1849).

Lulu. Opera in a prologue and three acts by Berg to his own libretto after Frank Wedekind's plays *Erdgeist* (1895) and *Die Büchse der Pandora* (1918) (Acts I and II, Zürich, 1937); Berg died before the final act was finished and it was completed by Friedrich Cerha (Paris, 1979).

Luonnotar. Tone-poem, op. 70 (1913), by Sibelius for soprano and orchestra; it is a setting of words from the *Kalevala* telling of the creation of the world.

Lustigen Weiber von Windsor, Die ('The Merry Wives of Windsor'). Opera (*komische-fantastische Oper*) in three acts by Nicolai to a libretto by Salomon Hermann Mosenthal after Shakespeare's play (?c.1597) (Berlin, 1849).

Lustige Witwe, Die ('The Merry Widow'). Operetta in three acts by Lehár to a libretto by Victor Léon and Leo Stein after Henri Meilhac's *L'Attaché d'ambassade* (1861) (Vienna, 1905).

Lux aeterna ('Eternal Light'). Work (1966) by Ligeti for 16 unaccompanied voices.

Lyric Suite. 1. Orchestral work (1904) by Grieg, arranged from four of his six *Lyric Pieces* (book 5) op. 54.

　　2. Work (1925–6) for string quartet by Berg.

Lyrische Symphonie. Zemlinsky's op. 18 (1922–3), seven songs for soprano, baritone, and orchestra, settings of the composer's German translations of poems by Rabindranath Tagore. It is dedicated to Berg, who quoted from it in his *Lyric Suite*.

Macbeth. 1. Opera in four acts by Verdi to a libretto by Francesco Maria Piave (with additional material by Andrea Maffei) after Shakespeare's play (1605–6) (Florence, 1847); Verdi revised and expanded it, using Piave's libretto translated into French by Charles-Louis-Étienne Nuitter and Alexandre Beaumont (Paris, 1865).
2. Tone-poem, op. 23 (1886–8), by Richard Strauss, revised in 1889–90.
3. Lyric drama in a prologue and three acts by Bloch to a libretto by Edmond Fleg after Shakespeare's play (Paris, 1910).

Madama Butterfly ('Madam Butterfly'). Opera (*tragedia giapponese*) in two acts by Puccini to a libretto by Giuseppe Giacosa and Luigi Illica after David Belasco's play *Madame Butterfly* (1900), itself based on John Luther Long's short story (1898), which in turn was based partly on Pierre Loti's story *Madame Chrysanthème* (Milan, 1904; revised Brescia, 1904).

Madam Press Died Last Week at Ninety. Work (1970) by Morton Feldman for eight players.

Mädchen mit den Schwefelhölzern, Das ('The Little Match Girl'). 'Music with images' by Helmut Lachenmann to a libretto by the composer after Hans Christian Andersen's fairy tale (1846) with extra material from Leonardo da Vinci and Gudrun Esslin (Hamburg, 1997).

Maddalena. Opera in one act by Prokofiev to his own libretto (concert performance, Manchester, 1978; staged Graz, 1981).

Madrigali guerrieri ed amorosi ('Madrigals of Love and War'). Monteverdi's eighth book of madrigals (1638).

Magic Flute, The. *See* ZAUBERFLÖTE, DIE.

Magnus liber organi ('Great Book of Organum'). A collection of two-voice plainchant settings for liturgical use, dating from the early Notre Dame period (*c*.1170). It has been attributed to Léonin and said to have been revised by Pérotin. The most important surviving work of the period, it is arranged for the church year in cycles of polyphonic settings of the Office and the Mass. Its title is taken from the description by the 13th-century theorist Anonymous IV: 'Magnus liber organi de graduali et antifonario'.

Mahagonny. 'Songspiel' in three parts by Weill after poems from Bertolt Brecht's *Hauspostille* (Baden-Baden, 1927); the title is also sometimes used to refer to **Aufstieg und Fall der Stadt Mahagonny*.

Maid of Orléans, The (*Orleanskaya deva*). Opera in four acts by Tchaikovsky to his own libretto after Friedrich von Schiller's tragedy (1801) translated by Vasily Andreyevich Zhukovsky, Jules Barbier's *Jeanne d'Arc*, and Auguste Mermet's libretto for his own opera, after Barbier (1876), with details from Henri Wallon's biography of Joan of Arc (St Petersburg, 1881).

Maid of Pskov, The (*Pskovityanka*). Opera in three acts by Rimsky-Korsakov to his own libretto after Lev Mey's play (1860), with additions by Vsevolod Krestovsky and Musorgsky (St Petersburg, 1873); it was revised (St Petersburg, 1895) and a prologue was added (Moscow, 1901).

Maid of the Mill, The. *See* SCHÖNE MÜLLERIN, DIE.

Mai-Dun. Symphonic rhapsody (1921) for orchestra by John Ireland; the title refers to Maiden Castle, Dorset.

Maja y el ruisenor, La ('The Lover and the Nightingale'). The fourth of Granados's *Goyescas* for piano; he later incorporated it as a song into scene 2 of his opera *Goyescas* and it is frequently heard as a separate concert aria with orchestra.

Makrokosmos. Two sets of fantasy pieces (1972, 1973) for amplified piano by George Crumb; both sets consist of 12 pieces after the signs of the zodiac, each portraying a friend of the composer's born under that sign. They are studies in avant-garde piano technique.

Makropulos Affair, The (*The Makropulos Case*; *Věc Makropulos*). Opera in three acts by Janáček to his own libretto after Karel Čapek's comedy *Věc Makropulos* (1922) (Brno, 1926).

Mamelles de Tirésias, Les ('The Breasts of Tiresias'). *Opéra bouffe* in a prologue and two acts by Poulenc to his own libretto after Guillaume Apollinaire's play (1917) (Paris, 1947).

Ma mère l'oye ('Mother Goose'). Suite for piano duet (1908–10) by Ravel, depicting characters from fairy tales by Charles Perrault and others; it was later orchestrated by Ravel, who added a prelude and four interludes to make a children's ballet (Paris, 1912).

Man and Boy: Dada. Chamber opera by Michael Nyman to a libretto by Michael Hastings (Karlsruhe, 2004). One of the characters in it is Kurt Schwitters, founder of the Dada movement.

Manfred. 1. Incidental music, op. 115 (1848–9), by Schumann for Byron's verse drama (1817), in a translation by K. A. Suckow (1852); it consists of an overture and 15 items.

2. Symphony (unnumbered), op. 58 (1885), by Tchaikovsky after Byron.

Manon. *Opéra comique* in five acts by Massenet to a libretto by Henri Meilhac and Philippe Gille after Antoine-François Prévost's novel *L'Histoire du chevalier Des Grieux et de Manon Lescaut* (1731) (Paris, 1884).

Manon Lescaut. Opera (*dramma lirico*) in four acts by Puccini to a libretto by Domenico Oliva and Luigi Illica after Antoine-François Prévost's novel *L'Histoire du chevalier Des Grieux et de Manon Lescaut* (1731) (Turin, 1893; revised Milan, 1894). Auber's *Manon Lescaut*, to a libretto by Eugène Scribe (Paris, 1856), Massenet's **Manon*, and Henze's **Boulevard Solitude* are also based on the story.

Mantra. Work by Stockhausen (1969–70) for two amplified, ring-modulated pianos with woodblock and crotales (played by the pianists); the whole score is based on one melodic formula.

Man Who Mistook his Wife for a Hat, The. Chamber opera in one act by Michael Nyman to a libretto by Christopher Rawlence after the case study by Oliver Sacks (1985) (London, 1986).

Manzoni Requiem. Title sometimes given to Verdi's Requiem (1874), composed in memory of the Italian novelist and poet Alessandro Manzoni (1785–1873) and first performed on the first anniversary of his death.

Maometto II ('Mahomet II'). Opera (*dramma*) in two acts by Rossini to a libretto by Cesare della Valle after his *Anna Erizo* (Naples, 1820). Rossini revised it as *Le Siège de Corinthe*.

Marcellus Mass. *See* MISSA PAPAE MARCELLI.

Marco Polo. 'An opera within an opera' by Tan Dun to a libretto by Paul Griffiths (Munich, 1996).

Mare nostrum ('Our Sea'). Music-theatre work by Kagel, for two singers and six players, subtitled 'discovery, pacification, and conversion of the Mediterranean by an Amazonian tribe' (Berlin, 1975).

Maria de Buenos Aires ('Maria of Buenos Aires'). Opera (*tango operita*) in two parts and 16 scenes by Astor Piazzolla to a libretto by Horacio Ferrer (Buenos Aires, 1968).

Maria di Rohan ('Maria of Rohan'). Opera (*melodramma tragico*) in three acts by Donizetti to a libretto by Salvadore Cammarano after Lockroy and Badon's play *Un duel sous le Cardinal de Richelieu* (1832) (Vienna, 1843).

Maria Golovin. Musical drama in three acts by Menotti to his own libretto (Brussels, 1958).

Maria Stuarda ('Mary Stuart'). Opera (*tragedia lirica*) in two or three acts by Donizetti to a libretto by Giuseppe Bardari after Andrea Maffei's translation (1830) of Friedrich von Schiller's *Maria Stuart* (1800) (Milan, 1835).

Marienleben, Das ('The Life of Mary'). Songs (1922–3) by Hindemith for soprano and piano, settings of poems by Rainer Maria Rilke; the 15 settings were revised between 1936 and 1948. Hindemith orchestrated four of them in 1938 and two more in 1948.

Mariés de la tour Eiffel, Les ('The Newly-Weds of the Eiffel Tower'). Ballet in one act by Auric, Honegger, Milhaud, Poulenc, and Tailleferre (five of Les Six, the other being Durey), to a scenario by Jean Cocteau; it was choreographed by Jean Börlin (Paris, 1921).

Marriage of Figaro, The. *See* NOZZE DI FIGARO, LE.

Marseillaise, La ('Allons enfants de la patrie'). French national anthem. It was written as a revolutionary marching song in 1792 by Claude-Joseph Rouget de Lisle (1760–1836) and was sung by a battalion from Marseilles when they entered Paris later that year. It was officially adopted in 1795 and has remained in use ever since, in spite of an attempt to replace it during the Second Empire of Napoleon III. The tune has been incorporated into works by several composers including Schumann, Wagner, Litolff, Liszt, Tchaikovsky, and Debussy.

Marteau sans maître, Le ('The Hammer without a Master'). Work (1953–5) by Boulez for contralto, alto flute, guitar, vibraphone, xylorimba, percussion, and viola, to a text by René Char; it was revised in 1957.

Martha (*Martha, oder Der Markt zu Richmond*; 'Martha, or The Market at Richmond'). Romantic comic opera in four acts by Flotow to a libretto by W. Friedrich after an idea by Jules-Henri Vernoy de Saint-Georges (Vienna, 1847).

Martyrdom of St Magnus, The. Chamber opera in nine scenes by Maxwell Davies to his own libretto after George Mackay Brown's novel *Magnus* (1973) (Kirkwall, 1977).

Martyre de Saint Sébastien, Le ('The Martyrdom of St Sebastian'). Incidental music (1911) by Debussy, for soprano, two contraltos, chorus, and orchestra, for a mystery play by Gabriele D'Annunzio; André Caplet assisted with the orchestration.

Mary of Egypt. Chamber opera ('Moving Icon') in one act by Tavener to a libretto by Mother Thekla after *The Account of the Life of Hallowed Mother Mary of Egypt* (Aldeburgh, 1992).

Mary, Queen of Scots. Opera in three acts by Musgrave to her own libretto after Amalia Elguera's play *Moray* (Edinburgh, 1977).

Masaniello. *See* MUETTE DE PORTICI, LA.

Maschinist Hopkins ('Hopkins the Engineer'). Opera in a prologue and three acts by Max Brand to his own libretto (Duisburg, 1929).

Maskarade ('Masquerade'). Comic opera in three acts by Nielsen to a libretto by Vilhelm Andersen after Ludvig Holberg's play *Mascarade* (1724) (Copenhagen, 1906).

Masked Ball, A. *See* BALLO IN MASCHERA, UN.

Mask of Orpheus, The. Opera ('lyric tragedy') in three acts by Birtwistle to a libretto by Peter Zinovieff (London, 1986).

Mask of Time, The. Choral work (1980–2) by Tippett for soprano, mezzo-soprano, tenor, and baritone soloists, chorus, and orchestra, a setting of his own text.

Masnadieri, I ('The Robbers'). Opera (*melodramma*) in four acts by Verdi to a libretto by Andrea Maffei after Friedrich von Schiller's play *Die Räuber* (1781) (London, 1847).

Masonic Funeral Music. *See* MAURERISCHE TRAUERMUSIK.

Masques et bergamasques. Divertissement (*comédie musicale*) by Fauré to a scenario by René Fauchois (Monte Carlo, 1919); Fauré made an orchestral suite (1920) from it.

Mass of Life, A (*Eine Messe des Lebens*). Choral work (1904–5) by Delius for soprano, alto, tenor, and bass soloists, chorus, and orchestra, to a German text selected by Fritz Cassirer from Friedrich Nietzsche's *Also sprach Zarathustra*. The second part was first performed in 1908 and the first complete performance (in English) was a year later.

Master and Margherita, The. *See* MEISTER UND MARGARITA, DER.

Mastersingers of Nuremberg, The. *See* MEISTERSINGER VON NÜRNBERG, DIE.

Match. Work (1964) by Kagel for two cellists (dressed as table-tennis players) and a percussionist (the referee); a film version followed in 1966 and it was televised the next year.

Materie, De ('Matter'). Music-theatre piece in four parts by Louis Andriessen to his own libretto after the Dutch Declaration of Independence and the writings of David Gorlaeus, Nicolaes Witsen, Hadewijch, Piet Mondrian, M. H. J. Schoenmakers, Marie Curie, and Willem Cloos (Amsterdam, 1989).

Mathis der Maler ('Mathis the Painter'). Opera in seven scenes by Hindemith to his own libretto (Zürich, 1938).

Matin, Le; Midi, Le; Soir, Le ('Morning'; 'Midday'; 'Evening'). Haydn's Symphonies nos. 6, 7, and 8, in D major, C major, and G major, composed *c.*1761; the last movement of *Le Soir* is known as 'La Tempête', the whole symphony sometimes being referred to as *Le Soir et la Tempête*.

Matrimonio segreto, Il ('The Secret Marriage'). Opera (*melodramma giocoso*) in two acts by Cimarosa to a libretto by Giovanni Bertati after George Colman the elder and David Garrick's play *The Clandestine Marriage* (1766) (Vienna, 1792).

Maurerische Trauermusik ('Masonic Funeral Music'). Work by Mozart, K477/479*a* (1785), for two oboes, clarinet, three basset horns, double bassoon, two horns, and strings; originally thought to have been composed for the funeral of two Viennese freemasons, it is dated several weeks before their death in Mozart's own catalogue.

Má vlast ('My Country'; 'My Fatherland'). Cycle of six symphonic poems (*c.*1872–9) by Smetana: *Vyšehrad* (the old citadel in Prague), *Vltava* (river Moldau), *Šárka* (a female Amazon warrior in Czech legend), *Z Českých luhů a hájů* (the woods and fields of Bohemia), *Tábor* (an ancient stronghold), and *Blaník* (a 'Valhalla' near Prague where slumbering heroes await their call to defend their nation).

Mavra. *Opéra bouffe* in one act by Stravinsky to a libretto by Boris Kochno after Aleksandr Pushkin's narrative poem *Domik v Kolomne* ('The Little House at Colomna', 1830) (Paris, 1922).

May Night (*Mayskaya noch'*). Opera in three acts by Rimsky-Korsakov to his own libretto after Nikolay Gogol's story *Mayskaya noch', ili Utoplennitsa* ('May Night, or The Drowned Maiden') from his *Evenings on a Farm near Dikanka* (i, 1831) (St Petersburg, 1880).

Mazeppa. 1. The title of several pieces by Liszt, taken from a poem of Victor Hugo. The earliest version of the musical material is the D minor study from the juvenile *Étude en douze exercices* (1825), revised in 1837 as *12 grandes études*; none of these pieces has any descriptive title. The D minor study from this set was elaborated ten years later and published separately with the title *Mazeppa*; it retained this appellation in the final revision of all 12 *études*, published in 1851 as *Études d'exécution transcendante*. Liszt also used an orchestrated version of this music as part of his symphonic poem *Mazeppa* (1851–4), which includes additional material from the *Arbeiterchor*.

2. Opera in three acts by Tchaikovsky to a libretto by Victor Burenin, revised by the composer with an aria to words by Vasily Kandaurov, after Aleksandr Pushkin's poem *Poltava* (1829) (Moscow, 1884).

Médée ('Medea'). *Opéra comique* in three acts by Cherubini to a libretto by François-Benoît Hoffman after Euripides (Paris, 1797). M.-A. Charpentier (1693), Benda (1775), Mayr (1813), Pacini (1843), Milhaud (1938), and Bryars (1984) wrote operas on the same subject and Barber wrote a ballet (1946) on it.

Méditations sur le Mystère de la Sainte Trinité ('Meditations on the Mystery of the Holy Trinity'). Organ work (1969) by Messaien.

Medium, The. 'Tragic opera' in two acts by Menotti to his own libretto (New York, 1946, revised 1947).

Meeresstille und glückliche Fahrt ('Calm Sea and Prosperous Voyage').
1. Overture, op. 27 (1828), by Mendelssohn, evoking two poems by Johann Wolfgang von Goethe.
2. Cantata, op. 112 (1814–15), by Beethoven, for chorus and orchestra, a setting of two poems by Goethe.

Mefistofele ('Mephistopheles'). Opera in a prologue, five acts, and an epilogue by Boito to his own libretto after Johann Wolfgang von Goethe's play *Faust* (Milan, 1868); Boito revised it into four acts (Bologna, 1875), then made a further revision (Venice, 1876).

Meistersinger von Nürnberg, Die ('The Mastersingers of Nuremberg'). Music drama in three acts by Wagner to his own libretto (Munich, 1868).

Meister und Margarita, Der ('The Master and Margarita'). Opera in a prologue and two acts by York Höller to his own libretto after Mikhail Bulgakov's novel (finished 1940) (Paris, 1989). Several composers have written operas on the subject, notably Rainer Kunad (Karlsruhe, 1986) and Sergey Slonimsky (concert 1989, staged Moscow, 1991).

Melancholic Songs of Love (*Melancholické písně o lásce*). Song cycle, op. 38 (1906), by Novák for mezzo-soprano and orchestra, settings of texts by Jaroslav Vrchlický, J. Borecký, and Pablo Neruda; originally for voice and piano, they were later orchestrated by Novák.

Melodien ('Melodies'). Orchestral work (1971) by Ligeti.

Men of Harlech (*Rhyfelgyrch Gwyr Harlech*). Song published in 1860, which has subsequently had a variety of lyrics, rallying the troops to defend Harlech castle; with its rousing march-like tune, it has become a Welsh anthem.

Mephistowalzer ('Mephisto Waltzes'). A series of works by Liszt, their title deriving from an abbreviation for 'Mephistopheles'. The first, *Der Tanz in der Dorfschenke* ('The Dance at the Village Inn') (1859), was originally for piano but was then orchestrated to become one of *Two Episodes from Lenau's Faust*. The second (1880–1) also exists in piano and orchestral versions. The third (1883, two versions) was composed for piano only, as was the fourth (1885). The *Bagatelle sans tonalité* was originally intended to be part of the series.

Mer, La ('The Sea'). Three symphonic sketches (1903–5) by Debussy: *De l'aube à midi sur la mer* ('From Dawn to Noon on the Sea'), *Jeux de vagues* ('Play of the Waves'), and *Dialogue du vent et de la mer* ('Dialogue of the Wind and the Sea').

Mercure. Ballet in three scenes by Satie to a scenario by Leonid Massine; it was choreographed by Massine, with designs by Pablo Picasso (Paris, 1924).

Merle noir, Le ('The Blackbird'). Work (1951) by Messiaen for flute and piano.

Merlin. Opera in three acts by Albéniz to a libretto by Francis Burdett Money-Coutts after Arthurian legend; it is the first part of a projected Arthurian trilogy and was completed in 1902. It had its premiere in Barcelona in 1950 and was revived in 1998.

Merrie England. Operetta in two acts by Edward German to a libretto by Basil Hood (London, 1902).

Merry Widow, The. *See* LUSTIGE WITWE, DIE.

Merry Wives of Windsor, The. *See* LUSTIGEN WEIBER VON WINDSOR, DIE.

Messages of the Late R. V. Trussova. Work (1980) by Kurtág for soprano and piano, settings of 21 poems by Rimma Dalos.

Messe de Nostre Dame. *See* NOTRE DAME MASS.

Messe des morts (Fr.). 'Mass for the dead', i.e. Requiem Mass.

Messiah. Oratorio by Handel to a text compiled by Charles Jennens from the Bible and the Prayer Book Psalter; it was first performed in Dublin in 1742. Handel revised it for subsequent performances and in the 19th century it became customary to perform it with enormous forces.

Métaboles. Orchestral work (1964) by Dutilleux; its title refers to the metabolic process by which the composer transforms the musical material during the work's five movements.

Metamorphosen. Study in C minor (1945) by Richard Strauss for 23 solo strings; it was composed as a lament for the wartime destruction of the German cultural world and quotes from Beethoven's 'Eroica' Symphony.

Metamorphoses after Ovid, Six. *See* SIX METAMORPHOSES AFTER OVID.

Michaels Reise um die Erde ('Michael's Journey Round the Earth'). Work (1978) by Stockhausen for trumpet and orchestra, Act II of his *Donnerstag aus Licht*, which is performable separately; Stockhausen made a reduced version of it (1978), for trumpet and nine instruments, and revised it in 1984.

Midi, Le. *See* MATIN, LE; MIDI, LE; SOIR, LE.

Midsummer Marriage, The. Opera in three acts by Tippett to his own libretto (London, 1955).

Midsummer Night's Dream, A. Opera in three acts by Britten to a libretto by the composer and Peter Pears after Shakespeare's play (1594–5) (Aldeburgh, 1960).

Mignon. *Opéra comique* in three acts by Ambroise Thomas to a libretto by Jules Barbier and Michel Carré after Johann Wolfgang von Goethe's novel *Wilhelm Meisters Lehrjahre* ('Wilhelm Meister's Apprenticeship', 1795–6) (Paris, 1866).

Mikado, The (*The Mikado; or, The Town of Titipu*). Operetta in two acts by Sullivan to a libretto by W. S. Gilbert (London, 1885).

Mikrokosmos ('Little World'). A collection of 153 piano pieces by Bartók, published in six volumes of progressive difficulty (with supplementary exercises), composed in 1926 and between 1932 and 1939; some of them exist in arrangements, by Bartók and Tibor Serly.

Mikrophonie I and II. Two works by Stockhausen; the first (1964) is for tam-tam (two players), two microphones, two filters, and potentiometers; the second (1965) is a setting of Helmut Heisenbüttel's *Einfache grammatische Meditationen* for six sopranos, six basses, Hammond organ, four ring modulators, and four-track tape.

'Military' Polonaise. Nickname of Chopin's Polonaise in A major op. 40 no. 1 (1838) for piano.

'Military' Symphony. Nickname of Haydn's Symphony no. 100 in G major (1793–4), so called because of its use in the Andante of a triangle, cymbals, and bass drum, in imitation of Turkish military music, and a trumpet call. Haydn made a setting of this movement for military band.

Mind of Winter, A. Work (1981) by Gerald Barry for soprano and orchestra, a setting of poems by Wallace Stevens.

Mines of Sulphur, The. Opera in three acts by Richard Rodney Bennett to a libretto by Beverley Cross (London, 1965).

'Minute' Waltz. Nickname of Chopin's Waltz in D♭ major op. 64 no. 1 (1846–7), for piano, so called because it can be played in one minute—but only if it is taken much too fast.

'Miracle' Symphony. Nickname of Haydn's Symphony no. 96 in D major (1791), so called because it was said (incorrectly) that at its first performance in London in 1791 the audience rushed forward at the end to congratulate the composer, thereby miraculously escaping being injured by a chandelier that fell on their seats. The incident in fact occurred during Haydn's second visit to London, in 1795, after a performance of his Symphony no. 102.

Miraculous Mandarin, The (*A csodálatos mandarin*). Pantomime in one act by Bartók to a scenario by Menyhért Lengyel (Cologne, 1926); because of censorship it was not performed in Budapest until 1946. Bartók arranged an orchestral suite from the score (1919 and 1927).

Mireille. Opera in five acts by Gounod to a libretto by Michel Carré after Frédéric Mistral's epic poem *Mirèio* (1859) (Paris, 1864).

Miroirs ('Mirrors'). Five piano pieces (1904–5) by Ravel: *Nocturelles* ('Moths'), *Oiseaux tristes* ('Sad Birds'), *Une barque sur l'océan* ('A Boat on the Ocean'), *Alborada del gracioso* ('The Fool's Morning Song'), and *La Vallée des cloches* ('The Valley of Bells'); Ravel orchestrated the third (1906, revised 1926) and fourth (1918).

Mirror of Whitening Light, A. Piece for chamber orchestra (1976–7) by Maxwell Davies.

Mirror on which to Dwell, A. Song cycle (1975) by Elliott Carter, settings of six poems by Elizabeth Bishop for soprano and instrumental ensemble.

Miserly Knight, The (*Skupoy rïtsar*). Opera in one act by Rakhmaninov to a shortened version of Aleksandr Pushkin's 'little tragedy' (1830) of the same title (Moscow, 1906).

Missa in tempore belli ('Mass in Time of War'). *See* PAUKENMESSE.

Missa Papae Marcelli. Mass for six voices by Palestrina, composed *c*.1561. It is dedicated to Pope Marcellus II, who established the Council of Trent which sought to reform the composition of polyphonic sacred music so that the words were intelligible. Romantic legend has it that, because of the clarity with which Palestrina treated the text, with this mass he 'saved church music'.

Missa solemnis ('Solemn Mass'). The name by which Beethoven's Mass in D major op. 123 is known; it was intended for the installation of Archduke Rudolph as Archbishop of Olmütz in 1820 but was not completed in its final version until 1823.

Miss Donnithorne's Maggot. Music-theatre piece by Maxwell Davies for soprano, flute, clarinet, piano, percussion, violin, and cello, a setting of a text by Randolph Stow (Adelaide, 1974); the ensemble includes four metronomes, bosun's whistle, and chamois leather rubbed on glass. In the 16th and 17th centuries 'maggot' was used as a title for a light piece of music, for example a dance, with a person's name attached.

Mitridate, re di Ponto ('Mithridates, King of Pontus'). Opera (*dramma per musica*) in three acts by Mozart to a libretto by Vittorio Amedeo Cigna-Santi after Giuseppe Parini's translation of Jean Racine's *Mithridate* (1673) (Milan, 1770).

Mittwoch aus Licht ('Wednesday from Light'). Opera in a greeting, four scenes, and a farewell by Stockhausen to his own libretto, the 'sixth day' of *Licht.

Mixtur. Work (1964) by Stockhausen for five orchestral groups, sine-wave generators, and four ring modulators; he revised it (1967) for five small orchestral groups with the same electronics.

Mlada. 'Magical opera-ballet' in four acts by Rimsky-Korsakov to his own libretto based on Viktor Krïlov's libretto *Mlada* (1872) (St Petersburg, 1892). The libretto (1872) was commissioned for an opera-ballet in four acts by Cui (Act I), Musorgsky and Rimsky-Korsakov (Acts II and III), and Borodin (Act IV), but it was never performed and much of the score was recycled into other works.

Mladi ('Youth'). Suite (1924) by Janáček for flute/piccolo, oboe, clarinet, horn, bassoon, and bass clarinet.

Moby Dick. Cantata (1936–8) by Bernard Herrmann, for two tenors, two basses, male chorus, and orchestra, to a text selected by W. Clark Harrington from Herman Melville's novel (1851).

Modern Painters. Opera in two acts by David Lang to a libretto by Manuela Hoelterhoff after John Ruskin's *The Seven Lamps of Architecture* (1848) (Santa Fe, NM, 1995).

Moïse et Pharaon (*Moïse et Pharaon, ou Le Passage de la Mer Rouge*; 'Moses and Pharaoh, or The Crossing of the Red Sea'). Opera in four acts by Rossini, derived from his *Mosè in Egitto* (1818), to a new libretto by Luigi Balocchi and Étienne de Jouy (Paris, 1827).

Moldau. *See* MÁ VLAST.

Molly Malone. *See* COCKLES AND MUSSELS.

Molly on the Shore. A British folksong arranged by Percy Grainger for two pianos and for various orchestral combinations; it has been arranged by others for numerous different ensembles, notably by Leopold Stokowski for orchestra.

Momente ('Moments'). Work (1961–4) by Stockhausen for soprano, four choral groups, four trumpets, four trombones, two electric organs, and three percussionists; it uses texts from the Song of Songs, Malinowski's *The Sexual Life of Savages*, onomatopoeic words, letters, and other sources, and consists of a series of 'moments', some of which need not be performed. It was expanded in 1964 and 1972.

Moments musicaux ('Musical Moments'). The title given by the publisher to Schubert's set of six piano pieces op. 94 D780 (1823–8), shown on the original title page as *Momens musicaux*. The term has been adopted by other composers for character pieces for piano.

Mondo della luna, Il ('The World on the Moon'). Opera (*dramma giocoso*) in three acts by Haydn to a libretto by Carlo Goldoni (Eszterháza, 1777). Goldoni's libretto was set by several composers, the first being Galuppi (1750).

Monsters of Grace. 'A digital opera in three dimensions' by Philip Glass, in collaboration with Robert Wilson, with words by Coleman Barks based on his translations of poems by the 13th-century Sufi poet Jalāl ad-Dīn ar-Rūmī (Los Angeles, 1998).

Montag aus Licht ('Monday from Light'). Opera in a greeting, three acts, and a farewell by Stockhausen to his own libretto (Milan, 1988), the 'third day' of *Licht.

Montezuma. Opera in three acts by Sessions to a libretto by Giuseppe Antonio Borgese based on the story of Hernán Cortez's conquest of the Aztecs and colonization of Mexico (West Berlin, 1964).

'Moonlight' Sonata. Nickname of Beethoven's Piano Sonata no. 14 in C♯ minor op. 27 no. 2 (1801), so called apparently because the poet Heinrich Rellstab (1799–1860) wrote in a review that it reminded him of a boat in the moonlight on Lake Lucerne.

Morceaux en forme de poire, Trois. *See* TROIS MORCEAUX EN FORME DE POIRE.

Morgenblätter ('Morning Papers'). Waltz, op. 279, by Johann Strauss (ii), composed for the Vienna Press Ball in 1864.

Mörike-Lieder ('Songs of Mörike'). 53 songs for voice and piano by Wolf, settings of poems by Eduard Friedrich Mörike (1804–75); most were composed in 1888 and they include *Elfenlied*, *Gesang Weylas*, *Der Feuerreiter*, and *An die Geliebte*.

Mort de Cléopâtre, La ('The Death of Cleopatra'). Lyric scene (1829) by Berlioz, for soprano or mezzo-soprano and orchestra, a setting of a text by P. A. Vieillard; it was part of a larger cantata *Cléopâtre*, an unsuccessful entry for the Prix de Rome.

Mortuos plango, vivos voco. Piece for tape (1980) by Jonathan Harvey.

Mosè in Egitto ('Moses in Egypt'). Opera (*azione tragica-sacra*) in three acts by Rossini to a libretto by Andrea Leone Tottola after the Old Testament and Francesco Ringhieri's *L'Osiride* (1760) (Naples, 1818); the famous prayer, sung by the Israelites before they cross the Red Sea, was added for the 1819 Naples revival. Rossini revised the opera as *Moïse et Pharaon.

Moses und Aron ('Moses and Aaron'). Opera in three acts by Schoenberg to his own libretto (Act III was not composed) (Zürich, 1957). 'The Dance Before the Golden Calf' (from Act II) was performed in concert in 1951, as were Acts I and II in 1954.

Mother Goose. *See* MA MÈRE L'OYE.

Mother of Us All, The. Opera in two acts by Virgil Thomson to a libretto by Gertrude Stein and a scenario by Maurice Grosser (New York, 1947).

Mourning Becomes Electra. Opera in three acts by Marvin David Levy to a libretto by Henry Butler after Eugene O'Neill's trilogy of plays (1931) (New York, 1967).

Mozart and Salieri. Opera ('dramatic scenes') in one act by Rimsky-Korsakov to an abridged version of Aleksandr Pushkin's 'little tragedy' (1830) (Moscow, 1898).

Mozartiana. Subtitle of Tchaikovsky's Suite no. 4 for orchestra (1887); three of its four movements are arrangements of music by Mozart and the fourth is of Gluck.

Muette de Portici, La ('The Mute Girl of Portici'; *Masaniello, ou La Muette de Portici*). Grand opera in five acts by Auber to a libretto by Eugène Scribe and Germain Delavigne (Paris, 1828).

Mulliner Book (London, British Library, Add. 30513). A collection of keyboard music copied by the organist Thomas Mulliner in the mid-16th century. It contains a wide variety of music, mostly for organ and including fantasias and transcriptions of anthems and secular songs; among the composers represented are Redford, Tallis, and Blitheman. One of the most valuable sources for the keyboard repertory, it has been published in the *Musica britannica* series in an edition by Denis Stevens (1951, revised 1954).

Musical Joke, A (*Ein musikalischer Spass*). Mozart's Divertimento in F major к522 (1787), for two horns and strings, a parody of composers and performers of popular music.

Musical Offering (*Musicalisches Opfer*). Collection of 13 works, вwv1079 (1747), by J. S. Bach (two ricercars, a trio sonata, and ten canons), some for keyboard and others for up to four instruments, on a theme by Frederick the Great, King of Prussia, to whom it is dedicated.

Musica transalpina. Title of two anthologies of Italian (i.e. transalpine) madrigals, with English words, edited by Nicholas Yonge and published in London by Thomas East. The first (1588) contains 57 madrigals, by Marenzio, Palestrina, Byrd, and Lassus, among others; the second (1597) contains 24, including examples by Ferrabosco, Marenzio, and Stefano Venturi. They were the first printed collections of Italian madrigals in England and had a great influence on English composers of the period.

Music for a While. Song by Henry Purcell, part of his incidental music to Dryden's play *Oedipus* (1692).

Music for 18 Musicians. Work (1974–6) by Reich for voices (wordless) and ensemble.

Music for Mallet Instruments, Voices, and Organ. Work (1973) by Reich for seven percussionists, three (wordless) female voices, and electronic organ.

Music in Twelve Parts. Instrumental piece (1971–4) by Philip Glass, composed for his own ensemble.

Musicircus. An 'environmental extravaganza' (1967) by Cage consisting of simultaneous performances of rock, jazz, electronic, piano, and vocal music, pantomime, and dance, with films and slide shows.

Music Makers, The. Ode, op. 69 (1911–12), by Elgar, a setting for contralto or mezzo-soprano, chorus, and orchestra of Arthur O'Shaughnessy's ode 'We are the Music-Makers' (1874); it includes several self-quotations (e.g. from the 'Enigma' Variations, Symphony no. 1, Violin Concerto). Kodály set the same ode for voices and orchestra (1964).

Music of the Spheres (*Sfaerernes musik*). Work (1918) by Rued Langgaard for mezzo-soprano, chorus, organ, and orchestra, setting text from Friedrich Nietzsche's *Jenseits von Gut und Böse* ('Beyond Good and Evil', 1886).

Musikalische Exequien. Work by Schütz for solo voices, chorus, and continuo, composed in 1636 for the funeral of Prince Heinrich Postumus of Reuss; the texts are those inscribed on the prince's coffin, the funeral oration, and the *Nunc dimittis* with biblical passages.

Musikalischer Spass, Ein. *See* MUSICAL JOKE, A.

Musikalische Opfer. *See* MUSICAL OFFERING.

My Country (*My Fatherland*). *See* MÁ VLAST.

My Ladye Nevells Booke. A manuscript collection of music for virginals completed in 1591 by John Baldwin. It consists of 42 keyboard pieces by Byrd, who was probably Lady Nevell's teacher. She, however, must quickly have relinquished the manuscript, for 'Lord Abergavenny, called the Deafe, presented it to the Queene' (Elizabeth I); it is now privately owned. There is a modern edition by Hilda Andrews (1926, reprinted 1969).

Mystery Sonatas. *See* ROSARY SONATAS.

Mystical Songs, Five. *See* FIVE MYSTICAL SONGS.

Naboth's Vineyard. Dramatic madrigal by Goehr with a text in Latin and English adapted from 1 Kings 21 (London, 1968); it forms a music-theatre triptych with *Shadowplay and *Sonata about Jerusalem.

Nabucco (*Nabucodonosor*). Opera (*dramma lirico*) in four parts by Verdi to a libretto by Temistocle Solera after Auguste Anicet-Bourgeois and Francis Cornu's play *Nabuchodonosor* (1836) and Antonio Cortesi's ballet *Nabuccodonosor* (1838) (Milan, 1842); it includes the famous choral lament of the Hebrews, 'Va pensiero'.

Nacht in Venedig, Eine ('A Night in Venice'). Operetta (*komische Oper*) in three acts by Johann Strauss (ii) to a libretto by F. Zell (Camillo Walzel) and Richard Genée after Eugène Cormon and Michel Carré's libretto *Château Trompette* (Berlin, 1883).

Naive and Sentimental Music. Orchestral work (1997–8) by John Adams.

Namensfeier ('Nameday'). Beethoven's overture op. 115, composed in 1814–15 for the nameday festivities of Emperor Franz II of Austria.

Namouna. Ballet in two acts by Lalo to a scenario by Charles Nuitter and Lucien Petipa, who choreographed it (Paris, 1882).

Nänie (Ger., from Lat.: *Naenie*, 'dirges'). Ode, op. 82 (1880–1) by Brahms, a setting for chorus and orchestra of a poem by Friedrich von Schiller.

Napoleon, Ode to. See ODE TO NAPOLEON BUONAPARTE.

Napoli (*Napoli, eller Fiskeren og hans Grud*; 'Napoli, or The Fisherman and his Bride'). Ballet in three acts by Holger Simon Paulli, Edvard Helsted, Niels Gade, and Hans Christian Lumbye, to a scenario by August Bournonville, who choreographed it (Copenhagen, 1842).

Nations, Les. A volume of trio sonatas (1726) by François Couperin, for two violins and continuo, divided into four sections: 'La Françoise', 'L'Espagnole', 'L'Impériale', and 'La Piémontoise'.

Nativité du Seigneur, La ('The Birth of the Lord'). Cycle of nine meditations for organ (1935) by Messiaen.

Nature, Life, and Love (*Příroda, život, a láska*). Cycle of overtures (1891–2) by Dvořák: *Amid Nature* (*In Nature's Realm*; *V přírodě*), *Carnival* (*Karneval*), and *Othello*.

Navarraise, La ('The Girl from Navarre'). Opera (*épisode lyrique*) in two acts by Massenet to a libretto by Jules Claretie and Henri Cain after Claretie's story *La Cigarette* (1890) (London, 1894).

Nearer, my God, to Thee. American and English hymns, both versions setting verses (1841) of Sarah Flower Adams (1805–48); the English hymn was composed by John Bacchus Dykes and the American one is sung to Lowell Mason's tune *Bethany* (1859). It has often been said to have been the hymn played and sung as the *Titanic* was sinking in 1912, but research has shown that to be false.

Nelsonmesse ('Nelson Mass'). Haydn's Mass no. 11 in D minor (1798); in his own catalogue of his works, Haydn headed it 'Missa in angustiis' and it is sometimes referred to as the 'Imperial Mass' or the 'Coronation Mass'. According to one story, it was written to celebrate Nelson's victory at Aboukir Bay; another claims that Nelson heard it at Eisenstadt in 1800.

Nerone ('Nero'). Opera (*tragedia*) in four acts by Boito to his own libretto (Milan, 1924).

New England Holidays. *See* HOLIDAYS.

New World, From the (*Z nového světa*). Dvořák's Symphony no. 9 (no. 5 in the earlier numbering) in E minor (1893); it was composed while the composer was in the USA and uses themes resembling African-American traditional melodies.

New Year. Opera in three acts by Tippett to his own libretto (Houston, TX, 1989).

Nibelung's Ring, The. *See* RING DES NIBELUNGEN, DER.

Night at the Chinese Opera, A. Opera in three acts by Judith Weir to her own libretto partly based on Chi Chun-Hsiang's *The Chao Family Orphan* (13th-century) (Cheltenham, 1987).

Nightingale, The (*Solovey; Le Rossignol*). Opera (lyric tale) in three acts by Stravinsky to a libretto by Stepan Mitusov after the tale by Hans Christian Andersen (Paris, 1914). At Serge Diaghilev's request, Stravinsky arranged music from the second and third acts as a ballet score, *Chant du rossignol* (Paris, 1920); the previous year it was given in concert, and it is now better known as a symphonic poem.

Nightingale's to Blame, The. Opera in a prologue and three scenes by Simon Holt to a libretto by the composer after David Johnston's translation of Federico García Lorca's lay *Amor de Don Perlimplín con Belisa su jardin* (1931) (Huddersfield, 1998).

Night on the Bare Mountain (*Ivanova noch' na Lïsoy gore;* 'St John's Night on Bald Mountain'). Orchestral work (1867) by Musorgsky, inspired by the witches' sabbath in Nikolay Gogol's story *St John's Eve*. He revised it as a choral piece for inclusion in the opera *Mlada* (1872), and again revised it as a choral introduction to Act III of *Sorochintsy Fair* (1874–80). This final version was freely revised and orchestrated by Rimsky-Korsakov, and though it is the most well known, it is no longer really Musorgsky's.

Night Ride and Sunrise (*Öinen ratsastus ja auringonnousu*). Tone-poem, op. 55 (1908), by Sibelius.

Nights in the Gardens of Spain. *See* NOCHES EN LOS JARDINES DE ESPAÑA.

Nimrod. The ninth of Elgar's 'Enigma' Variations, so called because it is a portrait of Elgar's friend A. J. Jaeger ('Jaeger' is the German for 'hunter'; Nimrod was the 'mighty hunter' of the Old Testament). The piece enshrines the day when the two men discussed Beethoven slow movements. It is often played separately as a commemorative item.

Nine Rivers. A cycle of nine pieces by James Dillon for various vocal, instrumental and electronic forces, composed between 1982 and 1996.

Niño, El. 'Nativity oratorio' in two acts by John Adams to a libretto (in English, Spanish, and Latin) by the composer from poems by Rosario Castellanos, Gabriela Mistral, Hildegard of Bingen, Sor Juana Inés de la Cruz, Rubén Darío, and Vicente Huidobro, an early English carol, texts from *The Play of the Annunciation* from the Wakefield mystery plays, Martin Luther's *Christmas Sermon*, the book of Haggai, Epistle of James, and other biblical sources (Paris, 2000).

Nixon in China. Opera in two acts by John Adams to a libretto by Alice Goodman (Houston, TX, 1987).

Nobilissima visione. Ballet by Hindemith to his own scenario, choreographed by Leonid Massine for the Ballets Russes de Monte Carlo (London, 1938).

Noces, Les (*Svadebka*; 'The Wedding'). Four choreographic scenes by Stravinsky to words adapted by the composer from Russian traditional sources, for soprano, mezzo-soprano, tenor, and bass soloists, chorus, four pianos, and 17 percussion instruments (including four timpani); it was choreographed by Bronislava Nijinska for Serge Diaghilev's Ballets Russes (Paris, 1923).

Noches en los jardines de España ('Nights in the Gardens of Spain'). Three symphonic impressions for piano and orchestra by Falla, composed 1911–15: *En el Generalife* ('In the Generalife'), *Danza lejana* ('Dance in the Distance'), and *En los jardines de la Sierra de Córdoba*.

Nocturnes. Three symphonic poems (1897–9) by Debussy: *Nuages* ('Clouds'), *Fêtes* ('Festivals'), and *Sirènes* ('Sirens', with women's voices). Debussy took the title from paintings by James McNeill Whistler.

Non nobis Domine. A celebrated vocal canon, usually sung in three parts, attributed (without evidence) to Byrd. It was traditionally sung at banquets as a 'grace after meat'. The opening phrase was common in music from the 16th to the 18th centuries: Handel used it in his 'Hallelujah Chorus'.

Norfolk Rhapsody. Orchestral work (1905–6) by Vaughan Williams, based on three folksongs he collected in Norfolk in 1905. He wrote two further *Norfolk Rhapsodies* in 1906, to make up a projected 'Norfolk Symphony', but they were later withdrawn.

Norma. Opera (*tragedia lirica*) in two acts by Bellini to a libretto by Felice Romani after Alexandre Soumet's verse tragedy *Norma* (1831) (Milan, 1831).

Nose, The (*Nos*). Opera in three acts by Shostakovich to a libretto by the composer, Yevgeny Zamyatin, Georgy Ionin, and Aleksandr Preys after the story by Nikolay Gogol (1835) (Leningrad, 1930).

Nostre Dame Mass. *See* NOTRE DAME MASS.

Notations. 12 piano pieces (1945) by Boulez; he began orchestrating them in 1978.

Notre Dame manuscripts. A collection of two-voice plainchant settings for liturgical use, dating from about 1170 and given the description **Magnus liber organi* by the 13th-century theorist Anonymous IV.

Notre Dame Mass (Nostre Dame Mass; Messe de Nostre Dame). Mass for four voices by Machaut, possibly dating from the 1360s, one of the earliest polyphonic settings of the Mass Ordinary.

Nouvelles Aventures. *See* AVENTURES; NOUVELLES AVENTURES.

Noveletten. Schumann's op. 21 (1838), a set of eight pieces for piano which make up a 'romantic story'; they were named after the singer Clara Novello. Several other composers (e.g. Niels Gade) adopted the title 'Novelette'.

November Steps. Work for biwa, shakuhachi, and orchestra (1967) by Takemitsu.

November Woods. Symphonic poem (1917) by Bax.

Now thank we all our God. *See* NUN DANKET ALLE GOTT.

Noye's Fludde. Dramatic work in one act by Britten to his own libretto, a setting of the Chester miracle play (Orford, 1958).

Nozze di Figaro, Le ('The Marriage of Figaro'). *Opera buffa* in four acts by Mozart to a libretto by Lorenzo Da Ponte after Beaumarchais's play *La Folle Journée, ou Le Mariage de Figaro* (1784) (Vienna, 1786).

Nuits d'été, Les ('Summer Nights'). Song cycle, op. 7, by Berlioz to poems by Théophile Gautier; it was composed in 1840–1 and revised in 1843 and 1856. The six songs are *Villanelle*, *Le Spectre de la rose*, *Sur les lagunes*, *Absence*, *Au cimetière*, and *L'Inconnue*.

Nunc. Work (1999) by Helmut Lachenmann for flute, trombone, men's voices (wordless), and orchestra, originally called *Nun*; the composer intended it for performance in the same programme as Strauss's *Eine Alpensinfonie*.

Nun danket alle Gott ('Now thank we all our God'). German hymn with words by the Lutheran bishop Martin Rinckart (1586–1649) and music by Johannes Crüger. J. S. Bach used the melody as the basis of his chorale prelude of that name, BWV657.

Nuove musiche, Le ('New Compositions'). The title of Giulio Caccini's first collection of monodic songs, published in Florence in 1602. In 1614 he issued a further volume, *Nuove musiche e nuova maniera di scriverle* ('New Compositions and New Way of Writing them').

Nutcracker (*Shchelkunchik*; *Casse-noisette*). Ballet in two acts and three scenes by Tchaikovsky to a scenario by Marius Petipa after Alexandre Dumas *père*'s version of E. T. A. Hoffmann's *Nussknacker und Mausekönig* ('Nutcracker and Mouse King'); it was choreographed by Lev Ivanov (St Petersburg, 1892). Tchaikovsky arranged an orchestral suite, op. 71*a* (1892), of eight numbers from the ballet.

Nymphs and Shepherds. Song by Purcell from the incidental music he wrote for Thomas Shadwell's play *The Libertine* (1692); it is often sung by a soprano but was made famous in a choral version recorded in 1929 by Manchester schoolchildren's choirs, conducted by Hamilton Harty.

Oberon (*Oberon, or The Elf King's Oath*). Opera in three acts by Weber to a libretto by James Robinson Planché after Christoph Martin Wieland's poem *Oberon* (1780), itself based on *Huon de Bordeaux*, a 13th-century French *chanson de geste* (London, 1826).

Oberto, conte di San Bonifacio. Opera (*dramma*) in two acts by Verdi to a libretto by Temistocle Solera from Antonio Piazza's libretto *Rocester* (Milan, 1839).

Oca del Cairo, L' ('The Goose of Cairo'). *Opera buffa* in two acts by Mozart to a libretto by Giovanni Battista Varesco (unfinished).

O Canada! Canadian national song by Calixa Lavallée (1839–1920) to French words by A. B. Routhier. An English text was written in 1908 by R. S. Weir. It is used as a patriotic song, particularly by French Canadians, but has never officially been adopted as a national anthem.

Oceanides, The (*Aallottarat*). Tone-poem, op. 73 (1914), by Sibelius. In Greek mythology the Oceanides were the 4000 daughters of Oceanus, the origin of all rivers and seas.

O Come, all ye Faithful. *See* ADESTE FIDELES.

Octandre. Work (1923) by Varèse for eight instruments; 'octandrous' flowers have eight stamens.

Ode for St Cecilia's Day. 1. Four choral works by Henry Purcell, two composed in 1683, one *c.*1685, and one in 1692.
   2. Choral work (1739) by Handel, a setting of John Dryden's poem (1798).
   3. Cantata (1889) by Hubert Parry for soprano, baritone, chorus, and orchestra, to a text (1713) by Alexander Pope.

Ode to Napoleon Buonaparte. Schoenberg's op. 41 (1942), for reciter, piano, and string quartet, a setting of Byron's poem (1814); it was later arranged for string orchestra.

Odyssey. Orchestral work (1972–87) by Nicholas Maw.

Oedipe ('Oedipus'). Opera (*tragédie lyrique*) in four acts by Enescu to a libretto by Edmond Fleg, partly after Sophocles' Oedipus plays (Paris, 1936).

Oedipus. Music-theatre piece by Wolfgang Rihm to his own libretto after Friedrich Hölderlin's German translation (1804) of *Oedipus tyrannus*, Friedrich Nietzsche's *Oedipus: Reden des letzten Philosophen mit sich selbst*, and Heiner Müller's *Oedipuskommentar* (Berlin, 1987).

Oedipus rex ('King Oedipus'). Opera-oratorio in two acts by Stravinsky to a text by Jean Cocteau after Sophocles' tragedy (*c.*430 BC) translated into Latin by Jean Daniélou; it was first performed as an oratorio in Paris in 1927 and staged in Vienna in 1928.

Offertorium. Work (1980; revised 1986) for violin and orchestra by Gubaidulina.

Offrandes oubliées, Les ('The Forgotten Offerings'). Orchestral work (1930) by Messiaen.

O God, our Help in Ages Past. Hymn of which the words, based on Psalm 90, are by Isaac Watts (1674–1748); it was first published in Watts's *Psalms of David* (1719). The tune is attributed to William Croft but first appeared anonymously, set to Psalm 42; it is known as 'St Anne', Croft being organist of St Anne's, Soho, in 1708. The first line is a stock 18th-century phrase found in J. S. Bach's organ fugue in E♭ major, which is therefore known in England as *'St Anne's Fugue'. The hymn is especially associated with Remembrance Day services.

O Haupt voll Blut und Wunden ('O sacred head sore wounded'). A chorale, a setting of Paul Gerhardt's hymn (1656) of that title to Hassler's melody *Mein G'müt ist mir verwirret*. It is often called the 'Passion Chorale' because Bach used it in his *St Matthew Passion*, but it also appears in the *Christmas Oratorio* and the cantatas nos. 135, 159, and 161.

Oiseau de feu, L'. *See* FIREBIRD, THE.

Oiseaux exotiques ('Exotic Birds'). Work by Messiaen for piano, 11 wind instruments, xylophone, glockenspiel, and two percussionists, composed in 1955–6.

Old Hundredth. Metrical psalm tune of uncertain origin. Its name indicates that it was set to the 100th psalm in the 'old' version of the metrical psalms. It is sung to the words 'All people that on earth do dwell', by William Kethe. Vaughan Williams made a ceremonial arrangement of it, for choir, congregation, orchestra, organ, and 'all available trumpets', for the coronation of Elizabeth II in 1953.

Olympians, The. Opera in three acts by Bliss to a libretto by J. B. Priestley (London, 1949).

On an Overgrown Path (*Po zarostlém chodníčku*). A series of 15 piano pieces (1901–8) by Janáček; they were published in two books, the first ten (which have titles) in book 1 (1911) and the last five in book 2 (1942).

Ondine. 1. Ballet in three acts and five scenes by Henze to a scenario by Frederick Ashton after Jean Giraudoux's play *Ondine* (1939), itself after Friedrich de la Motte Fouqué's *Undine* (1811); it was choreographed by Ashton (London, 1958).

2. The first piece of Ravel's **Gaspard de la nuit*.

3. Piano piece (1913) by Debussy, no. 8 of his *Préludes*, book 2.
See also UNDINE.

On Hearing the First Cuckoo in Spring. Tone-poem (1912) by Delius, the first of his Two Pieces for Small Orchestra (the second is *Summer Night on the River*).

On the Transmigration of Souls. Work (2002) for children's choir, chorus, orchestra, and pre-recorded soundtrack by John Adams, commemorating 11 September 2001.

Onward, Christian Soldiers. Hymn with words by the Revd Sabine Baring-Gould, first published in 1868 in an appendix to *Hymns Ancient and Modern*, and a tune by John Bacchus Dykes adapted from the slow movement of Haydn's Symphony no. 53. It became popular when set by Sullivan in 1871 as *Gertrude*; Holst set the same words in 1924.

On Wenlock Edge. Song cycle (1908–9) by Vaughan Williams, for tenor, string quartet, and piano, settings of six poems from A. E. Housman's *A Shropshire Lad* (1896), the first song being 'On Wenlock Edge'; Vaughan Williams arranged the cycle for tenor and orchestra (*c*.1923).

op. Abbreviation of *opus.

Ophelia Dances. Work (1975) by Oliver Knussen for nine instrumentalists.

opp. Abbreviated plural of *opus.

Oprichnik ('The Oprichnik'). Opera in four acts by Tchaikovsky to his own libretto after Ivan Lazhechnikov's tragedy (1834) (St Petersburg, 1874).

opus (Lat., usually abbreviated to op., plural opp.; Fr.: *oeuvre*; Ger.: *Opus*; It.: *opera*). 'Work'. The custom of numbering a composer's works as they appear—'opus 1' and so on—is useful in principle both as a means of identification and to show the place a particular work occupies in a composer's career. The term was used methodically from the early 17th century, when it customarily referred to a published volume containing several pieces; in the 19th century it began to be applied by composers to individual substantial works, but as the use of descriptive titles increased and abstract forms such as sonata and string quartet became relatively neglected the application of opus numbers grew less useful.

Because of the possibility of confusion (e.g. where publication of an early set of compositions was delayed) some scholars devised new systems of numbering works (*see*, for example, BWV; DEUTSCH; HOBOKEN; KIRKPATRICK; KÖCHEL; RYOM).

Opus clavicembalisticum. Piano piece (1929–30) by Sorabji; with a duration of nearly three hours, it is the longest non-repetitive piano work.

Oracolo, L' ('The Oracle'). Opera in one act by Franco Leoni to a libretto by Camillo Zanoni after Chester Bailey Fernald's story *The Cat and the Cherub* (1896) (London, 1905).

Orazi et i Curiazi, Gli ('The Horatii and the Curiatii'). Opera (*tragedia per musica*) in three acts by Cimarosa to a libretto by Simeone Antonio Sografi after Pierre Corneille's tragedy *Horace* (1640) (Venice, 1796).

Orb and Sceptre. March by Walton, composed for the coronation of Elizabeth II in 1953.

Orfeo, L'. Opera (*favola in musica*) in a prologue and five acts by Monteverdi to a libretto by Alessandro Striggio mainly after the Orpheus myth as told in Ovid's *Metamorphoses* though drawing on the account in Virgil's *Georgics* (Mantua, 1607).

Orfeo ed Euridice (*Orphée et Eurydice*). Opera (*azione teatrale*) in three acts by Gluck to a libretto by Ranieri Calzabigi (Vienna, 1762); Gluck made an expanded French version (*tragédie opéra*) to a libretto by Pierre Louis Moline after Calzabigi (Paris, 1774).

Organ Solo Mass. Mozart's *Missa brevis* in C major K259 (1776), so called because there is an important organ solo in the Benedictus.

Orgelbüchlein ('Little Organ Book'). Collection of 46 organ chorales, BWV599–644, by J. S. Bach; he intended to include 164 and conceived the collection partly as a teaching manual.

Orlando. Opera in three acts by Handel to a libretto adapted from Carlo Sigismondo Capece's *L'Orlando* (1711) after Ludovico Ariosto's *Orlando furioso* (1516) (London, 1733).

Orlando paladino ('The Paladin Orlando'). Opera (*dramma eroicomico*) in three acts by Haydn to a libretto by Nunziato Porta after Ludovico Ariosto's *Orlando furioso* (1516) (Eszterháza, 1782).

Ormindo. Opera (*favola regia per musica*) in three acts by Cavalli to a libretto by Giovanni Faustini (Venice, 1644).

Orphée aux enfers ('Orpheus in the Underworld'). *Opéra bouffon* in two acts by Offenbach to a libretto by Hector-Jonathan Crémieux and Ludovic Halévy after classical mythology (Paris, 1858); it was revised and expanded into four acts (Paris, 1874).

Orpheus. The myth of Orpheus has been the subject of many operas, notably Monteverdi's *L'*Orfeo*, Gluck's **Orfeo ed Euridice*, and Offenbach's **Orphée aux enfers*; others include those by Rossi (1647), Benda (1785), Naumann (1786), and Krenek (1926). The following are the principal musical works based on the Orpheus myth.

1. Symphonic poem by Liszt, originally composed as an introduction to his production of Gluck's *Orfeo ed Euridice* at Weimar in 1854.

2. Ballet in three scenes by Stravinsky, choreographed by George Balanchine (New York, 1948).

3. Ballet in two acts by Henze to a scenario by Edward Bond (Stuttgart, 1979).

Orpheus britannicus ('The British Orpheus'). Title given to two volumes of songs by Henry Purcell (the 'British Orpheus'), published posthumously (1698–1702) by Henry Playford, and to a volume of his songs published by John Walsh (1735). Britten and Peter Pears edited and arranged several for voice or voices and piano or orchestra.

Orpheus in the Underworld. *See* ORPHÉE AUX ENFERS.

Osud ('Fate'; 'Destiny'). Opera ('three novelesque scenes') by Janáček to a libretto by the composer and Fedora Bartošová; he completed it in 1907 for performance in Prague but that never took place. It was given in a version by Václav Nosek in Brno in 1958 and in its original form in Českě Budějovice in 1978.

Otello. 1. Opera (*dramma lirico*) in four acts by Verdi to a libretto by Arrigo Boito after Shakespeare's play *Othello, the Moor of Venice* (1603–4) (Milan, 1887).

    2. Opera (*dramma*) in three acts by Rossini to a libretto by Francesco Berio di Salsa after Shakespeare (Naples, 1816).

Othello. *See* NATURE, LIFE, AND LOVE.

Ottone (*Ottone, re di Germania*; 'Ottone, King of Germany'). Opera in three acts by Handel to a libretto adapted by Nicola Francesco Haym from Stefano Benedetto Pallavicino's *Teofane* (1719) (London, 1723).

Our Hunting Fathers. Symphonic song cycle, op. 8 (1936), by Britten, for soprano or tenor solo and orchestra, a setting of a text devised by W. H. Auden.

Our Man in Havana. Opera in three acts by Malcolm Williamson to a libretto by Sidney Gilliatt after Graham Greene's novel (1958) (London, 1963).

Ours, L' ('The Bear'). Nickname of Haydn's Symphony no. 82 in C major (1786), the first of the Paris symphonies, so called because of the 'growling' theme at the beginning of the last movement.

Outis. Opera ('musical action') in two parts by Berio to a libretto by the composer and Dario Del Corno (Milan, 1996).

Owen Wingrave. Opera in two acts by Britten to a libretto by Myfanwy Piper after Henry James's short story (1892) (BBC television, 1971; staged London, 1973).

'Oxford' Symphony. Nickname of Haydn's Symphony no. 92 in G major (1789), so called because it was performed when Haydn received an honorary doctorate from Oxford University in 1791 (though he did not compose it with Oxford in mind).

Oxyrhynchos Hymn. The earliest Christian hymn (AD *c*.300) for which the music is preserved (in Greek vocal notation). It takes its name from the place in Egypt where the papyrus was discovered.

Pacific 231. Orchestral work (1923) by Honegger, the first of his *Mouvements symphoniques*; it is named after a locomotive.

Padmâvatî. *Opéra-ballet* in two acts by Roussel to a libretto by Louis Laloy (Paris, 1923).

Paganini Variations. Two sets of piano studies, op. 35 (1862–3), by Brahms, variations on a theme from Paganini's *Caprice* no. 24 in A minor. Rakhmaninov (*see* RHAPSODY ON A THEME OF PAGANINI), Blacher (1947), Lutosławski (1941), and Rochberg (1970) wrote variations on the same theme. Schumann wrote two sets of piano studies (1832–3) on several themes from Paganini's *Caprices*, and Liszt used some of them in his **Études d'exécution transcendante d'après Paganini*.

Pagliacci ('Players'). Opera in a prologue and two acts by Leoncavallo to his own libretto based on a newspaper crime report (Milan, 1892); it is usually performed in a double bill with Mascagni's **Cavalleria rusticana*, the two operas being referred to popularly as 'Cav and Pag'.

Paladins, Les ('The Paladins'). Opera (*comédie lyrique*) in three acts by Rameau to a libretto attributed to, among others, Duplat de Monticourt (Paris, 1760).

Palestrina. Opera (*musikalische Legende*) in three acts by Pfitzner to his own libretto (Munich, 1917).

Palimpsest I and II. Orchestral works (2000, 2002) by Gerald Barry.

Pammelia (from Gk., 'all honey'). The first collection of vocal rounds, catches, and canons published in England. It contains 100 anonymous pieces, for from three to ten voices, and was published by Thomas Ravenscroft in 1609. A second part, **Deuteromelia*, was also published in 1609.

Panic. Work (1995) by Birtwistle for alto saxophone, drums, wind, and percussion.

Papillons ('Butterflies'). Schumann's op. 2 (1829–31), for solo piano, a set of 12 short dance pieces inspired by the masked-ball scene at the end of Jean Paul's *Flegeljahre* (1804–5) ('Age of Indiscretion').

Parade. Ballet in one act by Satie to a scenario by Jean Cocteau; it was choreographed by Leonid Massine, with designs by Pablo Picasso, for Serge Diaghilev's Ballets Russes (Paris, 1917).

Paradies und die Peri, Das ('Paradise and the Peri'). Cantata, op. 50 (1843), by Schumann, for soloists, chorus, and orchestra, a setting of a text based on a translation and adaptation of Thomas Moore's poem *Lalla*

Rookh (1817). In Persian mythology the Peri is a benign spirit seeking readmission to Paradise.

Paradise Lost. Opera (*sacra rappresentazione*) in two acts by Penderecki to a libretto by Christopher Fry after John Milton's poem (1667) (Chicago, 1978).

Paraphrases. Collection of piano duets (24 variations and 14 other pieces) based on the popular quick waltz tune *Chopsticks*; they were composed by Borodin, Cui, Lyadov, Rimsky-Korsakov, and Liszt, and were published in 1880.

Paride ed Elena ('Paris and Helen'). Opera (*dramma per musica*) in five acts by Gluck to a libretto by Ranieri Calzabigi (Vienna, 1770).

'Paris' Symphonies. Haydn's six symphonies, nos. 82–7 (1785–6), commissioned by the Comte d'Ogny for the Concert de la Loge Olympique in Paris; they include *L'*Ours*, *La *Poule*, and *La *Reine*. (Haydn's Symphonies nos. 90–2 were also written for Paris.)

'Paris' Symphony. Nickname of Mozart's Symphony no. 31 in D major к297/300a (1778), so called because it was written in Paris and first performed at the Concert Spirituel.

Paris: The Song of a Great City. Nocturne (1899) for orchestra by Delius. Frederick Ashton choreographed it (1936).

Paroles tissées ('Woven Words'). Work (1965) by Lutosławski for tenor and chamber orchestra to a text by Jean François Chabrun.

Parsifal. Opera (*Bühnenweihfestspiel*) in three acts by Wagner to his own libretto (Bayreuth, 1882).

Partenope. Opera in three acts by Handel to a libretto adapted anonymously from Silvio Stampiglia's *Partenope* (1699, revised 1708) (London, 1730).

Parthenia (Gk., 'virgin dances'). A collection of 21 pieces for virginals by Byrd, Bull, and Gibbons; it was presented to Prince Frederick and Princess Elizabeth on their marriage in 1613 as *Parthenia, or The Maydenhead of the First Musicke that ever was Printed for the Virginalls*. The pun in the title was reinforced in a companion volume, *Parthenia In-Violata* (1614), a collection of 20 anonymous pieces for virginals and bass viol. *Parthenia* was the first English music to be engraved on copper plates.

Pas d'acier, Le. *See* STEEL STEP, THE.

Passion and Resurrection. Church opera in 12 scenes by Jonathan Harvey to a text from Benedictine Latin church dramas (Winchester, 1981).

Passion Chorale. *See* O HAUPT VOLL BLUT UND WUNDEN.

Passione, La. Nickname of Haydn's Symphony no. 49 in F minor (1768), so called because it begins with an Adagio suggestive of Passion music.

'Pastoral' Sonata. Name given by the publisher to Beethoven's Piano Sonata no. 15 in D major op. 28 (1801), presumably because of the rustic rhythm in the finale.

'Pastoral' Symphony. 1. Beethoven's Symphony no. 6 in F major op. 68 (1808); it was published as *Sinfonia pastorale*, a programme symphony in which sounds of nature are imitated, its five movements being 'Awakening of Happy Feelings on Arriving in the Country', 'By the Brook', 'Merrymaking of the Country Folk', 'Storm', and 'Shepherds' Song: Joy and Gratitude after the Storm'.

2. A short orchestral movement in Handel's *Messiah*, referring to the shepherds who were told of Christ's birth.

Pastoral Symphony, A. Vaughan Williams's third symphony (1921); it has a wordless solo for soprano (or clarinet) in the last movement.

Pastor fido, Il ('The Faithful Shepherd'). Opera in three acts by Handel to a libretto by Giacomo Rossi after the play by Battista Guarini (1585) (London, 1712); Handel revised it with added choruses (London, 1734) and with the prologue *Terpsichore* and added dances (London, 1734). Salieri wrote a four-act opera with the same title, with a libretto by Lorenzo Da Ponte (Vienna, 1789).

'Pathetic' Symphony. See SYMPHONIE PATHÉTIQUE.

Pathétique Sonata ('Pathetic Sonata'). Beethoven's Piano Sonata no. 8 in C minor op. 13 (1797–8); the first edition (1799) is entitled 'Grande sonate pathétique', possibly Beethoven's own title.

Patience (*Patience; or, Bunthorne's Bride!*). Operetta in two acts by Sullivan to a libretto by W. S. Gilbert (London, 1881).

Patineurs, Les ('The Skaters'). Ballet in one act with music by Meyerbeer, choreographed by Frederick Ashton (London, 1937); the score was arranged by Constant Lambert using excerpts from Meyerbeer's operas *Le *Prophète* and *L'*Étoile du nord*. Waldteufel composed a waltz (1882) called *Les Patineurs*.

Paukenmesse ('Kettledrum Mass'). Haydn's Mass no. 9 in C major (1796); Haydn called it *Missa in tempore belli* ('Mass in Time of War') and it is sometimes referred to as *Kriegsmesse*.

Paukenwirbel-Symphonie. See 'DRUMROLL' SYMPHONY.

Paul Bunyan. Operetta in a prologue and two acts by Britten to a libretto by W. H. Auden (New York, 1941); Britten made a revised version (Snape, 1976).

Pavane. Fauré's op. 50 (1887) for orchestra, with optional mixed chorus.

Pavane pour une infante défunte ('Pavan for a Dead Infanta'). Piano piece (1899) by Ravel, which he orchestrated in 1910. It recalls the Spanish court custom of performing a solemn ceremonial dance at a time of royal mourning.

Pearl Fishers, The. See PÊCHEURS DE PERLES, LES.

Peasant Cantata (*Bauernkantate*). Bach's secular cantata no. 212, *Mer hahn en neue Oberkeet* ('We have a new regime', 1742), to a text by Picander, composed to mark the inauguration of the rule of Carl Heinrich von Dieskau (1706–82) over certain villages in the Leipzig area.

Péchés de vieillesse ('Sins of Old Age'). A collection of pieces by Rossini, for piano with and without voices, composed between 1857 and 1868 and grouped into 13 volumes, some with fanciful titles; they were not published until the 1950s.

Pêcheurs de perles, Les ('The Pearl Fishers'). Opera in three acts by Bizet to a libretto by Eugène Cormon and Michel Carré (Paris, 1863).

Peer Gynt. Incidental music by Grieg for Henrik Ibsen's play (1876). Some of it was later arranged as two orchestral suites: op. 46 (1888) and op. 55 (1891–2); these were then arranged for piano solo and duet. Saeverud also composed incidental music (1947) for the play, Egk wrote an opera on the subject (Berlin, 1938), and Schnittke a ballet (1986).

Pelléas et Mélisande ('Pelléas and Mélisande').
   1. Opera in five acts by Debussy after Maurice Maeterlinck's play (Paris, 1902).
   2. *Pelleas und Melisande*. Symphonic poem, op. 5 (1902–3), by Schoenberg.
   3. Suite of incidental music, op. 80 (1898), by Fauré for Maeterlinck's play.
   4. Incidental music, op. 46 (1905), by Sibelius for Maeterlinck's play; Sibelius arranged a suite from it the same year.

Pénélope. Opera (*poème lyrique*) in three acts by Fauré to a libretto by René Fauchois (Monte Carlo, 1913).

Penthesilea. Opera in one act by Othmar Schoeck to his own libretto after Heinrich von Kleist's tragedy (1808) (Dresden, 1927).

People United Will Never Be Defeated!, The. Piano work (1975) by Frederic Rzewski, 36 variations on a Chilean song by Sergio Ortega.

Perfect Fool, The. Opera in one act by Holst to his own libretto (London, 1923). The orchestral suite of the ballet music was first performed in 1920.

Péri, La ('The Peri'). Ballet (*poème dansé*) by Dukas, choreographed by Ivan Clustine (Paris, 1912). Dukas made an orchestral suite from the score.

Périchole, La. *Opéra bouffe* in two acts by Offenbach to a libretto by Henri Meilhac and Ludovic Halévy after Prosper Mérimée's comedy *Le Carrosse du Saint-Sacrement* (1830) (Paris, 1868); it was revised in three acts (Paris, 1874).

Perséphone. Melodrama in three scenes by Stravinsky to a libretto by André Gide; for narrator, tenor, chorus, children's chorus, and orchestra, it was choreographed by Kurt Jooss (Paris, 1934). Stravinsky revised it in 1949.

Peter and the Wolf (*Petya i volk*). Symphonic fairy tale for narrator and orchestra, op. 67 (1936), by Prokofiev; the characters in the story are represented by different solo instruments, the work having been conceived as a children's introduction to the orchestra.

Peter Grimes. Opera in a prologue and three acts by Britten to a libretto by Montagu Slater after George Crabbe's poem *The Borough* (1810) (London,

1945); Britten created an orchestral work, *Four Sea Interludes*, from the opera's descriptive orchestral numbers.

Petite Messe solennelle ('Little Solemn Mass'). Choral work (1863) by Rossini, a setting of the Mass text for soprano, mezzo-soprano, tenor, and baritone soloists, chorus, two pianos, and harmonium; Rossini arranged it for full orchestra (1867). The word 'petite' refers not to the work's size but to Rossini's modest evaluation of its importance.

Petites Liturgies de la Présence Divine, Trois. See TROIS PETITES LITURGIES DE LA PRÉSENCE DIVINE.

Petite suite ('Little Suite'). Work for piano duet (1886–9) by Debussy, its movements being 'En bateau', 'Cortège', 'Menuet', and 'Ballet'; it was arranged for piano solo by Jacques Durand (1906), for orchestra by Henri Busser (1907), and for small orchestra by Henri Mouton (1909).

Petits Riens, Les ('The Little Nobodies'). Ballet-divertissement by Mozart with a scenario by Jean-Georges Noverre, who also choreographed it (Paris, 1778). The music was lost until 1872, when it was found in the library of the Paris Opéra.

Petrushka. Ballet in four scenes by Stravinsky to a scenario by Alexandre Benois; it was choreographed by Mikhail Fokine for Serge Diaghilev's Ballets Russes (Paris, 1911). Stravinsky made an orchestral suite (1914) from the ballet; it was reorchestrated in 1947 as a suite in four parts with 15 movements. Stravinsky arranged three movements for piano (1921) and made a four-hand piano reduction of the score. Victor Babin made a version for two pianos and Theodor Szántó arranged five pieces into a piano suite.

Phaedra. 1. Dramatic cantata, op. 93 (1975), by Britten, a setting for mezzo-soprano and orchestra of extracts from Jean Racine's *Phèdre* (1677) translated by Robert Lowell.

 2. Monodrama in seven acts by George Rochberg to a libretto by Gene Rochberg after Robert Lowell's translation of Racine (Syracuse, NY, 1976).

Phantasiestücke ('Fantasy Pieces'). Schumann's op. 12 (1837), for piano, a set of eight pieces each with a descriptive title; he composed three further *Phantasiestücke* op. 111 (1851), but they have no titles and are described simply by their key signatures.

Philosopher, The (*Der Philosoph*). Nickname of Haydn's Symphony no. 22 in E♭ major (1764), so called because of the character of its opening Adagio.

Phoebus and Pan (*Der Streit zwischen Phoebus und Pan*, 'The Dispute between Phoebus and Pan'; *Geschwinde, geschwinde, ihr wirbelnden Winde*, 'Haste, haste, you whirling winds'). J. S. Bach's cantata no. 201 (1729), to a text by Picander after Ovid; it deals with the question of good and bad art, good music being represented by Phoebus, bad music by Pan. It has occasionally been staged.

Pictures at an Exhibition (*Kartinki s vystavki*). Suite for solo piano (1874) by Musorgsky, each of its ten movements inspired by pictures at a memorial exhibition for the Russian artist Victor Hartmann (1834–73) and with a

'Promenade' as a linking passage. There are several orchestral versions, by Henry Wood, Leopold Stokowski, and Elgar Howarth (brass and percussion) among others, but the most commonly heard is by Ravel (1922).

Pierrot lunaire ('Moonstruck Pierrot'). Schoenberg's op. 21 (1912), for female voice, flute, piccolo, clarinet, bass clarinet, violin, viola, cello, and piano; it is a cycle in three parts, each containing seven songs, which are settings of poems by Albert Giraud translated from French into German by O. E. Hartleben. The singer is required to use the technique of *Sprechgesang* ('speech-song').

Pigmalion (*Pygmalion*). *Acte de ballet* by Rameau to a libretto by Ballot de Sauvot after Antoine Houdar de Lamotte (1700) (Paris, 1748).

Pilgrim's Progress, The. Opera ('morality') in a prologue, four acts, and an epilogue by Vaughan Williams to his own libretto after John Bunyan's allegory (1674–9, 1684), with interpolations from the Bible and verse by Ursula Vaughan Williams (London, 1951). Act IV scene 2 is *The Shepherds of the Delectable Mountains*, a pastoral episode in one act (London, 1922). Granville Bantock wrote a choral piece on the same subject (1928).

Pineapple Poll. Ballet in one act and three scenes to music by Sullivan, arranged by Charles Mackerras, to a scenario by John Cranko (who choreographed it), based on W. S. Gilbert's Bab Ballad *The Bumboat Woman's Story* (London, 1951); a concert suite has been arranged from the score.

Pini di Roma ('Pines of Rome'). Symphonic poem (1923–4) by Respighi; its four sections are entitled 'Villa Borghese', 'A Catacomb', 'Janiculum', and 'Appian Way'. The score includes a recording of a nightingale.

Pique-Dame. *See* QUEEN OF SPADES, THE.

Pirata, Il ('The Pirate'). Opera (*melodramma*) in two acts by Bellini to a libretto by Felice Romani after Isidore J. S. Taylor's play *Bertram, ou Le Pirate*, a version of Charles Maturin's *Bertram* (1816) (Milan, 1827).

Pirates of Penzance, The (*The Pirates of Penzance; or, The Slave of Duty*). Operetta in two acts by Sullivan to a libretto by W. S. Gilbert (Paignton, 1879).

Pithoprakta. Orchestral work (1957) by Xenakis.

Planets, The. Orchestral suite, op. 32 (1914–16), by Holst. Its seven movements depict the astrological associations of seven planets: Mars, the Bringer of War; Venus, the Bringer of Peace; Mercury, the Winged Messenger; Jupiter, the Bringer of Jollity; Saturn, the Bringer of Old Age; Uranus, the Magician; Neptune, the Mystic (with wordless female chorus). It was first performed privately in 1918, publicly (without the second and seventh movements) in 1919, and complete in 1920. *See also* PLUTO, THE RENEWER.

Platée ('Plataea'). Opera (*comédie lyrique: ballet bouffon*) in a prologue and three acts by Rameau to a libretto by Adrien-Joseph Le Valois d'Orville after Jacques Autreau's play *Platée, ou Junon jalouse* (Versailles, 1745).

Playing Away. Opera in two acts by Benedict Mason to a libretto by Howard Brenton (Leeds, 1994).

Play of Daniel, The. A medieval liturgical drama which exists in several versions. The only one to have survived with the music complete was composed between 1227 and 1234 for Beauvais Cathedral, probably for Matins on 1 January. The first part deals with Daniel at Belshazzar's court, the second with Daniel's trials at the court of Darius.

Play of Robin and Marion, The. *See JEU DE ROBIN ET DE MARION, LE.*

Pleasure-Dome of Kubla Khan, The. Orchestral work, op. 8 (1917), by Charles T. Griffes, an arrangement of an earlier piano piece (1912).

Pléïades. Work (1978) by Xenakis for six percussionists.

Pli selon pli ('Fold upon Fold'). Work (1957–62) by Boulez for soprano and orchestra, subtitled 'Portrait de Mallarmé'.

Pluto, the Renewer. Orchestral work (2000) by Colin Matthews, commissioned as an addition to Holst's *The *Planets.*

Poème. Chausson's op. 25 (1896) for violin and orchestra, based on a short story by Ivan Turgenev.

Poème de l'amour et de la mer ('Poem of Love and the Sea'). Work (1882–90; revised 1893) for voice (usually mezzo-soprano) and orchestra or piano by Chausson, a setting of words by Maurice Bouchor.

Poème électronique. Work (1957–8) by Varèse for three-track tape; it was designed to fill Le Corbusier's Philips pavilion at the 1958 Brussels Exposition but the building has since been demolished.

Poèmes pour Mi ('Poems for Mi'). Song cycle (1936) by Messiaen for soprano and piano, settings of his own poems; Messiaen made an orchestral version in 1937. Mi was the composer's name for his first wife, the violinist Claire Delbos.

Poem of Ecstasy (*Poema ekstaza*; *Le Poème de l'extase*). Orchestral work, op. 54 (1905–8), by Skryabin; it was inspired by the composer's theosophical ideas on love and art.

Poem of Fire, The. *See PROMETHEUS, THE POEM OF FIRE.*

Poet and Peasant (*Dichter und Bauer*). Overture and incidental music by Suppé for Karl Elmar's play (1846).

Pohjola's Daughter (*Pohjolan tytär*). Symphonic fantasia, op. 49 (1906), by Sibelius; it is based on a legend from the *Kalevala.*

Poisoned Kiss, The (*The Poisoned Kiss, or The Empress and the Necromancer*). Opera ('romantic extravaganza') in three acts by Vaughan Williams to a libretto by Evelyn Sharp adapted from Richard Garnett's story *The Poison Maid* (1888) and Nathaniel Hawthorne's *Rapaccini's Daughter* (1844) (Cambridge, 1936); Vaughan Williams revised it in 1956–7 with new spoken dialogue by Ursula Vaughan Williams.

'Polish' Symphony. Nickname of Tchaikovsky's Symphony no. 3 in D major op. 29 (1875), so called because the finale is in polonaise rhythm.

Poliuto. Opera (*tragedia lirica*) in three acts by Donizetti to a libretto by Salvadore Cammarano after Pierre Corneille's play *Polyeucte* (1641) (Naples, 1848).

Polly. Ballad opera in three acts with musical arrangements attributed to Pepusch (with new songs for the first performance by Samuel Arnold) to a libretto by Gay (London, 1777); it was written as a sequel to Gay's *The Beggar's Opera*.

Polovtsian Dances. A sequence of choral and orchestral pieces forming a ballet scene in Act II of Borodin's opera **Prince Igor*. The Polovtsians were nomadic invaders of Russia who, in the opera, capture Igor and entertain him with these dances.

Pomo d'oro, Il ('The Golden Apple'). Opera (*festa teatrale*) in a prologue and five acts by Antonio Cesti to a libretto by Francesco Sbarra after the myth of the Judgment of Paris (Vienna, 1668).

Pomp and Circumstance. Five marches for orchestra, op. 39, by Elgar; nos. 1–4 were composed in 1901–7, no. 5 was completed by 1930. Elgar took the title from Shakespeare's *Othello* (Act III scene 3): 'Pride, pomp, and circumstance of glorious war!'. The trio section of the first march, slightly altered and with words by A. C. Benson beginning 'Land of Hope and Glory', became the finale of Elgar's *Coronation Ode*.

Pope Marcellus Mass. *See* MISSA PAPAE MARCELLI.

Porgy and Bess. Folk opera in three acts by Gershwin to a libretto by DuBose Heyward after his novel *Porgy* (1925), with lyrics by Heyward and Ira Gershwin (New York, 1935).

Poro (*Poro, re dell'Indie*; 'Porus, King of the Indians'). Opera in three acts by Handel to a libretto anonymously adapted from Pietro Metastasio's *Alessandro nell'Indie* (London, 1731).

Portsmouth Point. Overture (1924–5) by Walton after an etching by Thomas Rowlandson (1756–1827).

'Posthorn' Serenade. Nickname of Mozart's Serenade in D major K320 (1779), in which a posthorn is used in the second trio of the second minuet.

Postillon de Longjumeau, Le ('The Coachman of Longjumeau'). *Opéra comique* in three acts by Adolphe Adam to a libretto by Adolphe de Leuven and Brunswick (Léon Lévy) (Paris, 1836).

Poule, La ('The Hen'). Nickname of Haydn's Symphony no. 83 in G minor (1785), the second of the Paris symphonies, so called because of the 'clucking' second subject of the first movement (the title was acquired in the 19th century).

Powder her Face. Chamber opera in two acts by Thomas Adès to a libretto by Philip Hensher (Cheltenham, 1995).

'Prague' Symphony. Nickname of Mozart's Symphony no. 38 in D major K504 (1786), so called because it was first performed in Prague during Mozart's visit in 1787.

Prélude à 'L'Après-midi d'un faune'. *See* APRÈS-MIDI D'UN FAUNE', PRÉLUDE À 'L'.

Préludes. Piano pieces by Debussy, published in two books, each containing 12 (1910, 1912–13); the first includes *La *Fille aux cheveux de lin* and *La *Cathédrale engloutie*, and the second **Feux d'artifice*.

Préludes, Les. Symphonic poem by Liszt, in various versions composed between 1844 and 1854. It originated in 1844–5 as the overture to the choral work *Les Quatre Élémens* (to a text by Joseph Autran), for male voices and piano, and was first orchestrated by August Conradi in 1848. Liszt himself later revised both the musical structure and the orchestration, and appended a title and preface from one of Alphonse de Lamartine's *Nouvelles méditations poétiques* (1823), neither of which had any connection with the work as initially conceived.

Pribaoutki. Work by Stravinsky for male voice and flute, oboe, cor anglais, clarinet, bassoon, violin, viola, cello, and double bass, a setting of Russian traditional rhymes (London, 1918).

Prigioniero, Il ('The Prisoner'). Opera in a prologue and one act by Dallapiccola to his own libretto after Villiers de l'Isle-Adam's *La Torture par l'espérance* (1883) and Charles De Coster's *La Légende d'Ulenspiegel et de Lamme Goedzak* (1868) (Florence, 1950; broadcast 1949).

Prince Igor (*Knyaz' Igor'*). Opera in a prologue and four acts by Borodin to his own libretto after a scenario by Vladimir Stasov largely based on the anonymous, possibly 12th-century epic *Slovo o polku Igoreve* ('The Lay of the Host of Igor') (St Petersburg, 1890). Borodin worked on it from 1869 to 1887 but left it unfinished; Rimsky-Korsakov and Glazunov completed it and Rimsky orchestrated much of it. The *Polovtsian Dances form a ballet scene in Act II.

Prince of the Pagodas, The. Ballet in three acts by Britten to a scenario by John Cranko, who choreographed it (London, 1957). It has been choreographed several times since, notably by Kenneth MacMillan, with a revised scenario by Colin Thubron (London, 1989). Michael Lankester arranged a suite from the score (1979).

Princesse de Navarre, La ('The Princess of Navarra'). *Comédie-ballet* in three acts by Rameau to a libretto by Voltaire (Versailles, 1745).

Princess Ida (*Princess Ida; or, Castle Adamant*). Operetta in three acts by Sullivan to a libretto by W. S. Gilbert after Tennyson's *The Princess* (1847) (London, 1884).

Printemps ('Spring'). Symphonic suite by Debussy for orchestra and female chorus, composed in 1887; the original score was lost and in 1912 Henri Busser reorchestrated it from the piano version, under Debussy's supervision. It is not to be confused with *Rondes de printemps*; *see* IMAGES.

Prinz von Homburg, Der ('The Prince of Homburg'). Opera in three acts by Henze to a libretto by Ingeborg Bachmann after Heinrich von Kleist's play *Prinz Friedrich von Homburg* (1810) (Hamburg, 1960).

Prise de Troie, La. *See* TROYENS, LES.

Prodigal Son, The. Several composers have written works on this biblical subject, the best known being the following.
   1. Church parable, op. 81, by Britten to a text by William Plomer (Aldeburgh, 1968).
   2. Oratorio (1869) by Sullivan to his own text.
   3. Ballet by Prokofiev, choreographed by George Balanchine (Paris, 1929); its Russian title is *Bludnïy syn* but it is often known by its French title *L'Enfant prodigue*.
   4. Cantata by Debussy; *see* ENFANT PRODIGUE, L'.

Prolation. Orchestral work (1958) by Maxwell Davies; its title refers to the medieval system of mensural notation, the proportions of which the composer adopts.

Prometeo. 'A tragedy of listening' (*tragedia dell'ascolto*) by Nono to a text by Massimo Cacciari (Venice, 1984, revised 1985).

Prometheus. Symphonic poem by Liszt, originally composed in 1850 and orchestrated by Joachim Raff as the overture to a setting of choruses from Johann Gottfried Herder's *Prometheus Unbound*; Liszt revised and rescored it in 1855.

Prometheus, Die Geschöpfe des. *See* GESCHÖPFE DES PROMETHEUS, DIE.

Prometheus, the Poem of Fire (*Prometey, poema ogyna*; *Prométhée, le poème du feu*). Symphonic poem, op. 60 (1909–10), by Skryabin, for orchestra with piano, optional chorus, and 'light-keyboard' (projecting colours onto a screen).

Prophète, Le ('The Prophet'). Grand opera in five acts by Meyerbeer to a libretto by Eugène Scribe (Paris, 1849).

Proses lyriques ('Lyrics in Prose'). Four songs (1892–3) by Debussy for voice and piano, settings of his own texts.

Protecting Veil, The. Work (1987) for cello and strings by Tavener.

Proverb. 'Theatre of voices' (1995) by Reich for three sopranos, two tenors, vibraphones, and electronic organs, settings of a text from Ludwig Wittgenstein's *Culture and Value* (1946).

Prozession. Work (1967) by Stockhausen for four instruments, microphones, filters, and potentiometers; the performers are instructed to play 'events' from other works by Stockhausen.

'Prussian' Quartets. Mozart's last three string quartets, no. 21 in D major κ575 (1789), no. 22 in B♭ major κ589 (1790), and no. 23 in F major κ590 (1790), so called because they were commissioned by Friedrich Wilhelm II of Prussia, himself a cellist (hence the prominent cello parts). Haydn's six

String Quartets op. 50 (1787) are also known by this title because of their dedication.

Psalmus hungaricus. Work (1923) by Kodály for solo tenor, chorus, children's chorus ad libitum, orchestra, and organ, a setting of a text from the 16th-century Hungarian poet Mihály Kecskeméti Vég's paraphrase of Psalm 55; it was composed for the 50th anniversary of the union of Buda and Pest.

Pulcinella. Ballet with song in one act by Stravinsky to a scenario by Leonid Massine, who choreographed it for Serge Diaghilev's Ballets Russes with designs by Pablo Picasso (Paris, 1920); for soprano, tenor, bass, and chamber orchestra, it is an adaptation of works by Pergolesi or formerly attributed to him. Stravinsky made a suite from it for chamber orchestra (c.1922, revised 1947). His *Suite italienne* (1932) is also arranged from *Pulcinella*; he collaborated with Gregor Piatigorsky in a five-movement version for cello and piano and with Samuel Dushkin in a six-movement one for violin and piano.

Pulse Shadows. Work (1989–96) for soprano, chamber ensemble, and string quartet by Birtwistle.

Punch and Judy. Opera ('tragicomedy or comitragedy') in one act by Birtwistle to a libretto by Stephen Pruslin (Aldeburgh, 1968).

Purgatory. Opera in one act by Gordon Crosse to a libretto by the composer after William Butler Yeats's verse play (1939) (Cheltenham, 1966).

Puritani, I ('The Puritans'). Opera (*melodramma serio*) in three parts by Bellini to a libretto by Carlo Pepoli after the play by François Ancelot and Xavier (J. X. Boniface *dit* Saintine) *Têtes Rondes et Cavaliers* (1833), itself derived from Walter Scott's *Old Mortality* (1816) (Paris, 1835).

Putnam's Camp. Second movement of Ives's First Orchestral Set, *Three Places in New England*; it was composed in c.1914–15 and is sometimes performed separately.

Pygmalion. *See* PIGMALION.

Quartettsatz ('Quartet Movement'). Title given to an unfinished movement in C minor for string quartet by Schubert, D703 (1820); it was intended as the first movement of a whole quartet but only a fragment of the second movement was completed.

Quatro rusteghi, I (*Die vier Grobiane*; 'The Four Curmudgeons'; *School for Fathers*). Opera in three acts by Wolf-Ferrari to a libretto by Luigi Sugana and Giuseppe Pizzolato after Carlo Goldoni's play *I rusteghi* (1760) (Munich, 1906).

Quattro pezzi sacri ('Four Sacred Pieces'). Four choral works by Verdi, an *Ave Maria*, *Laudi alla Vergine Maria*, *Te Deum*, and *Stabat mater*, composed between 1889 and 1897 and published together in 1898.

Quattro stagioni, Le. *See* FOUR SEASONS, THE.

Quatuor pour la fin du temps ('Quartet for the End of Time'). Work (1940) by Messiaen for clarinet, piano, violin, and cello; he wrote it while he was in a Silesian prisoner-of-war camp, where it was performed the following year.

Queen, The. *See* REINE, LA.

Queen Mary's Funeral Music. *See* FUNERAL MUSIC FOR QUEEN MARY.

Queen of Spades, The (*Pikovaya dama*; *Pique-Dame*). Opera in three acts by Tchaikovsky to a libretto by Modest Tchaikovsky and the composer after Aleksandr Pushkin's novella (1833) (St Petersburg, 1890). *Pique-Dame*, popularly supposed to be the French title, is in fact German (the French term being *Dame de pique*).

Quickening. Work (1998) for soloists, children's choir, mixed choir, and orchestra by James MacMillan, settings of a text by Michael Symmons Roberts.

Quiet City. Orchestral work by Copland for trumpet, cor anglais, and strings, originally composed as incidental music for a play by Irwin Shaw (1939).

Quiet Flows the Don (*Tikhiy Don*, 'The Quiet Don'). Opera in four acts by Ivan Dzerzhinsky to a libretto by Leonid Dzerzhinsky on motifs from Mikhail Sholokhov's novel (Leningrad, 1935).

Quiet Place, A. Opera in one act by Bernstein to a libretto by Stephen Wadsworth (Houston, TX, 1983); Bernstein revised it into three acts (incorporating his *Trouble in Tahiti*, 1952) (Milan, 1984).

Radamisto. Opera in three acts by Handel to an anonymous libretto adapted from Domenico Lalli's *L'amor tirannico, o Zenobia* (1710, revised 1712) (London, 1720).

Radetzky March. March, op. 228 (1848), by Johann Strauss (i) (Radetzky was an Austrian field marshal).

Rage over a Lost Penny. Nickname of Beethoven's op. 129, a piano piece published posthumously (1828).

Rainbow in the Curved Air, A. Work (1968) by Terry Riley for electronic keyboard, dumbak, and tambourines.

'Raindrop' Prelude. Nickname of Chopin's Prelude in D♭ major for piano op. 28 no. 15 (1836–9), so called because the continuously repeated A♭ suggests the sound of raindrops.

Rake's Progress, The. Opera in three acts (nine scenes and an epilogue) by Stravinsky to a libretto by W. H. Auden and Chester Kallman after William Hogarth's series of paintings (1732–3) (Venice, 1951).

Rákóczi March. Hungarian popular march, probably set down by János Bihari (*c.*1810) in homage to Prince Ferenc Rákóczi II (1676–1735), who led the Hungarian revolt against Austria at the beginning of the 18th century. The melody has been used by several composers including Berlioz, who orchestrated it (1846) and incorporated it into *La Damnation de Faust*, Liszt (**Hungarian Rhapsody* no. 15), and Johann Strauss (ii) (*Der Zigeunerbaron*).

Ramifications. Work (1969) by Ligeti for string orchestra.

Rape of Lucretia, The. Opera in two acts by Britten to a libretto by Ronald Duncan after André Obey's play *Le Viol de Lucrèce* (1931), in turn based on Shakespeare's poem *The Rape of Lucrece* (1594) and on Livy's *Historiarum ab urbe condita libri* (Glyndebourne, 1946).

Rappresentatione di Anima, et di Corpo ('Drama of the Soul and the Body'). Sacred opera in a prologue and three acts by Cavalieri, to a text probably by Agostino Manni (Rome, 1600); it is the earliest opera of which all the music survives.

Rapsodie espagnole ('Spanish Rhapsody').
1. Orchestral work (1907–8) by Ravel in four movements: 'Prélude à la nuit', 'Malagueña', 'Habanera', and 'Feria'; the 'Habanera' was originally the first of the *Sites auriculaires* (1895–7) for two pianos.
2. Work for piano by Liszt (*c.*1863); it was arranged for piano and orchestra by Busoni.

Rasiermesserquartett. *See* 'RAZOR' QUARTET.

Rasumovsky Quartets. *See* 'RAZUMOVSKY' QUARTETS.

Raymonda. Ballet in three acts and four scenes by Glazunov to a scenario by Lydia Pashkova and Marius Petipa; it was choreographed by Petipa (St Petersburg, 1898).

'Razor' Quartet (*Rasiermesserquartett*). Nickname of Haydn's String Quartet in F minor op. 55 no. 2 (late 1780s), so called because he is said to have given it to the London publisher John Bland in exchange for a new English razor.

'Razumovsky' Quartets. Beethoven's String Quartets op. 59 no. 1 in F major, no. 2 in E minor, and no. 3 in C major (1805–6), so called because they are dedicated to Count Andrey Razumovsky, the Russian ambassador in Vienna, who was a keen quartet player; in the fourth movement of no. 1 and the third of no. 2 Beethoven used Russian folksongs (labelled 'Thème russe') from a collection published in 1790 by Johann Gottfried Pratsch (Ivan Prach). The set is also sometimes known as the 'Russian' Quartets.

Re cervo, Il. *See* KÖNIG HIRSCH.

Récitations. Work (1982) by Aperghis, a set of 14 pieces for solo voice in which disjointed words, phrases, and nonsense syllables are subjected to heightened rhythmic or playful declamation.

Red Poppy, The (*Krasnïy mak*). Ballet in three acts by Glière to a scenario by Mikhail Kurilko, choreographed by Lev Lashchilin and Vassily Tikhomirov (Moscow, 1927); Glière revised it as *The Red Flower* (*Krasnïy tsvetok*).

'Reformation' Symphony. Mendelssohn's Symphony no. 5 in D major (1832); it was written for (but not played at) the tercentenary in Augsburg of the foundation of the Lutheran Reformed Church, the first and last movements quoting the *'Dresden Amen' and the Lutheran chorale **Ein' feste Burg*.

Reigen ('Round Dance'). Opera in ten scenes by Philippe Boesmans to a libretto by Luc Bondy after Arthur Schnitzler's play *La Ronde* (1897) (Brussels, 1993).

Re in ascolto, Un ('A Listening King'). Opera (*azione musicale*) in two parts by Berio to a libretto he assembled from texts by Italo Calvino, W. H. Auden, Friedrich Einsiedel, and Friedrich Wilhelm Gotter (Salzburg, 1984).

Reine, La ('The Queen'). Nickname of Haydn's Symphony no. 85 in B♭ major (1785), the fourth of the Paris symphonies, so called because it was much admired by Marie Antoinette, 'La Reine de France'.

Rejoice in the Lamb (*Jubilate Agno*). Festival cantata, op. 30 (1943), by Britten for mixed chorus and organ, a setting of a text from Christopher Smart's *Jubilate Agno* (1758–63).

Rejoice in the Lord Alway. *See* 'BELL' ANTHEM.

Relâche ('No Show'; 'Theatre Closed'). Ballet in two acts by Satie to a scenario by Francis Picabia, with a cinematographic entr'acte by René Clair; it was choreographed by Jean Börlin (Paris, 1924).

Renard (*Bayka pro lisu, petukha, kota da barana*; 'Fable of the Fox, the Cock, the Cat, and the Ram'). Burlesque in song and dance in one act by Stravinsky to his own libretto after Russian folk tales; it was choreographed by Bronislava Nijinska for Serge Diaghilev's Ballets Russes (Paris, 1922).

Rencontre imprévue, L' ('The Unexpected Meeting'). *Opéra comique* in three acts by Gluck to a libretto after Alain-René Lesage and D'Orneval's *opéra comique Les pèlerins de la Mecque* (1726) as revised by Louis Hurtaut Dancourt (Vienna, 1764).

Rendering. Orchestral work (1989) by Berio, based on Schubert's sketches for a tenth symphony.

Re pastore, Il ('The Shepherd King'). Serenata in two acts by Mozart to a libretto by Pietro Metastasio (Salzburg, 1775). The libretto was used by several composers including Gluck (1756).

Requiem Canticles. Work (1965–6) by Stravinsky for alto, bass, chorus, and orchestra, a setting of extracts of the most important parts of the Roman Catholic Requiem Mass, with instrumental prologue, interlude, and postlude; he composed it with his own death in mind, and it was his last major composition.

Requiem Mass (Fr.: *Messe des morts*; Ger.: *Totenmesse*; It.: *Messa per i defunti*; Lat.: *Missa pro defunctis*). The votive Mass for the dead of the Roman rite, the Tridentine version of which begins with the Introit 'Requiem aeternam dona eis Domine' ('Give them eternal rest, O Lord'). There are notable settings for non-liturgical use by Mozart (completed after his death by Süssmayr and with some additions by Eybler), Cherubini (in C minor, 1816, and D minor, 1836), Berlioz (**Grande Messe des morts*, 1837), Bruckner (an early work; 1848–9), Verdi (1874), Fauré (1887–8), Dvořák (1890), Pizzetti (1922–3), and Duruflé (1947, revised 1961). Schütz's **Musikalische Exequien* (1636) and Brahms's **A *German Requiem* (1865–8) are Protestant memorial works. *See also* CELTIC REQUIEM; WAR REQUIEM.

Resurrection. Opera by Tod Machover to a libretto by Laura Harrington after Tolstoy's novella (1899) (Houston, TX, 1999).

'Resurrection' Symphony. Popular name for Mahler's Symphony no. 2 in C minor (1888–94, revised 1903), so called because the finale is a setting for soprano and alto soloists, chorus, and orchestra of Friedrich Gottlieb Klopstock's poem *Aufersteh'n* ('Resurrection').

Réveil des oiseaux ('The Birds' Awakening'). Work (1953) by Messiaen for piano and orchestra.

Revelation and Fall. Music-theatre piece by Maxwell Davies to a text from Georg Trakl's *Offenbarung and Untergang* (London, 1968).

'Revolutionary' Étude. Nickname of Chopin's *Étude* in C minor for piano op. 10 no. 12 (1830), so called because it is said that he composed it as a patriotic reaction to hearing that Warsaw had been captured by the Russians.

Rhapsody in Blue. Work (1924) by Gershwin for piano and orchestra, orchestrated by Ferde Grofé, who reorchestrated it in 1926 and 1942 (the version most often used).

Rhapsody on a Theme of Paganini. Rakhmaninov's op. 43 (1934) for piano and orchestra, 24 variations on Paganini's *Caprice* no. 24 in A minor for violin.

Rheingold, Das ('The Rhinegold'). Opera (*Vorabend*) in four scenes by Wagner to his own libretto, the 'preliminary evening' of *Der *Ring des Nibelungen*.

'Rhenish' Symphony. Schumann's Symphony no. 3 in E♭ major (1850) (his fourth in order of composition); the fourth of its five movements was inspired by the installation of a cardinal at Cologne on the Rhine.

Rhinegold, The. *See* RHEINGOLD, DAS.

Richard Coeur-de-lion ('Richard the Lionheart'). Opera (*comédie mise en musique*) in three acts by Grétry to a libretto by Michel-Jean Sedaine after an anonymous account in the *Bibliothèque universelle des romans*, ii (1776) (Paris, 1784); it was revised into four acts (Fontainebleau, 1785).

Riders to the Sea. Opera in one act by Vaughan Williams to his own libretto, an almost verbatim setting of J. M. Synge's play (1904) (London, 1937).

Rienzi der Letzte der Tribunen ('Rienzi, the Last of the Tribunes'). Opera (*grosse tragische Oper*) in five acts by Wagner to his own libretto after Edward Bulwer-Lytton's novel (1835) (Dresden, 1842).

Rigoletto. Opera (*melodramma*) by Verdi in three acts with a libretto by Francesco Maria Piave after Victor Hugo's play *Le Roi s'amuse* (1832) (Venice, 1851).

Rinaldo. Opera in three acts by Handel to a libretto by Giacomo Rossi based on an outline by Aaron Hill after Torquato Tasso's *Gerusalemme liberata* (1581) (London, 1711); Handel revised it substantially (London, 1731).

Ring des Nibelungen, Der ('The Nibelung's Ring'). *Bühnenfestspiel* ('stage festival play') for three days and a preliminary evening by Wagner to his own libretto; it was first performed as a cycle on 13, 14, 16, and 17 August 1876 at the Festspielhaus, Bayreuth. The four operas of the *Ring* cycle are *Das Rheingold*, the preliminary evening, in four scenes (Munich, 1869); *Die Walküre*, the first day, in three acts (Munich, 1870); *Siegfried*, the second day, in three acts (Bayreuth, 1876); and *Götterdämmerung*, the third day, in three acts (Bayreuth, 1876).

Ringed by the Flat Horizon. Orchestral work (1980) by George Benjamin.

Rio Grande, The. Work (1927) by Constant Lambert for solo piano, chorus, and orchestra, a setting of a poem by Sacheverell Sitwell.

Rise and Fall of the City of Mahagonny. *See* AUFSTIEG UND FALL DER STADT MAHAGONNY.

Rising of the Moon, The. Opera in three acts by Nicholas Maw to a libretto by Beverley Cross (Glyndebourne, 1970).

Rite of Spring, The (*Vesna svyashchennaya*; *Le Sacre du printemps*). Ballet ('scenes of pagan Russia') in two parts by Stravinsky to a scenario by Nicholas Roerich; it was choreographed by Vaslav Nijinsky for Serge Diaghilev's Ballets Russes (Paris, 1913). It is in two parts, 'The Adoration of the Earth' and 'The Sacrifice'. Stravinsky made a four-hand piano reduction of the score.

Ritorno d'Ulisse in patria, Il ('The Return of Ulysses to his Homeland'). Opera (*dramma per musica*) in a prologue and three acts by Monteverdi, to a libretto in five acts by Giacomo Badoaro after Homer's *Odyssey* (Venice, 1640).

Ritual Dances from 'The Midsummer Marriage'. Orchestral work (with chorus ad lib) by Tippett, comprising four dances from his opera *The *Midsummer Marriage*. The first three are from Act II and the fourth is from Act III; they are *The Earth in Autumn* ('The Hound Chases the Hare'), *The Waters in Winter* ('The Otter Pursues the Fish'), *The Air in Spring* ('The Hawk Swoops on the Bird'), and *Fire in Summer* (a celebration of carnal love). They were first performed in 1953.

Ritual Fire Dance (*Danza ritual del fuego*). Dance from Falla's ballet *El *amor brujo* (1915); it became popular in Falla's piano arrangement and has been arranged for other instruments, including the cello.

Roaratorio. 'An Irish Circus on Finnegans Wake' (1979) by Cage for any ensemble and tape.

Robert le diable ('Robert the Devil'). *Grand opéra* in five acts by Meyerbeer to a libretto by Eugène Scribe and Germain Delavigne (Paris, 1831).

Roberto Devereux (*Roberto Devereux, ossia Il conte di Essex*; 'Robert Devereux, or The Earl of Essex'). Opera (*tragedia lirica*) in three acts by Donizetti to a libretto by Salvadore Cammarano after François Ancelot's tragedy *Élisabeth d'Angleterre* (Naples, 1837).

Robin et Marion. *See* JEU DE ROBIN ET DE MARION, LE.

Rock of Ages, Cleft for Me. Hymn of which the words were written by the Revd Augustus Montague Toplady (1740–78), vicar of Broadhembury, Devon; the tune is by Richard Redhead, from *Church Hymn Tunes, Ancient and Modern* (1853).

Rococo Variations. *See* VARIATIONS ON A ROCOCO THEME.

Rodelinda (*Rodelinda, regina de' longobardi*; 'Rodelinda, Queen of the Lombards'). Opera in three acts by Handel to a libretto by Nicola Francesco Haym adapted from Antonio Salvi's *Rodelinda, regina de' longobardi* (1710), after Pierre Corneille's play *Pertharite, roi des Lombards* (1651) (London, 1725).

Rodeo. Ballet in one act by Copland to a scenario by Agnes de Mille, who choreographed it (New York, 1942); it is subtitled 'The Courting at Burnt Ranch' and uses traditional songs. Copland arranged four dance episodes from it for orchestra (1942) and arranged the work for piano (1962).

Rodrigue et Chimène. Unfinished opera in three acts by Debussy to a libretto by Catulle Mendès; it was reconstructed by Richard Langham Smith (extracts, with piano accompaniment, Paris, 1987).

Roi Arthus, Le ('King Arthur'). Opera (*drame lyrique*) in three acts by Chausson to his own libretto (Brussels, 1903).

Roi David, Le ('King David'). Dramatic psalm in five parts by Honegger, for narrator, soprano, mezzo-soprano, tenor, chorus, and orchestra, a setting of a text by René Morax (Mézières, 1921); Honegger revised and reorchestrated it in three parts (1923) and arranged an orchestral suite from it.

Roi de Lahore, Le ('The King of Lahore'). Opera in five acts by Massenet to a libretto by Louis Gallet (Paris, 1877).

Roi d'Ys, Le ('The King of Ys'). Opera in three acts by Lalo to a libretto by Édouard Blau (Paris, 1888).

Roi malgré lui, Le ('The King in Spite of Himself'). *Opéra comique* in three acts by Chabrier to a libretto by Émile de Najac and Paul Burani (Paris, 1887).

Roman Carnival, The. *See* CARNAVAL ROMAIN, LE.

Roman de Fauvel. *See* FAUVEL, ROMAN DE.

'Romantic' Symphony. Bruckner's Symphony no. 4 in E♭ major, composed in 1874 and revised in 1878–80 and 1886.

Romeo and Juliet. Shakespeare's tragedy (1594 or 1595) has been the subject of many musical works, of which the best known are:

1. *Roméo et Juliette*. Dramatic symphony, op. 17 (1839), by Berlioz, for alto, tenor, and bass soloists, chorus, and orchestra, to a text by Émile Deschamps.

2. *Roméo et Juliette*. Opera in five acts by Gounod to a libretto by Jules Barbier and Michel Carré (Paris, 1867).

3. *Romeo i Dzhulyetta*. Fantasy overture by Tchaikovsky; it was composed in 1869 and revised in 1870 and 1880.

4. *Romeo i Dzhulyetta*. Ballet in a prologue, three acts, and an epilogue by Prokofiev to a scenario by Leonid Lavrovsky, the composer, and Sergey Radlov; it was choreographed by Ivo Psota (Brno, 1938). Prokofiev arranged three orchestral suites from the score: no. 1, op. 64*b* (1936), in seven movements; no. 2, op. 64*c* (1937), in seven movements; no. 3, op. 101 (1946), in six movements.

Among other operas on the subject are those by Benda (1776), Dalayrac (1792), Steibelt (1793), Zingarelli (1796), Bellini (I *Capuleti e i Montecchi*, 1830), Zandonai (1922), Sutermeister (1940), Blacher (1950), and Malipiero (1950). Bernstein's *West Side Story* (1957) is an updated version of the same story.

Rondine, La ('The Swallow'). Opera (*commedia lirica*) in three acts by Puccini to a libretto by A. M. Willner and Heinz Reichert (Monte Carlo, 1917).

Rosa. 'A horse drama' in 12 scenes by Louis Andriessen to a libretto by Peter Greenaway (Amsterdam, 1994).

Rosamunde, Fürstin von Cypern ('Rosamund, Princess of Cyprus'). Play (1823) by Helmina von Chézy for which Schubert wrote the overture and musical interludes; the overture played at the first performance was the one already composed for *Alfonso und Estrella. The overture now known as the *Rosamunde* overture (D644) was composed for G. E. Hoffmann's melodrama *Die Zauberharfe* ('The Magic Harp') (1820).

Rosary [Mystery] **Sonatas.** Sonatas (?1674) by Biber for violin and continuo.

Rose Lake, The. 'Song without words' for orchestra (1991–3) by Tippett.

Rosen aus dem Süden ('Roses from the South'). Waltz, op. 388 (1880), by Johann Strauss (ii); it was originally written for his opera *Das Spitzentuch der Königin* ('The Queen's Lace Handkerchief').

Rosenkavalier, Der ('The Knight of the Rose'). Opera (*Komödie für Müsik*) in three acts by Richard Strauss to a libretto by Hugo von Hofmannsthal (Dresden, 1911).

Roses from the South. *See* ROSEN AUS DEM SÜDEN.

Rossignol, Le. *See* NIGHTINGALE, THE.

Rothko Chapel. Work by Morton Feldman for soprano, alto, chorus (all wordless), and three players, composed for the inauguration of the Rothko Chapel in Houston, Texas, in 1971.

Royal Hunt of the Sun, The. Opera in three acts by Iain Hamilton to his own libretto after Peter Shaffer's play (1964) (London, 1977).

Roxolane, La. Nickname of Haydn's Symphony no. 63 in C major (1779), so called because the second movement uses material from Haydn's incidental music to the play *Soliman II, oder Die drei Sultaninnen*, in which the heroine was Roxolane.

Royall Consort, The. A collection of 66 dance pieces by William Lawes, originally for two violins, two bass viols, and continuo, arranged in large suites.

Rrrrrrr.... 'Radio fantasy' (1981–2) by Kagel; he arranged it as a radio play (1982) and as the television play *Er* (1984).

Rückert-Lieder. Five songs with orchestra (1901–2) by Mahler to poems by Friedrich Rückert (1788–1866); they are *Ich atmet' einen linden Duft!* ('I Breathed a Delicate Fragrance'), *Blicke mir nicht in die Lieder* ('Do not Look into my Songs'), *Ich bin der Welt abhanden gekommen* ('I am Lost to the World'), *Um Mitternacht* ('At Midnight'), and *Liebst du um Schönheit* ('If you Love for Beauty').

Ruddigore (*Ruddigore* [originally *Ruddygore*]; *or, The Witch's Curse*). Operetta in two acts by Sullivan to a libretto by W. S. Gilbert (London, 1887).

Rugby. Orchestral work (1928) by Honegger, the second of his *Mouvements symphoniques*.

Ruinen von Athen, Die ('The Ruins of Athens'). Incidental music by Beethoven, op. 113 (1811), for a play by August von Kotzebue given at the first night of the German theatre in Budapest (1812); it includes an overture, choruses, an aria, and a Turkish march (adapted from his variations for piano op. 76).

Rule, Britannia! Song by Arne from his masque *Alfred*, with words by James Thomson and David Mallett (Cliveden, 1740); *Alfred* was not given in London until 1745, when threat of rebellion led 'Rule, Britannia!' to provoke patriotic fervour among the audiences. In 1746 Handel introduced the tune into his *Occasional Overture*; Beethoven wrote a set of piano variations on it (1803) and introduced it into his *Wellingtons Sieg* (1813). It also appears in Attwood's anthem *O Lord, Grant the King a Long Life*, and Wagner and Alexander Mackenzie wrote overtures based on it.

Rusalka. 1. Opera ('lyric fairy tale') in three acts by Dvořák to a libretto by the Czech writer Jaroslav Kvapil (i) after Friedrich de la Motte Fouqué's *Undine* (1811) (Prague, 1901).

2. Romantic opera in four acts by Dargomïzhsky to his own libretto after Aleksandr Pushkin's poem (1837) (St Petersburg, 1856).

Ruslan and Lyudmila. 'Magic' opera in five acts by Glinka to a libretto by Valerian Fyodorovich Shirkov (with minor contributions by others) after Aleksandr Pushkin's poem (1820) (St Petersburg, 1842).

Russian Easter Festival. Overture (1888) by Rimsky-Korsakov, based on Russian Orthodox Church melodies.

'Russian' Quartets. Haydn's six String Quartets op. 33 (1781), so called because later editions bear a dedication to the Grand Duke Pavel Petrovich, who visited Haydn in Vienna in 1781; they are also known as *Gli scherzi*, because their minuets are headed 'Scherzo', and as the 'Maiden' Quartets (*Jungfernquartette*), because a female figure is depicted on the title page of the 1782 Hummel edition. Beethoven's *Razumovsky' Quartets are sometimes known as the 'Russian' Quartets.

Rustle of Spring (*Frühlingsrauschen*). Piano piece by Sinding, the third of his Six Pieces op. 32 (1896); it exists in many arrangements.

Ruy Blas. Overture, op. 95 (1839), by Mendelssohn, written for a German performance of Victor Hugo's play of that name (1838).

RV. Abbreviation for *Ryom-Verzeichnis, used as a prefix to the numbers of Vivaldi's works as given in the standard thematic catalogue of Peter Ryom.

Ryom. Abbreviation for the standard thematic catalogue of the works of Vivaldi drawn up by the Danish scholar Peter Ryom (*b* 1937). Vivaldi's works are commonly referred to by Ryom number (often further abbreviated to rv, standing for Ryom-Verzeichnis).

Sabre Dance. A movement from Khachaturian's ballet *Gayané*.

Sacre du printemps, Le. *See* RITE OF SPRING, THE.

Sadko. Opera (*opera bïlina*, operatically treated heroic ballad) in three or five acts by Rimsky-Korsakov to his own libretto compiled (with the help of Vladimir Stasov and Vladimir Bel'sky among others) from *Sadko, bogatïy gosti* and other ancient ballads and tales (Moscow, 1897). Rimsky-Korsakov had earlier (1867) written a symphonic poem with the same title.

Saga, En. *See* EN SAGA.

St Anne. Hymn tune, probably by William Croft; it has always been ascribed to him, though it was first published in an anonymous collection (1708) and is usually sung to the words 'O God, our help in ages past'. J. S. Bach's Fugue in E♭ major for organ, the last item in the *Clavier-Übung* book 3, is known as the 'St Anne Fugue' because it begins with the same notes as the hymn tune.

'St Anthony' Variations. *See* VARIATIONS ON A THEME BY HAYDN.

Saint François d'Assise ('St Francis of Assisi'; *Scènes franciscains*, 'Franciscan Scenes'). Opera in three acts by Messiaen to his own libretto (Paris, 1983).

St John Passion (*Johannes-Passion*). Setting by J. S. Bach, BWV245, of the Passion story to an anonymous text adapted from Barthold Heinrich Brockes's poem *Der für die Sünde der Welt gemarterte und sterbende Jesus* ('Jesus, Martyred and Dying for the Sins of the World') after St John's Gospel; for soloists, chorus, and orchestra, it was first performed on Good Friday 1724. Selle (1623), Schütz (1666), Telemann (several), and Pärt (1982) also wrote *St John Passion* settings.

St John's Night on Bald Mountain. *See* NIGHT ON THE BARE MOUNTAIN.

St Luke Passion (*Passio et mors domini nostri Jesu Christi secundum Lucam*). Oratorio (1966) by Penderecki, for soprano, baritone, and bass soloists, boys' chorus, three mixed choruses, and orchestra, after St Luke's Gospel.

St Matthew Passion (*Matthäus-Passion*). Setting by J. S. Bach, BWV244, of the Passion story to a text by Picander after St Matthew's Gospel; for soloists, chorus, and orchestra, it was probably first performed on Good Friday 1727. Richard Davy (late 15th century) and Schütz (1666) also wrote *St Matthew Passion* settings.

St Nicolas. Cantata, op. 42, by Britten for tenor, chorus, women's semi-chorus, four boy singers, strings, piano duet, percussion, and organ; a setting of a text by Eric Crozier telling the life of St Nicolas of Myra, it had its premiere in 1948 at the first Aldeburgh Festival.

St Paul (*Paulus*). Oratorio, op. 36 (1836), by Mendelssohn, for soprano, contralto, tenor, and bass soloists, chorus, and orchestra, a setting of a text by Julius Schubring after the Acts of the Apostles.

St Paul's Suite. Suite for string orchestra, op. 29 no. 2 (1912–13), by Holst, written for St Paul's Girls' School, Hammersmith, where Holst was director of music from 1905.

St Thomas Wake. Foxtrot (1969) by Maxwell Davies for dance band and orchestra on a pavan by John Bull.

Sakuntala. Opera in three acts by Weingartner to his own libretto after Kalidasa's drama *Abhijñasakuntala* (*c*.400 BC) (Weimar, 1884). Alfano wrote a three-act opera on the same subject (Bologna, 1921), Ernest Reyer wrote a ballet *Sacountala* (1858), and Goldmark wrote an overture *Sakuntala* (1865).

Salammbô. Projected grand opera in four acts by Musorgsky to his own libretto after Gustave Flaubert's novel (1862) (concert performance of fragments, Milan, 1980).

Salome. Opera (*Musikdrama*) in one act by Richard Strauss to Hedwig Lachmann's German translation of Oscar Wilde's play (1893) (Dresden, 1905).

'Salomon' Symphonies. *See* 'LONDON' SYMPHONIES.

Salón México, El. Orchestral work (1933–6) by Copland; it is named after a dance hall in Mexico City that Copland visited in 1932 and includes Mexican folksongs.

Salut d'amour (*Liebesgruss*; 'Love's Greeting'). Piece by Elgar, originally for solo piano (1888); it was orchestrated in 1889, and later arranged for violin and piano and for many other combinations.

Samson. Oratorio (1743) by Handel to a text adapted by Newburgh Hamilton from John Milton's *Samson Agonistes* and other poems.

Samson et Dalila. Opera in three acts by Saint-Saëns to a libretto by Ferdinand Lemaire after Judges 14–16 (Weimar, 1877).

Samstag aus Licht ('Saturday from Light'). Opera in a greeting and four scenes by Stockhausen to his own libretto (Milan, 1984), the 'second day' of **Licht*.

Samuel Beckett: What is the Word? Two works by Kurtág to texts by Samuel Beckett; the first, op. 30*a* (1990), is for soprano and piano, and the second, op. 30*b* (1991), is for speaker, chorus, and chamber ensemble.

Sancta civitas ('Holy City'). Oratorio (1923–5) by Vaughan Williams, to a text from Revelation with additions from Taverner's Bible (1539) and other sources, for tenor, baritone, chorus, semi-chorus, and orchestra.

San Francisco Polyphony. Orchestral work (1974) by Ligeti.

Sanguine Fan, The. Ballet in one act by Elgar to a scenario by Ian Lowther based on a fan design drawn in sanguine (red crayon) by Charles Conder; it was first performed as a mimed play (London, 1917), in aid of war charities, and was staged as a ballet (under the title *L'Éventail*), choreographed by Ronald Hynd (London, 1976).

Sapho. Opera (*pièce lyrique*) in five acts by Massenet to a libretto by Henri Cain and Arthur Bernède after Alphonse Daudet's novel (1884) (Paris, 1897).

Šárka. Opera in three acts by Fibich to a libretto by Anežka Schulzová (Prague, 1897). Janáček wrote an unfinished opera on the same subject.

Satyagraha. Opera in three acts by Philip Glass to a libretto by the composer and Constance DeJong after the *Bhagavad Gītā* (Rotterdam, 1980).

Saul. Oratorio (1739) by Handel to a text by Charles Jennens.

Saul og David ('Saul and David'). Opera in four acts by Nielsen to a libretto by Einar Christiansen (Copenhagen, 1902).

Sāvitri. Chamber opera in one act by Holst to his own libretto adapted from an incident in the *Mahābhārata* (London, 1916).

Savoy operas. Name by which the operas of Gilbert and Sullivan are known because from *Iolanthe* (1882) onwards they were first produced at the Savoy Theatre, London.

Sayings of Péter Bornemisza, The. Work (1968; revised 1976) by Kurtág for soprano and piano, settings of texts by Bornemisza (1535–84).

Scala di seta, La ('The Silken Ladder'). Opera (*farsa comica*) in one act by Rossini to a libretto by Giuseppe Maria Foppa after F.-A.-E. de Planard's libretto for Pierre Gaveaux's *L'Échelle de soie* (1808) (Venice, 1812).

Scaramouche. Suite for two pianos (1937) by Milhaud; it is based on the incidental music he wrote for Molière's *Le Médecin volant* ('The Flying Doctor') for a production at the Théâtre Scaramouche, hence its title.

Scardinelli-Zyklus. Sequence of choral songs and solo instrumental and ensemble pieces by Holliger, to texts by Friedrich Hölderlin, composed between 1975 and 1991.

Scènes de ballet. Ballet divertissement in 11 numbers by Stravinsky. It was first performed, with choreography by Anton Dolin, in abbreviated form because of disagreements between the composer and the producers (New York, 1944). It was then staged complete, with choreography by Frederick Ashton (London, 1948).

Scenes from a Novel (*Stseni iz romana*). Work (1979–82) by Kurtág for soprano, violin, double bass, and cimbalom, settings of 15 poems by Rimma Dalos.

Scenes from Childhood. *See* KINDERSZENEN.

Scenes from Comus. Work (1965) by Hugh Wood for soprano and tenor soloists and orchestra, to a text from Milton's masque *Comus* (1634).

Scenes from Goethe's 'Faust'. *See* 'FAUST', SCENES FROM GOETHE'S.

Scenes from Schumann. Seven paraphrases for orchestra (1970, revised 1986) by Robin Holloway.

Schafe können sicher weiden. *See* SHEEP MAY SAFELY GRAZE.

Schauspieldirektor, Der ('The Impresario'). *Singspiel* in one act by Mozart to a libretto by Gottlieb Stephanie the younger (Schönbrunn, 1786).

Schéhérazade. *See* SHEHERAZADE.

Scherzi, Gli. *See* 'RUSSIAN' QUARTETS.

Scherzi musicali ('Musical Jokes'). Two sets of madrigal-like songs by Monteverdi, influenced by the French style; the first (1607) contains 15 songs for three voices, and the second (1632) ten for one or two voices with continuo.

Schicksalslied ('Song of Destiny'). Choral work, op. 54 (1868–71), by Brahms, a setting of a poem by Friedrich Hölderlin.

Schlachthof 5 ('Slaughterhouse Five'). Opera in two acts by Hans-Jürgen von Bose to his own libretto after Kurt Vonnegut's novel *Slaughterhouse-Five; or, The Children's Crusade* (1969) (Munich, 1996).

Schneewitchen ('Snow White'). Opera in a prologue, five scenes, and an epilogue by Holliger to his own libretto after Robert Walser's play (1901) (Zürich, 1998).

Schöne Melusine, Die ('The Beautiful Melusina'). Overture, op. 32 (1833), by Mendelssohn inspired by Conradin Kreutzer's opera *Melusine* (1833; a setting of Franz Grillparzer's libretto *Melusina*).

Schöne Müllerin, Die ('The Beautiful Maid of the Mill'). Song cycle, D795 (1823), for male voice and piano by Schubert, settings of 20 poems (1821) by Wilhelm Müller.

Schoolmaster, The (*Der Schulmeister*). Nickname of Haydn's Symphony no. 55 in E♭ major (1774), so called because the dotted figure in the slow movement has been thought to suggest a schoolmaster's admonishing finger.

Schöpfung, Die. *See* CREATION, THE.

Schöpfungsmesse. *See* 'CREATION' MASS.

'Schübler' Chorales. Popular name for six of Bach's chorale preludes for organ, BWV645–50, published (*c.*1748–9) by Johann Schübler; five of them are arrangements of arias from Bach's cantatas.

Schulmeister, Der. *See* SCHOOLMASTER, THE.

Schwanda the Bagpiper (*Švanda dudák*). Opera in two acts by Jaromír Weinberger to a libretto by Miloš Kareš after an old Czech children's story (Prague, 1927).

Schwanengesang ('Swan Song'). Collection of songs for voice and piano by Schubert, D957 (1828), settings of seven poems by Ludwig Rellstab, six by Heinrich Heine, and one by Johann Gabriel Seidl, published posthumously as a 'cycle' under this title by Tobias Haslinger.

Schwarze Maske, Die ('The Black Mask'). Opera in three acts by Penderecki to a libretto by Harry Kupfer and the composer after Gerhart Hauptmann's play (1928) (Salzburg, 1986).

Schweigsame Frau, Die ('The Silent Woman'). Opera (*komische Oper*) in three acts by Richard Strauss to a libretto by Stefan Zweig after Ben Jonson's play *Epicoene* (1609) (Dresden, 1935).

Scipione ('Scipio'). Opera in three acts by Handel to a libretto by Paolo Antonio Rolli based on Antonio Salvi's *Publio Cornelio Scipione* (1704) after Livy's *Historiarum ab urbe condita libri* (London, 1726).

Scottish Fantasy (*Schottische Fantasie*). Fantasia on Scottish folk tunes (1879–80) for violin and orchestra by Bruch.

Scottish Symphony. Mendelssohn's Symphony no. 3 in A minor, composed between 1830 and 1842; it was inspired by a visit to Holyrood, Edinburgh, in 1829 and is dedicated to Queen Victoria.

Scythian Suite (*Ala i Lolly*; 'Ala and Lolly'). Orchestral work, op. 20 (1914–15), by Prokofiev.

Sea Drift. Work (1903–4) by Delius, a setting for baritone, chorus, and orchestra of an extract from Walt Whitman's *Out of the Cradle Endlessly Rocking*.

Sea Interludes, Four. *See* FOUR SEA INTERLUDES.

Sea Pictures. Song cycle, op. 37 (1897–9), by Elgar, for alto and orchestra, settings of poems by Roden Noel, Caroline Alice Elgar, Elizabeth Barrett Browning, Richard Garnett, and Adam Lindsay Gordon.

Seasons, The. 1. (*Die Jahreszeiten*). Oratorio (1799–1801) by Haydn, for soprano, tenor, and bass soloists, chorus, and orchestra, to a text by Gottfried van Swieten after an English poem by James Thomson (1700–48) translated by Barthold Heinrich Brockes.

2. Ballet in one act and four scenes by Glazunov to a scenario by Marius Petipa, who choreographed it (St Petersburg, 1900).

See also FOUR SEASONS, THE.

Sea Symphony, A. Vaughan Williams's first symphony, for soprano and baritone soloists, chorus, and orchestra, to a text taken from poems by Walt Whitman; it was composed between 1903 and 1909 and later revised, the last revision being in 1923.

Second Mrs Kong, The. Opera in two acts by Birtwistle to a libretto by Russell Hoban (Glyndebourne, 1994).

Secret, The (*Tajemství*). Comic opera in three acts by Smetana to a libretto by Eliška Krásnohorská (Prague, 1878).

Secret Marriage, The. *See* MATRIMONIO SEGRETO, IL.

Secret Theatre. Work (1984) for 14 instruments by Birtwistle.

Sederunt principes. A four-voice chant setting (*organum quadruplum*) by Pérotin, a gradual for St Stephen composed *c.*1200.

Seejungfrau, Die ('The Mermaid'). Tone-poem (1902–3) by Zemlinsky after Hans Christian Andersen's fairy tale.

Segreto di Susanna, Il (*Susannens Geheimnis*; 'Susannah's Secret'). Opera ('intermezzo') in one act by Wolf-Ferrari to a libretto by Enrico Golisciani (Munich, 1909).

Se la face ay pale. Chanson for three voices by Dufay, composed probably in the 1430s; he later used its tenor part as the tenor cantus firmus of a mass for four voices. David Lang based his *Face So Pale* (1992) for six pianos on the same melody.

Sellinger's Round, Variations on an Elizabethan Theme. Work for string orchestra by Arthur Oldham, Tippett, Lennox Berkeley, Britten, Humphrey Searle, and Walton, composed to celebrate the coronation of Elizabeth II in 1953; it consists of six variations on the Elizabethan tune *Sellinger's Round*. Tippett expanded his contribution into his *Divertimento on Sellinger's Round* (1953–4), the tune appearing in all five movements.

Semele. Opera in three acts by Handel to a libretto by William Congreve after Ovid's *Metamorphoses* (London, 1744).

Semiramide ('Semiramis'). Opera (*melodramma tragico*) in two acts by Rossini to a libretto by Gaetano Rossi after Voltaire's *Sémiramis* (1748) (Venice, 1823). It is the subject of numerous operas, notably by Porpora (1729), Vivaldi (1732), Hasse (1744), Gluck (1748), Galuppi (1749), Paisiello (1772), Salieri (1782), Catel (1802), Meyerbeer (1819), and Respighi (1910), many of them settings of a libretto by Pietro Metastasio.

Semyon Kotko. Opera in five acts by Prokofiev to a libretto by the composer and Valentin Katayev after Katayev's novella *Ya-sïn trudovogo naroda* ('I am a Son of the Labouring Masses') (Moscow, 1940).

Sensemayá. Orchestral work (1938) by Revueltas; it is based on the Cuban Nicolás Guillén's poem *Sensemayá: Canto para matar una culebra*, an incantatory 'song for the killing of a snake'.

Séquence. Work (1955) by Barraqué for soprano and ten players, a setting of a text by Friedrich Nietzsche.

Sequenza ('Sequence'). Title given by Berio to a series of short virtuoso works for solo instruments (flute, harp, trombone, oboe, etc.) begun in the 1950s. Some have been developed into larger works; for example *Sequenza VI* for viola (1967) was expanded to become *Chemins II* (1967) for nine instruments and *Chemins III* (1968) for large orchestra, and *Sequenza X* (1984) for trumpet grew into *Kol-Od* (1996) for trumpet and ensemble.

Seraglio, The Abduction from the. *See* ENTFÜHRUNG AUS DEM SERAIL, DIE.

Serenade for Tenor, Horn, and Strings. Song cycle, op. 31 (1943), by Britten in which a prologue and epilogue for solo horn enclose settings of six poems on the theme of evening, by Charles Cotton, Tennyson, William Blake, an anonymous one (*The Lyke-Wake Dirge*), Ben Jonson, and John Keats; it was written for Peter Pears and Dennis Brain.

Serenade to Music. Work by Vaughan Williams for four sopranos, four altos, four tenors, four basses, and orchestra, a setting of a passage from Shakespeare's *The Merchant of Venice* (1596–7); it was composed for Henry Wood's golden jubilee (1938) as a conductor. Vaughan Williams arranged it for four soloists and orchestra, for chorus and orchestra, and for orchestra alone.

Serenata notturna ('Nocturnal Serenade'). Mozart's Serenade no. 6 in D major K239 (1776), for two small groups of strings.

Serious Songs, Four. *See* VIER ERNSTE GESÄNGE.

Sermon, a Narrative, and a Prayer, A. Cantata (1960–1) by Stravinsky for alto and tenor soloists, narrator, chorus, and orchestra; the text of the Sermon is from Romans 8 and Hebrews 11 and 12, the Narrative from the Acts of the Apostles, and the Prayer is a setting of a text by the 17th-century playwright Thomas Dekker.

Serse ('Xerxes'). Opera in three acts by Handel to an anonymous revision of Silvio Stampiglia's libretto *Il Xerse* (1694) based on Nicolo Minato's *Il Xerse* (1654) (London, 1738).

Serva padrona, La ('The Maid as Mistress'). Opera (intermezzo) by Pergolesi to a libretto by Gennaro Antonio Federico after Jacopo Angelo Nelli's play (Naples, 1733); it was first performed between the two acts of Pergolesi's *opera seria Il prigioniero superbo*.

Seven Deadly Sins, The. *See* SIEBEN TODSÜNDEN DER KLEINBÜRGER, DIE.

Seven Last Words of Our Saviour on the Cross. Work by Haydn composed in 1785 or 1786, a series of Easter meditations ('passioni istrumentale') commissioned by Cádiz Cathedral for performance on Good Friday 1786 or 1787; it was published as 'Seven Sonatas, with an Introduction, and at the end an Earthquake', the 'sonatas' being Adagios. It appeared in four versions: for orchestra (1785); for string quartet (1787); for harpsichord or piano (1787), arranged not by Haydn but with his approval; as a choral work (by 1796) for soloists, chorus, and orchestra (with a text by Joseph Friebert, revised by Haydn and Gottfried von Swieten).

The 'Seven Last Words', the final utterances of Christ on the Cross drawn from the four Gospels, have been used as texts for other Passion music, for example Schütz's *Die sieben Worte* (*c*.1645), Gounod's *Les Sept Paroles de N. S. Jésus-Christ sur la croix* (1858), and James MacMillan's *Seven Last Words on the Cross* (1993).

Shadow of Night, The. Orchestral work (2001) by Birtwistle.

Shadowplay. Piece by Goehr for tenor, narrator, and ensemble, a setting of a text by Kenneth Cavander after book 7 of Plato's *Republic* (London, 1970); it forms a music-theatre triptych with **Naboth's Vineyard* and **Sonata about Jerusalem*.

Shadows of Time, The. Orchestral work (1995–7) by Dutilleux, composed in response to the commemorations of the 50th anniversary of the liberation of Paris at the end of World War II; its five movements are 'Les Heures' ('Hours'), 'Ariel maléfique' ('Evil Ariel'), 'Mémoire des ombres' ('Memory of Shadows'), 'Vagues de lumière' ('Waves of Light'), and 'Dominante bleue?' ('Blue Dominant?').

Shadowtime. 'Scenic action' in five sections by Brian Ferneyhough to a libretto by Charles Bernstein (Munich, 2004).

Shaker Loops. Work (1978) for string septet by John Adams; he made a version for string orchestra (1983).

Sheep May Safely Graze. English title of the soprano aria 'Schafe können sicher weiden' from J. S. Bach's cantata no. 208, *Was mir behagt, ist nur die muntre Jagd* ('The cheerful hunt is all that pleases me'; probably 1713). Several arrangements have been made, notably Mary Howe's for two pianos (1935) and piano solo (1937), Percy Grainger's transcription *Blithe Bells*, Walton's arrangement as the seventh number of his ballet *The Wise Virgins* (the fifth movement of the ballet suite), and John Barbirolli's for cor anglais and strings.

Sheherazade. **1**. Symphonic suite (1888) by Rimsky-Korsakov based on tales from *The Thousand and One Nights*; it was choreographed by Mikhail Fokine for Serge Diaghilev's Ballets Russes (Paris, 1910).

2. *Schéhérazade*. Song cycle (1903) by Ravel, for mezzo-soprano and orchestra, settings of three poems by Tristan Klingsor (the pseudonym of Léon Leclère) inspired by *The Thousand and One Nights*. Ravel had earlier (1898) written an overture with the same title.

Shepherd on the Rock, The. *See* HIRT AUF DEM FELSEN, DER.

Shepherds Hey! A British folksong arranged by Percy Grainger for several different combinations including two pianos and orchestra; it has been arranged by other composers for numerous different ensembles, notably by Leopold Stokowski for orchestra.

Shepherds of the Delectable Mountains, The. *See* PILGRIM'S PROGRESS, THE.

Short Ride in a Fast Machine. Orchestral work (1986) by John Adams.

Shropshire Lad, A. Song cycle (1911) by Butterworth, settings of six poems from A. E. Housman's book (1896); he based an orchestral rhapsody (1912), with the same title, on a theme from the song *Loveliest of Trees*. Several other composers have set poems from Housman's collection, notably Vaughan Williams (*On Wenlock Edge*), John Ireland, Ivor Gurney, Arthur Somervell, and C. W. Orr.

Sicilian Vespers, The. *See* VÊPRES SICILIENNES, LES.

Sieben letzten Worte, Die. *See* SEVEN LAST WORDS OF OUR SAVIOUR ON THE CROSS.

Sieben Todsünden der Kleinbürger, Die ('The Seven Deadly Sins of the Bourgeoisie'). Ballet in a prologue, seven scenes, and an epilogue by Weill to a libretto by Bertolt Brecht; it includes songs for soprano, male quartet, and orchestra and was choreographed by George Balanchine (Paris, 1933).

Siège de Corinthe, Le (*L'assedio di Corinto*; 'The Siege of Corinth'). Opera (*tragédie lyrique*) in three acts by Rossini to a libretto by Luigi Balocchi and Alexandre Soumet after Cesare della Valle's libretto for Rossini's *Maometto II* (1820) (Paris, 1826).

Siege of Rhodes, The. Heroic opera in five acts by Henry Cooke, Henry Lawes, Matthew Locke, Charles Coleman, and George Hudson, to a libretto by William Davenant, first performed in London in 1656; it was the first all-sung English opera but the music is now lost.

Siegfried. Opera in three acts by Wagner to his own libretto, the 'second day' of Der *Ring des Nibelungen*.

Siegfried Idyll. Orchestral work by Wagner, composed in 1870 as a birthday present for his wife Cosima and first performed on Christmas morning 1870, her 33rd birthday. It was played by about 15 musicians in their house at Tribschen and never intended for public performance, but financial hardship forced Wagner to sell it for publication, for which he expanded the orchestration. It includes themes from the opera *Siegfried*, on which Wagner was working when his son Siegfried was born, and the lullaby 'Schlaf, Kindlein, schlaf' ('Sleep, Baby, Sleep').

Siegfrieds Tod ('Siegfried's Death'). Proposed opera by Wagner to his own libretto. From it developed the idea of a four-opera cycle on the legend of Siegfried and the Nibelung's ring; much revised, *Siegfrieds Tod* eventually became *Götterdämmerung*.

Signor Bruschino, Il (*Il Signor Bruschino, ossia Il figlio per azzardo*; 'Mr Bruschino, or Son by Accident'). Opera (*farsa giocosa*) in one act by Rossini to a libretto by Giuseppe Maria Foppa after Alissan de Chazet and E. T. Maurice Ourry's play *Le Fils par hasard, ou Ruse et folie* (1809) (Venice, 1813).

Si j'étais roi ('If I Were King'). *Opéra comique* in three acts by Adolphe Adam to a libretto by Adolphe Philippe d'Ennery and Jules Brésil (Paris, 1852).

Silbersee, Der (*Der Silbersee: Ein Wintermärchen*; 'The Silverlake: A Winter's Fairy Tale'). Play with music in three acts by Weill to a libretto by Georg Kaiser (Leipzig, Erfurt, and Magdeburg, 1933).

Silbury Air. Work (1977) by Birtwistle for 15 instruments.

Silken Ladder, The. See SCALA DI SETA, LA.

Silver Tassie, The. Opera in four acts by Mark-Anthony Turnage to a libretto by Amanda Holden after Sean O'Casey's play (1928) (London, 2000).

Simon Boccanegra. Opera in a prologue and three acts by Verdi to a libretto by Francesco Maria Piave (with additions by Giuseppe Montanelli) after Antonio García Gutiérrez's play *Simón Bocanegra* (1843) (Venice, 1857); Verdi revised it, with a libretto revised by Arrigo Boito, adding the famous Council Chamber scene (Milan, 1881).

Simple Gifts ('The Gift to be Simple'). Shaker hymn, probably composed in 1848 by Joseph Brackett (1797–1882) in the Shaker community in Alfred, Maine. Copland quoted it in **Appalachian Spring* and arranged it in his first set of *Old American Songs* (1950).

Simple Symphony. Britten's op. 4 (1934), for string orchestra (or quartet), based on tunes he wrote in 1925 when he was 12.

Sinfonia antartica. Vaughan Williams's seventh symphony (1949–52), for soprano solo, women's chorus, and orchestra; it is based on the music he wrote for the film *Scott of the Antarctic* (1948) and contains a part for wind machine.

Sinfonia da requiem. Orchestral work, op. 20 (1940), by Britten, composed in memory of his parents.

Sinfonia espansiva ('Expansive Symphony'). Subtitle of Nielsen's Symphony no. 3 op. 27 (1910–11); the score includes parts for soprano and baritone soloists.

Sinfonia semplice ('Simple Symphony'). Subtitle of Nielsen's Symphony no. 6 op. posth. (1924–5).

Sinfonie capricieuse ('Capricious Symphony'). Berwald's second symphony, in D major (1842).

Sinfonie sérieuse ('Serious Symphony'). Berwald's first symphony, in G minor (1842).

Sinfonie singulière ('Curious Symphony'). Berwald's third symphony, in C major (1845).

Singet dem Herrn ein neues Lied ('O sing unto the Lord a new song'). Motet (BWV225, ?1726–7) by Bach for double chorus on a text from Psalm 149 and Johann Gramann's hymn *Nun lob, mein Seel, den Herren* and an anonymous text. Bach also wrote a cantata (BWV190, 1724) with the same title.

Sinking of the Titanic, The. Work by Gavin Bryars; its original, indeterminate version (1969) was for digital tapes and flexible ensemble but Bryars revised it (1997) for digital tapes and orchestra.

Sirius. Work (1975–7) by Stockhausen for soprano, bass, trumpet, bass clarinet, and electronics; he made four versions for electronics alone: 'Früh-lings-Version', 'Sommer-Version', 'Herbst-Version', and 'Winter-Version'.

Sir John in Love. Opera in four acts by Vaughan Williams to his own libretto after Shakespeare's play *The Merry Wives of Windsor* (?1597) with interpolations from other Elizabethan texts (London, 1929).

Six épigraphes antiques ('Six Ancient Inscriptions'). Work (1914) by Debussy for piano duet, incorporating music from his **Chansons de Bilitis*.

Six Metamorphoses after Ovid. Work, op. 49 (1951), by Britten for solo oboe; its movements are Pan, Phaeton, Niobe, Bacchus, Narcissus, and Arethusa.

Skaters' Waltz, The. *See* PATINEURS, LES.

Skye Boat Song. Song (1884) by Harold Boulton, the opening line of which is 'Speed bonnie boat, like a bird on the wing'; the first half of the tune is said to be an old sea shanty and the second part is attributed to Annie MacLeod. It commemorates the escape in disguise of 'Bonnie Prince Charlie', the Young Pretender, who in 1745 crossed in a small boat from Uist to Skye with the help of Flora MacDonald (1722–90).

Slaughterhouse Five. *See* SCHLACHTHOF 5.

Slavonic Dances. Two sets of eight dances by Dvořák for piano duet, op. 46 (1878) and op. 72 (1886), often heard in the composer's orchestral versions.

Slavonic Rhapsodies. Three orchestral works, op. 45 (1878), by Dvořák.

Sleeping Beauty, The (*Spyashchaya krasavitsa*). Ballet in a prologue and three acts by Tchaikovsky to a scenario by Marius Petipa and Ivan Vsevo-lozhsky after Charles Perrault's fairy tale; it was choreographed by Petipa (St Petersburg, 1890). Serge Diaghilev staged it as *The Sleeping Princess* (London, 1921); the last act is sometimes performed separately as *Aurora's Wedding*.

Snow Maiden, The (*Snegurochka*). Opera (*vesennyaya skazka*, 'springtime tale') in a prologue and four acts by Rimsky-Korsakov to his own libretto after Aleksandr Ostrovsky's play (1873) (St Petersburg, 1882). Tchaikovsky wrote incidental music (1873) for Ostrovsky's play.

Socrate ('Socrates'). Symphonic drama (1918) by Satie, for one or more voices with piano or chamber orchestra, settings of texts by Plato translated by Victor Cousin.

Soir, Le. *See* MATIN, LE; MIDI, LE; SOIR, LE.

Soirées musicales ('Musical Evenings'). A collection of salon pieces (songs and duets) by Rossini, published in 1835. Britten orchestrated five of them under the same title (op. 9, 1936) and the rest were orchestrated by Respighi for his ballet *La *Boutique fantasque*.

Soldaten, Die ('The Soldiers'). Opera in four acts by Bernd Alois Zimmermann to a libretto by the composer after Jakob Michael Reinhold Lenz's play (1776) (Cologne, 1965).

Soldier's Tale, The. *See* HISTOIRE DU SOLDAT.

Soleil des eaux, Le ('The Sun of the Waters'). Work by Boulez originally composed in 1948 for a radio play by René Char; Boulez revised it in 1950 as a cantata, in 1958 for larger forces, and in 1965 for soprano and chorus.

Solemn Melody. Work (1908) for organ and strings by Walford Davies.

Solomon. Oratorio (1749) by Handel to a biblical text by an unknown author.

Sombrero de tres picos, El (*Le Tricorne*; 'The Three-Cornered Hat'). Ballet in two scenes by Falla to a scenario by Gregorio Martínez Sierra after Pedro Antonio de Alarcón's novel (1874); it was choreographed by Leonid Massine, with designs by Pablo Picasso, and first produced by Serge Diaghilev's Ballets Russes (London, 1919). It is an expanded version of Sierra and Falla's pantomime *El corregidor y la molinera* ('The Magistrate and the Miller's Daughter') (Madrid, 1917) and has the same plot as Wolf's *Der Corregidor*. Falla arranged two orchestral suites from the score (1919).

Sonata about Jerusalem. Cantata by Goehr to texts adapted by Recha Freier and the composer from the autobiography of Obadiah the Proselyte and the Chronicle of Samuel de Yahya ben al Maghribi (12th century) (Tel Aviv, 1971); it forms a music-theatre triptych with *Naboth's Vineyard and *Shadowplay.

Sonata 1.x.05 (*Z ulice*; 'From the Street'). Piano sonata (1905) by Janáček in two movements ('The Presentiment' and 'The Death'); it was composed in response to the death on 1 October 1905 of a student named František Pavlík who was killed in Brno during demonstrations protesting at the Germans' refusal to allow the Czech minority to establish their own university.

Sonata pian e forte (alla quarta bassa). Work for eight instruments by Giovanni Gabrieli, published in his *Sacrae symphoniae* (1597). Written for St Mark's, Venice, it exploits contrast and dialogue.

Sonatas for String Quartet. Work (1967) by Brian Ferneyhough.

Song of Destiny. *See* SCHICKSALSLIED.

Song of the Earth, The. *See* LIED VON DER ERDE, DAS.

Song of the Flea (*Pesnya Mefistofelya o blokhe*). Song (1879) by Musorgsky for voice and piano, a setting of Mephistopheles' song in Goethe's *Faust*.

Song of the High Hills. Work (1911) by Delius for orchestra and (wordless) chorus, with solo parts for soprano and tenor (from the chorus).

Song of the Night, The (*Pieśń o nocy*). Subtitle of Szymanowski's Symphony no. 3 (1914–16), for tenor or soprano solo, chorus, and orchestra, a setting of words by the 13th-century Sufi poet Jalāl ad-Dīn ar-Rūmī.

Song of the Volga Boatmen. Russian work-song made famous through Fyodor Chaliapin's recording and Stravinsky's arrangement (1917) for wind and brass.

Songs and Dances of Death (*Pesni i plyaski smerti*). Song cycle by Musorgsky (1877) for voice and piano, settings of four poems by Arseny Golenishchev-Kutuzov.

Songs My Mother Taught Me. Song for high voice and piano by Dvořák, to words by Adolf Heyduk, no. 4 of his *Gypsy Songs* op. 55 (1880).

Songs of a Wayfarer. *See* LIEDER EINES FAHRENDEN GESELLEN.

Songs of Farewell. 1. Six unaccompanied secular motets (1916–18) by Hubert Parry to texts by Henry Vaughan, John Davies, Thomas Campion, J. G. Lockhart, and John Donne, and from Psalm 39.
   2. Five songs (1930) by Delius, settings of poems by Walt Whitman for chorus and orchestra.

Songs of the Sea. Five songs, op. 91 (1904), by Stanford, for baritone, male chorus, and orchestra, settings of poems by Henry Newbolt.

Songs without Words. *See* LIEDER OHNE WORTE.

Sonnambula, La ('The Sleepwalker'). Opera (*melodramma*) in two acts by Bellini to a libretto by Felice Romani after Eugène Scribe and J.-P. Aumer's ballet-pantomime *La Sonnambule, ou L'Arrivée d'un nouveau seigneur* (1827) (Milan, 1831).

Sonntag aus Licht ('Sunday from Light'). Projected opera by Stockhausen to his own libretto, the 'seventh day' of *Licht*.

Sophie's Choice. Opera in four acts by Nicholas Maw to a libretto by Paul Bentley after William Styron's novel (1979) (London, 2002). Maw arranged a concert suite (2004) from the score.

Sorceror, The. Operetta in two acts by Sullivan to a libretto by W. S. Gilbert (London, 1877).

Sorcerer's Apprentice, The. *See* APPRENTI SORCIER, L'.

Sorochintsy Fair (*Sorochinskaya yarmarka*). Opera in three acts by Musorgsky to his own libretto (with Arseny Golenishchev-Kutuzov) after a story by Nikolay Gogol from his collection *Evenings on a Farm near Dikanka* (i, 1831). It was left incomplete at the composer's death and was finished and orchestrated by Lyadov, Vyacheslav Karatïgin, and others (Moscow, 1913). It was also completed and orchestrated by Cui (St Petersburg, 1917), by Tcherepnin (Monte Carlo, 1923), and by Shebalin (Moscow, 1932), this last becoming the standard version.

Sosarme (*Sosarme, re di Media*; 'Sosarmes, King of Media'). Opera in three acts by Handel to a libretto anonymously adapted from Antonio Salvi's *Dionisio re di Portogallo* (1707) (London, 1732).

Souvenirs de Bayreuth ('Memories of Bayreuth'). 'Fantasy in the form of a quadrille' for piano duet by Fauré and Messager on themes from Wagner's *Der *Ring des Nibelungen*; it was published in 1930. Gustave Samazeuilh made an arrangement of it for solo piano.

Spanisches Liederbuch ('Spanish Songbook'). Collection of 44 songs (1889–90) for voice and piano by Wolf, settings of German translations by Paul Heyse and Emanuel Geibel of 16th- and 17th-century Spanish poems. Five were later orchestrated by Wolf.

Spanish Capriccio. Orchestral work, op. 34 (1887), by Rimsky-Korsakov; it is often known by the mixed Italian and French title 'Capriccio espagnol'.

Spanish Lady, The. Opera in two acts by Elgar to a libretto by Barry Jackson after Ben Jonson's *The Devil is an Ass* (1616); Elgar began it in 1932, drawing on sketches from 50 years earlier, but it was still in fragmentary form when he died two years later. Percy M. Young edited two songs and a suite for strings from it and made a performing version (Cambridge, 1994).

Spartacus *(Spartak)*. Ballet in four acts by Khachaturian to a scenario by Nikolay Volkov; it was choreographed by Leonid Jacobson (Leningrad, 1956). Khachaturian revised the score in 1968.

Spectre de la rose ('Phantom of the Rose'). Ballet in one act to a scenario by Jean-Louis Vaudoyer, choreographed by Mikhail Fokine to Weber's **Aufforderung zum Tanz* (Monte Carlo, 1911).

Spem in alium numquam habui ('In no other is my hope'). A motet in 40 parts (eight five-voice choirs) by Tallis; it was commissioned to rival Striggio's 40-part motet *Ecce beatam lucem* and was first performed in 1568 or 1569.

Spiral. Work (1969) by Stockhausen for soloist and short-wave receiver.

'Spring' Sonata *(Frühlingssonate)*. Nickname of Beethoven's Violin Sonata in F major op. 24 (1801).

Spring Song *(Frühlingslied)*. Mendelssohn's *Lied ohne Worte* no. 30 in A major for piano (op. 62; book 5, 1844).

'Spring' Symphony. Schumann's Symphony no. 1 in B♭ major (1841).

Spring Symphony, A. Choral work, op. 44 (1949), by Britten, for soprano, alto, and tenor soloists, boys' choir, chorus, and orchestra, settings of poems by Robert Herrick, W. H. Auden, Richard Barnfield, George Peele, William Blake, Francis Beaumont and John Fletcher, Thomas Nashe, Henry Vaughan, Edmund Spenser, John Clare, and John Milton, and two anonymous verses.

Staat, De ('The Republic'). Work (1976) by Louis Andriessen for four female singers and orchestra, a setting of a text by Plato from *The Republic*.

Staatstheater ('State Theatre'). Music-theatre piece *(szenische Komposition)* by Kagel (Hamburg, 1971). In nine sections for various forces, it is described by the composer as 'not just the negation of opera, but of the whole tradition of music-theatre'; 'Repertoire' is an assemblage of ironic incidents and 'Ensemble' is a 16-part *a cappella* choral piece satirizing the history of opera.

Star-child. A 'parable' (1977) by George Crumb for soprano, children's chorus, male speaking chorus, bell ringers, and orchestra, setting texts from the *Dies irae*, *Massacre of the Innocents* (13th century), and the Bible (John 12: 36).

Star Clusters, Nebulae, and Places in Devon. Work (1971) by David Bedford for two eight-part choirs and brass, a setting of a text by the composer.

Starlight Express, The. Incidental music by Elgar for Violet Pearn's play based on Algernon Blackwood's *A Prisoner in Fairyland* (London, 1915).

Star-Spangled Banner, The ('O say, can you see by the dawn's early light?'). National anthem of the USA. The music is by John Stafford Smith and the words are by Francis Scott Key (1779–1843), who wrote them in 1814 on board a British frigate in Baltimore Harbour as he watched the British bombardment of Fort McHenry. Smith's melody, to which Key created his verses, was sung in Anacreontic societies in England and the USA to the words 'To Anacreon in Heaven'. It was adopted as the American national anthem in 1831.

Stations of the Sun, The. Orchestral work (1998) by Julian Anderson.

Steel Step, The (*Stal'noy skok*; *Le Pas d'acier*). Ballet in two scenes by Proko-fiev to a scenario by the composer and Georgy Yakulov, choreographed by Leonid Massine (Paris, 1927). Prokofiev arranged an orchestral suite (1926) from the score.

Stele. Orchestral work (1994) by Kurtág; the title is from the Greek word for a monumental pillar or inscription, and the last of the three movements is an expansion of a piano piece (1993) Kurtág composed in memory of his friend the cellist András Mihály.

Stiffelio. Opera in three acts by Verdi to a libretto by Francesco Maria Piave after Émile Souvestre and Eugène Bourgeois's play *Le Pasteur, ou L'Évangile et le foyer* (1849) (Trieste, 1850).

Stimmung ('Tuning'). Work (1968) by Stockhausen for two sopranos, mezzo-soprano, tenor, baritone, and bass; the six unaccompanied singers, each with a microphone, vocalize without words for 75 minutes.

Stone Flower, The (*Kamenniy tsvetko*). Ballet in a prologue and three acts by Prokofiev to a scenario by Mira Mendelson (Prokof'yeva) and Leonid Lavrovsky, who choreographed it (Moscow, 1954); Yuri Grigorovich rechor-eographed it (Leningrad, 1957).

Stone Guest, The (*Kamenniy gost'*). Opera in three acts by Dargomïzhsky, a setting of Aleksandr Pushkin's play (1830) on the Don Juan story; begun in the 1860s and nearly finished at the time of the composer's death, it was completed by Cui and orchestrated by Rimsky-Korsakov (St Petersburg, 1872).

Story of Vasco. Opera in three acts by Gordon Crosse to a libretto by Ted Hughes after Georges Schéhadé's play *L'Histoire de Vasco* (1956) (London, 1974).

Straniera, La ('The Stranger'). Opera (*melodramma*) in two acts by Bellini to a libretto by Felice Romani after Victor-Charles Prévôt's novel *L'Étrangère* (1825) (Milan, 1829).

Strathclyde Concertos. A series of ten concertos by Maxwell Davies. Nos. 1–8 are for solo instrument(s) with orchestra: no. 1, for oboe (1987); no. 2, for cello (1988); no. 3, for horn and trumpet (1989); no. 4, for clarinet (1990); no. 5, for violin and viola (1991); no. 6, for flute (1991); no. 7, for double bass (1992); no. 8, for bassoon (1993). No. 9 is for six woodwind instruments and string orchestra (1994); no. 10, for orchestra (1996).

Stravaganza, La ('The Extraordinary'). Title of Vivaldi's op. 4, 12 violin concertos published in two books (Amsterdam, *c.*1712–13).

Street Scene. American opera in two acts by Weill to a libretto by Elmer Rice after his own play (1929), with lyrics by Langston Hughes and Rice (Philadelphia, 1946).

Structures. Two pieces (1952, 1961) for two pianos by Boulez.

Suite bergamasque. Piano work by Debussy, composed in 1890 and revised in 1905; the first, second, and fourth movements were orchestrated by Gustave Cloez, the third, 'Clair de lune', by André Caplet.

Sumer is icumen in. A mid-13th-century infinite canon (or round) at the unison for four tenor voices over a texted ground (or *pes*) also in canon at the unison. It is sometimes known as the 'Reading Rota' because it has been ascribed to John of Fornsete, a monk of Reading. A Latin text ('Perspice christicola') written below the English in the only extant manuscript may have been added later. It is one of the earliest surviving secular works.

Summer Night on the River. Tone-poem by Delius, the second of his Two Pieces for Small Orchestra (the first is *On Hearing the First Cuckoo in Spring*); it is not to be confused with his *Two Songs to be Sung of a Summer Night on the Water* (1917), textless works for chorus.

'Sun' Quartets. Nickname of Haydn's six String Quartets op. 20 (1772), so called because of the design of the title page of the first edition (1774).

Suns Dance. Work for ten players (1985) by Colin Matthews.

Sun-Treader. Orchestral work (1926–31) by Carl Ruggles; 'sun-treader' was Robert Browning's epithet for Percy Bysshe Shelley.

Suor Angelica ('Sister Angelica'). Opera in one act by Puccini to a libretto by Giovacchino Forzano, the second part of Puccini's *Il *trittico* (New York, 1918).

. . . sur incises . . . . Work (1998) by Boulez for solo piano and seven instruments (two pianos, three harps, marimba, and two vibraphones).

'Surprise' Symphony. Nickname of Haydn's Symphony no. 94 in G major (1791), so called because of the sudden *fortissimo* in the slow movement. Haydn incorporated this movement into the aria 'Schon eilet' in *The Seasons*.

Surrogate Cities. Suite for sampler and orchestra (1994) by Heiner Goebbels, portraying a 'vertical' slice of city life.

Survivor from Warsaw, A. Schoenberg's op. 46 (1947), for narrator, male voices, and orchestra, a setting of his own text.

Susanna. Oratorio (1749) by Handel to an anonymous biblical text.

Susannah. Opera ('musical drama') in two acts by Carlisle Floyd to his own libretto (Tallahassee, FL, 1955).

Svanda the Bagpiper. *See* SCHWANDA THE BAGPIPER.

Swan Lake (*Lebedinoye ozero*; *Le Lac des cygnes*). Ballet in four acts by Tchaikovsky to a scenario by Vladimir Begichev and Vasily Geltser; it was choreographed by Wenzel Reisinger (Moscow, 1877) and later by Marius Petipa and Lev Ivanov (St Petersburg, 1895).

Swan of Tuonela, The (*Tuonelan joutsen*). Symphonic legend, op. 22 no. 3, by Sibelius, composed in 1893 and revised in 1897 and 1900; it was written as a prelude to an unfinished opera but was published as the third symphonic poem of the **Lemminkäinen Suite*. A cor anglais represents the swan; Tuonela is the Finnish Hades.

Sylphide, La ('The Sylph'). Ballet in two acts by Jean Schneitzhoeffer to a scenario by Adolphe Nourrit, choreographed by Filippo Taglioni (Paris, 1832). August Bournonville choreographed it, to a score by Herman Løvenskjold (Copenhagen, 1836), a production that has been frequently revived.

Sylphides, Les ('The Sylphs'). Ballet in one act to music by Chopin; originally called *Chopiniana*, it was choreographed by Mikhail Fokine (St Petersburg, 1907).

Sylvia, ou La Nymphe de Diane. Ballet in three acts and five scenes by Delibes to a scenario by Jules Barbier and Baron de Reinach; it was choreographed by Louis Mérante (Paris, 1876).

Symphonia antarctica. *See* ANTARCTIC SYMPHONY.

Symphonia domestica ('Domestic Symphony'). Tone-poem, op. 53 (1902–3), by Richard Strauss, depicting a day in the life of the Strauss family, with themes representing the composer, his wife Pauline, and their baby son.

Symphonic Dances. Orchestral work, op. 45 (1940), by Rakhmaninov.

Symphonic Metamorphoses on Themes of Weber. Orchestral work (1943) by Hindemith; the second of its four movements is a '*Turandot*

Scherzo' based on a tune Weber wrote for a performance in 1809 of Friedrich von Schiller's *Turandot*.

Symphonic Variations. Work (1885) for piano and orchestra by Franck.

Symphonie espagnole ('Spanish Symphony'). Work (1874) for violin and orchestra by Lalo.

Symphonie fantastique ('Fantastic Symphony'). Symphony, op. 14, by Berlioz, composed in 1830 and revised 1831–45. Subtitled 'Épisode de la vie d'un artiste' ('Episode in the Life of an Artist'), it is in five movements: 'Rêveries, passions' ('Dreams, Passions'), 'Un bal' ('A Ball'), 'Scène aux champs' ('Scene in the Fields'), 'Marche au supplice' ('March to the Scaffold'), and 'Songe d'une nuit du Sabbat' ('Dream of a Witches' Sabbath'). The work was inspired by Berlioz's love for the Irish actress Harriet Smithson, and this is symbolized by a recurring theme (an *idée fixe*) used in a similar way to a Wagnerian leitmotif. *See also* LÉLIO.

Symphonie funèbre et triomphale ('Funereal and Triumphal Symphony'). Orchestral work by Berlioz, commissioned in 1840 by the French government to mark the tenth anniversary of the 1830 Revolution. It was originally scored for large military band and intended for outdoor performance, but Berlioz added parts for optional string orchestra (1842) and later for chorus, a setting of a patriotic text by Antoni Deschamps. The work is sometimes known as *Grande Symphonie funèbre et triomphale*.

Symphonie liturgique. Honegger's Symphony no. 3 (1945–6).

Symphonie pathétique. Subtitle of Tchaikovsky's Symphony no. 6 in B minor op. 74 (1893), so called at his brother Modest's suggestion. (The Russian word *patetichesky* means 'passionate' or 'emotional' rather than 'pathetic'.)

Symphonies of Wind Instruments. Work (1920) by Stravinsky composed in memory of Debussy.

Symphonie sur un chant montagnard français ('Symphony on a French Mountain Song'). Work for piano and orchestra, op. 25 (1886), by d'Indy; it is subtitled 'Symphony cévenole' because the theme comes from the Cévennes region. (The composer described it as a work 'for orchestra and piano'.)

Symphony in Three Movements. Orchestral work (1942–5) by Stravinsky.

'Symphony of a Thousand'. Nickname of Mahler's Symphony no. 8 in E♭ major (1906); it was so named for publicity purposes by Emil Guttmann, the impresario who organized its premiere (Munich, 1910), because of the huge vocal and orchestral forces engaged to perform it.

Symphony of Psalms. Work for chorus and orchestra (without violins and violas) by Stravinsky to a Latin text from Psalms 38, 39, and 150; it was composed in 1930 and revised in 1948.

Symphony of Sorrowful Songs. Subtitle of Górecki's Symphony no. 3 (1976) for soprano and orchestra; each of its three movements includes a setting of an anonymous lament (one from the 15th century) on the theme of motherhood.

Symphony of Three Orchestras, A. Work (1976) by Elliott Carter for three orchestral groups.

Syringa. Work (1978) by Elliott Carter for mezzo-soprano, baritone, and 11 players, settings of texts by John Ashbery and from ancient Greek sources.

Syrinx. Work for solo flute (1913) by Debussy.

S

Tabarro, Il ('The Cloak'). Opera in one act by Puccini to a libretto by Giuseppe Adami after Didier Gold's play *La Houppelande* (1910), the first part of Puccini's *Il *trittico* (New York, 1918).

Tafelmusik (*Musique de table*; 'Table Music'). A collection (1733) of instrumental works by Telemann; it is in three 'productions', each comprising an *ouverture*-suite, a quartet, a concerto, a trio, a solo, and a 'conclusion' (with the instrumentation of the *ouverture*). *Tafelmusik* was a genre of instrumental and vocal music composed specifically for performance during meals.

Tale of Tsar Saltan, The (*The Tale of Tsar Saltan, of his Son the Renowned and Mighty Bogatïr Prince Guidon Saltanovich, and of the Beautiful Swan-Princess*; *Skazka o Tsare Saltane o sine ego slavnom i moguchem bogatïre knyaze Gvidone Saltanoviche i o prekrasnoy Tsarevna Lebedi*). Opera in a prologue and four acts by Rimsky-Korsakov to a libretto by Vladimir Bel'sky after Aleksandr Pushkin's imitation folk poem (1832) (Moscow, 1900).

Tales from the Vienna Woods (*Geschichten aus dem Wienerwald*). Waltz, op. 325 (1868), by Johann Strauss (ii).

Tales of Hoffmann, The. *See* CONTES D'HOFFMANN, LES.

Tallis's Canon. The eighth of nine tunes composed for Archbishop Parker's *The Whole Psalter Translated into English Metre* (*c*.1567). The canon is formed by the tenor and treble voices and was originally attached to Psalm 67. Most of the tunes in the psalter are in use as hymn tunes.

Tamara (*Thamar*). Symphonic poem (1866–82) by Balakirev after a poem by Mikhail Lermontov. It was choreographed as a one-act ballet by Mikhail Fokine, with a scenario by Léon Bakst, for Serge Diaghilev's Ballets Russes (Paris, 1912).

Tamerlano. Opera in three acts by Handel to a libretto by Nicola Francesco Haym adapted from Agostin Piovene's *Tamerlano* (1711) and from *Bajazet* (1719), a revised version of the same libretto prepared by Ippolito Zanelli and Francesco Borosini, after Jacques Prodon's play *Tamerlan, ou La Mort de Bajazet* (1675) (London, 1724).

Tancredi. Opera (*melodramma eroico*) in two acts by Rossini to a libretto by Gaetano Rossi after Voltaire's *Tancrède* (1760) (Venice, 1813).

Tannhäuser (*Tannhäuser und der Sängerkrieg auf Wartburg*; 'Tannhäuser and the Singers' Contest on the Wartburg'). Opera (*grosse romantische Oper*) in three acts by Wagner to his own libretto (Dresden, 1845).

Tapfere Soldat, Der ('The Brave Soldier'; *The Chocolate Soldier*; *Der Praliné-Soldat*, 'The Chocolate-Cream Soldier'). Operetta in three acts by Oscar

Straus to a libretto by Rudolf Bernauer and Leopold Jacobson after George Bernard Shaw's play *Arms and the Man* (1894) (Vienna, 1908).

Tapiola. Tone-poem, op. 112 (1926), by Sibelius; it is based on a legend from the *Kalevala. Tapio was the god of Finnish forests.

Taras Bulba. Rhapsody for orchestra (1915–18) by Janáček after Nikolay Gogol's story about Bulba, the Ukrainian Cossack leader.

Tasso: Lamento e trionfo. Symphonic poem by Liszt, after a poem by Byron. Sketches for it exist from 1841–5; the first version was completed in 1849, orchestrated by August Conradi, and performed as an overture to Johann Wolfgang von Goethe's play *Torquato Tasso*. It was revised in 1850–1, reorchestrated by Joachim Raff, and given its final version by Liszt himself in 1854.

Taverner. Opera in two acts by Maxwell Davies to his own libretto after 16th-century letters and documents concerning the life of the composer John Taverner (London, 1972).

Te Deum laudamus (Lat., 'We praise you, O God'). The long hymn that constitutes the supreme expression of rejoicing in the Roman Catholic, Anglican, and other Christian Churches. The traditional plainchant to the Latin hymn is of a magnificent character. Many settings from the late 17th century onwards have been on extended lines, with solos, choruses, and orchestral accompaniment. Important settings have been made by Purcell (for St Cecilia's Day, 1694), Handel (for the Peace of Utrecht, 1713, and for the victory of *Dettingen, 1743), Graun (written after the Battle of Prague, 1757), Bortnyansky (14 settings for single or double chorus *a cappella* written for the Russian imperial chapel after 1779), Berlioz (for the Paris Exhibition of 1855, and composed on a huge scale, with three choirs and large instrumental forces), Bruckner (1885), Dvořák (1896), Verdi (1898), Stanford (1898), Hubert Parry (1900; also another for the coronation of George V in 1911), Kodály (for the 250th anniversary of the end of the Turkish occupation of Buda, 1936), Britten (1934), and Walton (for the coronation of Elizabeth II, 1953).

Tehillim. Work (1981) by Reich for voices and ensemble or voices and orchestra, a setting of Hebrew texts from Psalms 19, 34, 18, and 150.

Telemusik. Work (1966) for four-track tape by Stockhausen.

Telephone, The (*The Telephone, or L'Amour à trois*; 'The Eternal Triangle'). *Opera buffa* in one act by Menotti to his own libretto (New York, 1947).

Tempest, The. Shakespeare's play (1610 or 1611) has been the subject of many musical works, and several composers have written incidental music for it, or have set texts from it as songs. Among the best known are:

    1. *The Tempest.* Incidental music by Sibelius for soloists, chorus, harmonium, and orchestra (Copenhagen, 1926); Sibelius made two orchestral suites from it.

    2. *The Tempest.* Symphonic fantasy for orchestra (1863) by Tchaikovsky.

3. *Der Sturm.* Opera in three acts by Frank Martin to a libretto adapted from August Wilhelm von Schlegel's German translation of the play (Vienna, 1956).

4. *Die Zauberinsel* ('The Magic Island'). Opera in two acts by Sutermeister to his own libretto (Dresden, 1942).

5. *The Tempest, or The Enchanted Island.* Semi-opera with music by John Weldon and a text by William Davenant, John Dryden, and Thomas Shadwell (London, ?1712).

6. *The Magic Island.* Symphonic prelude (1953) by William Alwyn.

7. *The Tempest.* Opera in three acts by John C. Eaton to a libretto by Andrew Porter (Santa Fe, NM, 1985).

8. Opera in three acts by Thomás Adès to a libretto by Meredith Oakes (London, 2004).

Templar und die Jüdin, Der ('The Templar and the Jewess'). Opera (*grosse romantische Oper*) in three acts by Marschner to a libretto by Wilhelm August Wohlbrück after various plays based on Walter Scott's novel *Ivanhoe* (1819) (Leipzig, 1829).

Temps restitué, Le ('Restored Time'). Work (1968) by Barraqué for soprano, chorus, and large ensemble, a setting of texts from Hermann Broch's *Der Tod des Vergil* (1945; translated by Albert Kohn) and by the composer.

Tender Land, The. Opera in three acts by Copland to a libretto by Horace Everett (Erik Johns) after James Agee's book *Let Us Now Praise Famous Men* (1941) (New York, 1954); Copland arranged an orchestral suite from it in 1956.

Terpsichore. Michael Praetorius's collection (1612) of some 300 dance tunes used in the French court of Henri IV; Praetorius harmonized them and arranged them for from four to six parts. Terpsichore is one of the nine Muses of Greek mythology who came to be associated with lyric poetry and dance.

Terre est un homme, La ('Earth is a Man'). Orchestral work (1979) by Brian Ferneyhough.

Teseo ('Theseus'). Opera in five acts by Handel to a libretto by Nicola Francesco Haym adapted from Philippe Quinault's *Thésée* (1675) (London, 1713).

Thaïs. Opera (*comédie lyrique*) in three acts by Massenet to a libretto by Louis Gallet after Anatole France's novel (1890) (Paris, 1894). The 'Méditation' from Act II is often played as a separate item.

Thamar. *See* TAMARA.

Theodora. Oratorio (1750) by Handel to a text by Thomas Morell after Robert Boyle's *The Martyrdom of Theodora and Didymus.*

Thérèse. Opera in one act by Tavener to a libretto by Gerald McLarnon (London, 1979).

Theresienmesse ('Theresa Mass'). Haydn's Mass no.12 in B♭ major (1799), its title a reference to the consort of Emperor Franz II of Austria.

Theseus Game. Work (2002) by Birtwistle for large ensemble and two conductors.

Thieving Magpie, The. *See* GAZZA LADRA, LA.

Three-Cornered Hat, The. *See* SOMBRERO DE TRES PICOS, EL.

Threepenny Opera, The. *See* DREIGROSCHENOPER, DIE.

Three Places in New England. Orchestral work by Ives, also known as the First Orchestral Set (or *A New England Symphony*). Its three movements are *The Saint-Gaudens in Boston Common* (*c.*1916–17), *Putnam's Camp, Redding, Connecticut* (*c.*1914–15, *c.*1919–20), and *The Housatonic at Stockbridge* (*c.*1912–17, revised *c.*1921).

Three Screaming Popes (after Francis Bacon). Orchestral work (1989) by Mark-Anthony Turnage.

Three Sisters. Opera in a prologue and three sequences by Peter Eötvös to a libretto by the composer and Claus H. Henneberg after Anton Chekhov's play (1901) (Lyons, 1998).

Three Tales. Documentary video opera in three parts by Reich, with Beryl Korot (complete, Vienna, 2002); the three parts are *Hindenburg*, *Bikini*, and *Dolly*.

Threni: id est Lamentationes Jeremiae Prophetae ('Threni: that is, The Lamentations of the Prophet Jeremiah'). Choral work (1958) by Stravinsky, a setting of a biblical text for soprano, alto, two tenor, and two bass soloists, chorus, and orchestra.

Threnody 'to the Victims of Hiroshima'. Work (1960) by Penderecki for 52 strings.

Thus Spake Zarathustra. *See ALSO* SPRACH ZARATHUSTRA.

Tiefland ('The Lowlands'). Opera (*Musikdrama*) in a prologue and two acts by d'Albert to a libretto by Rudolph Lothar (Rudolph Spitzer) after Angel Guimerá's Catalan drama *Terra baixa* (Prague, 1903).

Tijd, Der ('Time'). Work (1981) by Louis Andriessen for female chorus and large ensemble, a setting of a text by St Augustine.

Till Eulenspiegels lustige Streiche (nach alter Schelmenweise—in Rondeauform) ('Till Eulenspiegel's Merry Pranks, after an Old Rogue's Tune—in Rondo Form'). Tone-poem, op. 28 (1894–5), by Richard Strauss. It has been used for several ballets, including one by Vaslav Nijinsky for Serge Diaghilev's Ballets Russes (New York, 1916) and one by George Balanchine (New York, 1951).

Till Eulenspiegel has also been the subject of an opera *Til' Ulenshpigel'* by Karetnikov to a libretto after Charles De Coster (1993). Flor Alpaerts (1927), Jan Blockx (1920), Otakar Jeremiáš (1949), Rezniček (1902), and

Maximilian Steinberg (1936) are among composers who have used the same subject.

Time and Motion Study I–III. Three pieces by Brian Ferneyhough: *I* (1971–7) is for bass clarinet; *II* (1973–6) is for cello and live electronics; and *III* (1974) is for 16 solo voices, percussion, and live electronics.

Tintagel. Tone-poem (1919) by Bax.

Tipperary. A song by Harry J. Williams and Jack Judge; it begins 'It's a long way to Tipperary' and became extremely popular during World War I.

Tiramisu. Work (1995) by Julian Anderson for ten instruments.

Tod Jesu, Der ('The Death of Jesus'). Passion cantata by Graun to a text by Karl Wilhelm Ramler; it was first performed in 1755 in Berlin, where it was given annually until well into the 20th century.

Tod und das Mädchen, Der ('Death and the Maiden'). Song (1817) by Schubert to a poem by Matthias Claudius; Schubert used the theme for variations in the second movement of his String Quartet no. 14 in D minor D810 (1824), which is known by the song's title.

Tod und Verklärung ('Death and Transfiguration'). Tone-poem, op. 24 (1888–9), by Richard Strauss; in four sections, it depicts an artist's deathbed visions.

Tombeau de Couperin, Le ('The Tomb of Couperin'). Suite for piano (1914–17) by Ravel; it is in six movements, each dedicated to the memory of a friend who died in World War I. Ravel orchestrated nos. 1, 3, 5, and 4 (in that order) in 1919.

Tom Jones. Operetta in three acts by Edward German to a libretto by Alexander M. Thompson and Robert Courtneidge, with lyrics by Charles H. Taylor, after Henry Fielding's novel (1748) (Manchester, 1907). Philidor wrote an opera based on Henry Fielding (1765, revised 1766).

Tosca. Opera (*melodramma*) in three acts by Puccini to a libretto by Giuseppe Giacosa and Luigi Illica after Victorien Sardou's play *La Tosca* (1887) (Rome, 1900).

'Tost' Quartets. 12 string quartets by Haydn, op. 54 nos. 1–3, op. 55 nos. 1–3, and op. 64 nos. 1–6 (1788–90), so called because they are dedicated to the Viennese violinist Johann Tost.

Totentanz (Ger., 'dance of death'). Work for piano and orchestra by Liszt, after a poem by Johann Wolfgang von Goethe; it was planned as early as 1839 but first composed in 1849, with revised versions in 1853 and 1859. The final version is a paraphrase on the *Dies irae*, with some material taken from Mozart's Requiem; the early versions also incorporate music from Liszt's 1834 setting of the psalm *De profundis*.

Tote Stadt, Die ('The Dead City'). Opera in three acts by Korngold to a libretto by Paul Schott (Julius and E. W. Korngold) after Georges Rodenbach's novel *Bruges la morte* (1892) (Hamburg and Cologne, 1920).

Toussaint (*Toussaint, or The Aristocracy of the Skin*). Opera in three acts by David Blake to a libretto by Anthony Ward (London, 1977).

Tout un monde lointain ('A Whole Distant World'). Concerto for cello and orchestra (1967–70) by Dutilleux; it was inspired by the poetry of Charles Baudelaire, each of its five movements being headed by a quotation from *Les Fleurs du mal* (1857).

Toward the Unknown Region. Song (1905–6) for chorus and orchestra by Vaughan Williams, a setting of words by Walt Whitman from *Whispers of Heavenly Death* (1870).

'Toy' Symphony (*Kindersymphonie*; *La Foire des enfants*; *Symphonie burlesque*). A Symphony in C major, for first and second violins, double bass, keyboard instrument, and a series of toy instruments (including cuckoo, quail, and nightingale, trumpet, drum, rattle, and triangle), long attributed to Haydn but now thought to be by Leopold Mozart, possibly with Michael Haydn and Leopold Angerer. Other composers have written symphonies incorporating toy instruments, notably Sigmund Romberg and Mendelssohn.

Tragic Overture (*Tragische-Ouvertüre*). Brahms's op. 81, composed in 1880 and revised in 1881.

'Tragic' Symphony. Schubert's Symphony no. 4 in C minor D417 (1816), his own title. It is also applied to Mahler's Symphony no. 6 in A minor (1903–4, revised 1906 and later) and Bruckner's Symphony no. 5 in B♭ major (1875–6).

Tragoedia. Work (1965) by Birtwistle for wind quintet, harp, and string quartet.

Trahison orale, La (*Der mündliche Verrat*; 'Oral Treason'). Work (1983) by Kagel for three speakers and seven players, a 'music-epic about the devil' (*Musikepos über den Teufel*); he arranged it as a radio play (1987).

Transcendental Studies. *See* ÉTUDES D'EXÉCUTION TRANSCENDANTE D'APRÈS PAGANINI.

Transfiguration de notre Seigneur Jésus-Christ, La ('The Transfiguration of our Lord Jesus Christ'). Work (1965–9) by Messiaen for 100 voices and orchestra, settings of texts from the Bible and the missal, and by St Thomas Aquinas.

Transit. Work (1975) for six amplified voices, amplified flute, oboe, clarinet, and ensemble by Brian Ferneyhough.

Trauermusik ('Mourning Music'). Work (1936) by Hindemith for viola (or violin or cello) and orchestra; he composed it a few hours after he heard of the death of King George V, and it was performed at a concert the next day.

Trauersinfonie ('Mourning Symphony'). Popular name for Haydn's Symphony no. 44 in E minor, apparently so called because its third movement, an Adagio, was performed at a memorial concert in Berlin in 1809.

Träumerei ('Reverie'). Piano piece by Schumann, no. 7 of his *Kinderszenen* op. 15 (1838).

Traviata, La ('The Fallen Woman'). Opera in three acts by Verdi to a libretto by Francesco Maria Piave after Alexandre Dumas *fils*'s play *La Dame aux camélias* (1852) (Venice, 1853).

Treemonisha. Opera in three acts by Scott Joplin to his own libretto. It was completed in 1911 but Joplin's orchestration was lost; modern orchestrations have been made by T. J. Anderson, William Bolcom, and Gunther Schuller. The opera was first staged in Atlanta, Georgia, in 1972.

Trial by Jury. Operetta in one act by Sullivan to a libretto by W. S. Gilbert (London, 1875).

Trial of Lucullus, The. Opera in one act by Sessions, a setting of Bertolt Brecht's radio play *Das Verhör des Lukullus* (1939), translated by H. R. Hays (Berkeley, CA, 1947).

Tricorne, Le. *See* SOMBRERO DE TRES PICOS, EL.

Triduum. Triptych for orchestra by James MacMillan, comprising *The World's Ransoming* (1996), a Cello Concerto (1996), and a symphony *Vigil* (1997).

Trillo del diavolo, Il. *See* 'DEVIL'S TRILL' SONATA.

Trilogy of the Last Day. Work (1996–7) by Louis Andriessen for two sopranos, two mezzo-sopranos, two tenors, two baritones, children's chorus, piano, koto, and large ensemble, settings of texts by Lucebert and Lao Tse; its three movements are 'The Last Day', 'The Way', and 'Dancing on the Bones'.

Trionfi ('Triumphs'). Theatrical triptych by Orff comprising *Carmina burana*, *Catulli carmina*, and *Trionfo d'Afrodite* (Salzburg, 1953).

Trionfo di Afrodite ('Triumph of Aphrodite'). Opera (*concerto scenico*) by Orff, for soloists, chorus, and orchestra, a setting of Latin and Greek texts by Catullus, Sappho, and Euripides (Milan, 1953); it is the third part of his trilogy *Trionfi*.

Tristan und Isolde ('Tristan and Isolda'). Opera (*Handlung*) in three acts by Wagner to his own libretto (Munich, 1865).

Trittico, Il ('The Triptych'). The collective title Puccini gave his three one-act operas *Il *tabarro*, *Suor Angelica*, and *Gianni Schicchi*; they are not connected in subject matter, unlike the component parts of a trilogy, but were intended to be performed together as one evening's entertainment.

Triumphes of Oriana, The. A collection of 25 English madrigals for five and six voices by Morley, Weelkes, and 21 others, published by Morley in 1601. It is assumed to be in praise of Elizabeth I, each piece ending with the line 'Long live fair Oriana', a feature modelled on the Italian collection *Il trionfo di Dori* (1592).

Triumph of Beauty and Deceit, The. Opera in two acts by Gerald Barry to a libretto by Meredith Oakes after Benedetto Pamphili's *The Triumph of Time and Truth* (1757) (televised 1995).

Triumph of Neptune, The. 'English pantomime' in 12 scenes with music by Berners to a libretto by Sacheverell Sitwell, choreographed by George Balanchine (London, 1926); some of it was scored by Walton. Berners arranged an orchestral suite from it (1926–7); a longer suite was arranged by Roy Douglas.

Triumph of Time, The. Orchestral work (1971–2) by Birtwistle.

Troades ('The Trojan Women'). Opera in one act by Aribert Reimann to a libretto by Gerd Albrecht and the composer after Franz Werfel's translation of Euripides' play (Munich, 1986).

Troilus and Cressida. Opera in three acts by Walton to a libretto by Christopher Hassall after Geoffrey Chaucer and other sources (but not Shakespeare) (London, 1954); it was revised in 1963 and again in 1976.

Trois morceaux en forme de poire ('Three Pear-Shaped Pieces'). Work for piano duet (1890–1903) by Satie, a set of six (*sic*) pieces; they were orchestrated by Roger Desormière.

Trois Petites Liturgies de la Présence Divine ('Three Little Liturgies of the Divine Presence'). Work (1945) by Messiaen for chorus, piano, and orchestra, settings of three contemplative texts by the composer.

Trojans, The. *See* TROYENS, LES.

Trout, The. *See* FORELLE, DIE.

'Trout' Quintet. Nickname of Schubert's Piano Quintet in A major D667 (1819), so called because the fourth of its five movements, an Andantino, is a set of variations on the melody of his song *Die *Forelle* ('The Trout').

Trovatore, Il ('The Troubadour'). Opera (*dramma*) in four parts by Verdi to a libretto by Salvadore Cammarano (and Leone Emanuele Bardare) after Antonio García Gutiérrez's play *El trovador* (1836) (Rome, 1853); it includes the famous Gypsies' 'Anvil Chorus'.

Troyens, Les ('The Trojans'). Opera in five acts by Berlioz to his own libretto after Virgil's *Aeneid*; it was composed between 1856 and 1858. In order to get it performed (it was extremely long), Berlioz divided it into two parts, the first called *La Prise de Troie* (Acts I–II), the second *Les Troyens à Carthage* (Acts III–V); the latter was first performed in Paris in 1863, and the opera was first given complete in Karlsruhe in 1890.

Trumpet Voluntary. The title of a transcription by Henry Wood for organ, brass, and drums of a keyboard piece originally attributed to Henry Purcell but now known to be by Jeremiah Clarke; it survives in a version for harpsichord entitled *The Prince of Denmark's March* and in a suite for wind.

Tryst. Work (1989) for chamber orchestra by James MacMillan.

Tsar's Bride, The (*Tsarskaya nevesta*). Opera in four acts by Rimsky-Korsakov to a libretto by Il'ya Tyumenev based on a scenario by the composer after Lev Aleksandrovich Mey's play (1849) (Moscow, 1899).

Tudor Portraits, Five. See FIVE TUDOR PORTRAITS.

Turandot. 1. Opera (*dramma lirico*) in three acts by Puccini to a libretto by Giuseppe Adami and Renato Simoni after Carlo Gozzi's dramatic fairy tale (1762) (Milan, 1926); it was completed by Alfano.

   2. Opera (*chinesisches Fabel*) in two acts by Busoni to his own libretto after Gozzi (Zürich, 1917).

Turangalîla-symphonie. Symphony (1946–8; revised 1990) by Messiaen for large orchestra; its title comes from the Sanskrit *turanga* ('the passage of time, movement, rhythm') and *lîla* ('play in the sense of divine action on the cosmos, also the play of creation, destruction, life and death, also love'). It is the largest of Messiaen's three works inspired by the legend of Tristan and Isolda, the others being *Cinq rechants* and *Harawi*.

Turco in Italia, Il ('The Turk in Italy'). Opera (*dramma buffo*) in two acts by Rossini to a libretto by Felice Romani after Caterino Mazzolà's *Il turco in Italia* set by Franz Seydelmann (1788) (Milan, 1814).

Turn of the Screw, The. Opera in a prologue and two acts by Britten to a libretto by Myfanwy Piper after Henry James's story (1898) (Venice, 1954).

Twilight of the Gods, The. See GÖTTERDÄMMERUNG.

Two Organa. Work for chamber orchestra (1995) by Oliver Knussen.

Two Widows, The (*Dvě vdovy*). Comic opera in two acts by Smetana to a libretto by Emanuel Züngel after P. J. Félicien Mallefille's play *Les Deux Veuves* (1860) (Prague, 1874); it was revised with recitatives and extra numbers (Prague, 1878).

Tzigane (Fr., 'Gypsy'). Concert rhapsody (1924) by Ravel for violin and piano; it was later orchestrated by the composer.

t

Ubu rex. *Opera buffa* in two acts by Penderecki to a libretto by Jerzy Jarocki and the composer after Albert Jarry's play *Ubu roi* (1896) (Munich, 1991).

Uccelli, Gli ('The Birds'). Suite for small orchestra (1927) by Respighi, based on bird pieces for lute and harpsichord by 17th- and 18th-century composers (including Rameau and Pasquini).

'Ukrainian' Symphony. Nickname of Tchaikovsky's Symphony no. 2 in C major op. 17 (1872), so called because it uses folksongs from Ukraine; it is also known as the *'Little Russian' Symphony.

Ulisse ('Ulysses'). Opera in a prologue and two acts by Dallapiccola to a libretto by the composer after Homer's *Odyssey* and other sources (Berlin, 1968, as *Odysseus*).

Ultimos ritos ('Last Rites'). Work (1969–72) by Tavener, for soprano, alto, tenor, and bass soloists, five male speakers, chorus, large brass ensemble, and orchestra, to a text by St John of the Cross and the Crucifixus from the Nicene Creed.

Unanswered Question, The. Work (1908) for chamber orchestra by Ives; it is the first of *Two Contemplations*, the other being *Central Park in the Dark*, and was revised *c*.1930–5.

Undina. Opera in three acts by Tchaikovsky to a libretto by Vladimir Sollogub after Friedrich Heinrich Carl de la Motte Fouqué's story *Undine* (1811), translated by Vasily Zhukovsky; it was composed in 1869 but rejected for performance. Tchaikovsky destroyed most of it but incorporated some of its numbers into The *Snow Maiden*, the *'Little Russian' Symphony, and *Swan Lake*.

Undine. 1. Opera (*Zauberoper*: 'magic opera') in three acts by E. T. A. Hoffmann to a libretto by Friedrich Carl de la Motte Fouqué after his own story (1811) (Berlin, 1816).
   2. Opera (*romantische Zauberoper*) in four acts by Albert Lortzing to a libretto by the composer after Fouqué (Magdeburg, 1845).
   See also ONDINE.

'Unfinished' Symphony. Schubert's Symphony no. 8 in B minor D759 (1822), of which two movements and the sketch of a third survive. There are many unfinished symphonies, for example by Tchaikovsky, Mahler, Elgar, and Shostakovich, but the title is generally taken to refer only to Schubert's.

Unity Capsule. Piece for solo flute (1975–6) by Brian Ferneyhough.

Universal Prayer. Cantata (1970) by Panufnik, a setting for soprano, contralto, tenor, and bass soloists, three harps, organ, and mixed chorus of a poem by Alexander Pope.

Utopia Limited (*Utopia Limited; or, The Flowers of Progress*). Comic opera in two acts by Sullivan to a libretto by W. S. Gilbert (London, 1893).

Utrecht Te Deum and Jubilate. Choral settings by Handel, composed to celebrate the Peace of Utrecht and first performed in 1713 in St Paul's Cathedral, London.

Utrenja. Work (1969–71) by Penderecki for five vocal soloists, two choruses, boys' chorus, and orchestra; it is in two parts—'The Entombment' and 'The Resurrection'. *Utrenia* is the Russian Orthodox Matins.

u

Vaganza. Work (1985) by John Casken for large ensemble including chamber organ.

Vakula the Smith (*Kuznets Vakula*). Opera in three acts by Tchaikovsky to a libretto by Yakov Polonsky after Nikolay Gogol's story *Noch' pered rozhdestvom* ('Christmas Eve') in *Evenings on a Farm near Dikanka* (ii, 1832) (St Petersburg, 1876); Tchaikovsky revised it as **Cherevichki*.

VALIS. Opera in two parts by Tod Machover to a libretto by the composer (with contributions from others) after Philip K. Dick's novel (1981) (Paris, 1987).

Valkyrie, The. *See* WALKÜRE, DIE.

Vallée d'Obermann ('Obermann Valley'). Work for solo piano by Liszt, originally part of *Album d'un voyageur*, later revised as no. 6 of book 1 of *Années de pèlerinage*.

Valse, La ('The Waltz'). Orchestral work ('choreographic poem') by Ravel, composed in 1919–20; he arranged it for two pianos (1921) and Lucien Garban arranged it for piano duet. It was used for a one-act ballet, choreographed by Bronislava Nijinska (Paris, 1928), and has since been choreographed by George Balanchine (1951) and Frederick Ashton (1958).

Valses nobles et sentimentales ('Noble and Sentimental Waltzes'). Work (1911) by Ravel for piano solo; he orchestrated it the following year. The score was used for the ballet *Adélaïde, ou Le Langage des fleurs*, to Ravel's own scenario, choreographed by Ivan Clustine (Paris, 1912), and it has since been choreographed by Serge Lifar (1938), Frederick Ashton (1947), Kenneth MacMillan (1966), and Ronald Hynd (1975).

Valse triste ('Sad Waltz'). Waltz, op. 44 (1903), by Sibelius, composed as part of the incidental music for Arvid Järnefelt's play *Kuolema* ('Death'); it was originally for strings but Sibelius revised the orchestration in 1904 and also arranged it for piano.

Vampyr, Der ('The Vampire'). Opera (*grosse romantische Oper*) in two acts by Marschner to a libretto by Wilhelm August Wohlbrück after plays based on John W. Polidori's story *The Vampyre* (1819), a revision of Byron's *Fragment of a Novel* (sometimes called *Augustus Darvell*) (Leipzig, 1828). Lindpaintner wrote a three-act opera on the same subject (Stuttgart, 1828).

Vanda. Grand opera in five acts by Dvořák to a libretto by Václav Beneš-Šumavský and František Zákrejs after a story by Julian Surzycki (Prague, 1876); Dvořák revised it into four acts.

Vanessa. Opera in four acts by Samuel Barber to a libretto by Gian Carlo Menotti after a story in Isak Dinesen's (Karen Blixen's) *Seven Gothic Tales* (1934) (New York, 1958).

Vanishing Bridegroom, The. Opera in three parts by Judith Weir to her own libretto after J. F. Campbell of Islay's *Popular Tales of the West Highlands* (ii, 1860) and *Carmina gadelica*, edited by Alexander Carmichael (ii, 1900) (Glasgow, 1990).

Vanitas. Opera ('natura morta') in one act by Salvatore Sciarrino to a libretto assembled by the composer from anonymous sources, Sempronius, and others (Milan, 1981).

Variations. Eight works by Cage in which indeterminacy is taken to extraordinary limits. The score of *Variations I* (1958), for example, consists of transparent plastic sheets inscribed with lines and dots which the performer or performers superimpose in any way and play on any instrument or instruments; *Variations VIII* (1978) is for 'no music or recordings'.

Variations and Fugue on a Theme by Handel. Brahms's op. 24 (1861), for solo piano; the theme is from the first suite in B♭ major from the *Suites de pieces de clavecin* (1733).

Variations and Fugue on a Theme of Henry Purcell. *See* YOUNG PERSON'S GUIDE TO THE ORCHESTRA, THE.

Variations on 'America'. Work (1891–2) by Ives for organ; the composer added polytonal interludes *c.*1909–10. It was arranged for orchestra by William Schuman in 1964 and for concert band by Schuman and William E. Rhoads.

Variations on a Rococo Theme. Tchaikovsky's op. 33 (1876), for cello and orchestra, an introduction, theme, and eight variations. Wilhelm Fitzenhagen (1848–90), the cellist for whom it was written, made many changes to the solo part, transferred the cadenza and the third and fourth variations to the end of the work, and omitted the last variation, claiming that Tchaikovsky authorized his revisions; it is his version that is usually heard today, though the original was revived in 1941 and has been recorded.

Variations on a Theme by Haydn. Orchestral work by Brahms, op. 56*a* (1873), a set of eight variations and a finale on a theme often called 'St Anthony's Chorale', from the second movement of a divertimento for wind probably not by Haydn; Brahms arranged the work for two pianos (op. 56*b*).

Variations on a Theme of Corelli. Rakhmaninov's op. 42 (1931), for solo piano; the theme is *La folia*, which was at one time mistakenly thought to be by Corelli.

Variations on a Theme of Frank Bridge. Britten's op. 10 (1937), for string orchestra; the theme is from Bridge's *Idyll* no. 2 for string quartet.

Variations on a Waltz by Diabelli. *See* DIABELLI VARIATIONS.

Variations symphoniques. *See* SYMPHONIC VARIATIONS.

Veil of the Temple, The. Choral and orchestral work by Tavener for soprano, tenor, two baritones, and two basses, massed choirs, duduk, organ, and brass, settings of chants, prayers, and psalms of many faiths in eight liturgical cycles. It was conceived as an all-night vigil (a 'journey to the centre of the Cosmos') and its first performance (2003) lasted seven hours, but Tavener made a shortened concert version (2004).

Venetian Games (*Gry weneckie*; *Jeux vénitiens*). Work (1960–1) for chamber orchestra by Lutosławski, the first in which he used aleatory procedures.

Veni, Veni, Emmanuel. Percussion concerto (1992) by James MacMillan.

Venus and Adonis. 1. Tragic opera in a prologue and three acts by Blow to a libretto by an unknown author (London or Windsor, *c.*1683); it is the earliest surviving English opera.
2. Masque in two interludes by Pepusch to a libretto by Colley Cibber after book 10 of Ovid's *Metamorphoses* (London, 1715).

Vêpres siciliennes, Les (*I vespri siciliani*; 'The Sicilian Vespers'). Opera in five acts by Verdi to a libretto by Eugène Scribe and Charles Duveyrier after their libretto *Le Duc d'Albe* (1838) (Paris, 1855); it was translated into Italian by Eugenio Caimi, as *Giovanni di Guzman*, and is now most often given in this version but under the title *I vespri siciliani*.

Vera costanza, La ('True Constancy'). Opera (*dramma giocoso*) in three acts by Haydn to a libretto by Francesco Puttini (Eszterháza, 1779).

Vera storia, La ('The True Story'). Opera in two acts by Berio to a libretto by Italo Calvino (Milan, 1982).

Verklärte Nacht ('Transfigured Night'). Schoenberg's op. 4 (1899), for two violins, two violas, and two cellos, based on a poem (from *Weib und Welt*) by Richard Dehmel; Schoenberg arranged it for string orchestra in 1917 and made a second version in 1943.

Verratene Meer, Das ('Treacherous Oceans'). Opera (*Musikdrama*) in two parts by Henze to a libretto by Hans-Ulrich Treichel after Yukio Mishima's *Gogo no eiko* ('The Sailor Who Fell from Grace with the Sea', 1963) (Berlin, 1990).

Vesalii icones ('Images of Vesalius'). Theatre piece by Maxwell Davies for male dancer, solo cello, and ensemble of five players (including parts for out-of-tune piano, knife grinder, and saucepan) (London, 1969).

Vesperae solennes de confessore ('Solemn Vespers of the Confessor'). Work by Mozart, K339 (1780), for soprano, alto, tenor, and bass soloists, chorus, organ, and orchestra.

Vespri siciliani, I. *See* VÊPRES SICILIENNES, LES.

Vespro della Beata Vergine ('Vespers of the Blessed Virgin'). A collection of motets (1610) by Monteverdi, composed for performance at Mantua; for different vocal and instrumental combinations, they are *Domine ad* *adiuvandum*, *Dixit Dominus*, *Nigra sum*, *Laudate pueri*, *Pulchra es*, *Laetatus sum*, *Duo seraphim*, *Nisi Dominus*, *Audi coelum*, *Lauda, Jerusalem*, *Sonata sopra 'Sancta Maria'*, *Ave maris stella*, and two *Magnificat* settings.

Vestale, La ('The Vestal Virgin'). Opera (*tragédie lyrique*) in three acts by Spontini to a libretto by Étienne de Jouy (Paris, 1807).

Vexations. Piano piece (*c.*1893) by Satie consisting of a short passage repeated 840 times.

Viaggio a Reims, Il (*Il viaggio a Reims, ossia L'albergo del giglio d'oro*; 'The Journey to Reims, or The Hotel of the Golden Lily'). Opera (*dramma giocoso*) in one act by Rossini to a libretto by Luigi Balocchi partly derived from Madame de Staël's novel *Corinne, ou L'Italie* (1807) (Paris, 1825). It was composed as an entertainment for the coronation of Charles X, and Rossini later used some of the music from it in *Le Comte Ory*.

Vida breve, La ('The Short Life'). Opera ('lyric drama') in two acts and four scenes by Falla to a libretto by Carlos Fernández Shaw (Nice, 1913).

Viderunt omnes. A four-voice chant setting (*organum quadruplum*) by Pérotin, a gradual for Christmas and Circumcision composed *c.*1200.

Vie parisienne, La ('Parisian Life'). *Opéra bouffe* in five (later four) acts by Offenbach to a libretto by Henri Meilhac and Ludovic Halévy (Paris, 1866).

Vier ernste Gesänge ('Four Serious Songs'). Song cycle, op. 121 (1896), by Brahms for voice and piano, four settings of extracts from Martin Luther's translation of the Bible. They were arranged for voice and orchestra by Malcolm Sargent and in English are sometimes known as 'Four Biblical Songs'.

Vier letzte Lieder ('Four Last Songs'). Title given by the publisher to songs (1946–8) by Richard Strauss for soprano or tenor solo and orchestra, settings of poems by Joseph von Eichendorff and Hermann Hesse. In order of composition they are 1. *Im Abendrot* ('At Twilight'), 2. *Frühling* ('Spring'), 3. *Beim Schlafengehen* ('Falling Asleep'), 4. *September*; Strauss is said to have favoured the order 3, 4, 2, 1, but they are published and usually performed 2, 4, 3, 1.

View from the Bridge, A. Opera in two acts by William Bolcom to a libretto by Arnold Weinstein and Arthur Miller after Miller's play (1955, revised 1957) (Chicago, 1999).

Vigil. *See* TRIDUUM.

Village Romeo and Juliet, A (*Romeo und Julia auf dem Dorfe*). Opera ('lyric drama') in six pictures (or scenes) by Delius to his own libretto after Gottfried Keller's story from his collection *Die Leute von Seldwyla* (1856) (Berlin, 1907). The intermezzo before the final scene is *The *Walk to the Paradise Garden*. Eric Fenby arranged an orchestral suite (1948) from the score of the opera.

Villi, Le ('The Wilis'). *Opera-ballo* in two acts by Puccini to a libretto by Ferdinando Fontana after Alphonse Karr's short story *Les Willis* (1852) (Milan, 1884; revised Turin, 1884).

Vingt regards sur l'enfant Jésus ('20 Looks at the Child Jesus'). Work (1944) by Messiaen for piano; each of its 20 movements has a title, for example 'Regard du Père', 'Regard des anges'.

Viola in My Life, The. Four pieces by Morton Feldman: I (1970) for viola, flute, percussion, piano, violin, and cello; II (1970) for viola, flute, clarinet, percussion, piano, violin, and cello; III (1970) for viola and piano; IV (1971) for viola and orchestra.

Visage nuptial, Le ('The Bridal Face'). Work by Boulez for soprano, alto, female chorus, and orchestra, a setting of a text by René Char; Boulez composed an earlier version, for soprano and alto soloists and chamber orchestra, in 1946, then expanded it in 1952 and revised it in 1989.

Vision of St Augustine, The. Work (1963–5) by Tippett, for baritone, chorus, and orchestra, a setting of texts from St Augustine's *Confessions* and from the Bible.

Visions de l'Amen. Suite for two pianos (1943) by Messiaen.

Visions fugitives ('Fleeting Visions'). 20 pieces for solo piano, op. 22 (1915–17), by Prokofiev.

Visitation, The (*Die Heimsuchung*). Opera in three acts by Gunther Schuller to his own libretto after Franz Kafka's novel *Der Prozess* ('The Trial', 1925) (Hamburg, 1966).

Visit of the Old Lady, The. *See* BESUCH DER ALTEN DAME, DER.

Vltava ('River Moldau'). Symphonic poem by Smetana, the fourth of his cycle *Má vlast and often played separately.

Vocalise. A melody sung without text but to one or more vowel sounds. Several composers have written vocalises as concert pieces, notably Spohr (Sonatina for voice and piano, 1848), Ravel (*Vocalise-étude en forme de habanera*, 1907), Rakhmaninov (*Vocalise* op. 34 no. 14, 1912, revised 1915), Medtner (*Sonata-Vocalise mit einem Motto 'Geweihter Platz'*, 1922–3, and *Suite-Vocalise*, 1926), and Vaughan Williams (*Three Vocalises* for soprano and clarinet, 1958).

Voces intimae ('Friendly Voices'). Subtitle of Sibelius's String Quartet in D minor op. 56 (1909).

Voci (*Folksongs II*). Work (1984) by Berio for viola and two ensembles.

Vögel, Die ('The Birds'). Opera in two acts by Walter Braunfels to his own libretto after Aristophanes (Munich, 1920).

Voix humaine, La ('The Human Voice'). Opera (*tragédie lyrique*) in one act by Poulenc to a libretto by Jean Cocteau after his play (1928) (Paris, 1959); it is a monodrama for soprano and orchestra.

Von heute auf morgen ('From One Day to the Next'). Opera in one act by Schoenberg to a libretto by Max Blonda (pseudonym of Gertrud Schoenberg) (Frankfurt, 1930).

Votre Faust ('Your Faust'). Opera (*fantaisie variable genre opéra*) in two parts by Henri Pousseur to a libretto by Michel Butor after various Faust sources (Milan, 1969, revised 1981).

Voyage, The. Opera in a prologue, three acts, and an epilogue by Philip Glass to a libretto by David Henry Hwang after Glass's story (New York, 1992); it was commissioned to commemorate the 500th anniversary of Christopher Columbus's arrival in America.

Voyevoda ('The Provincial Governor'). Opera in three acts by Tchaikovsky to a libretto by Aleksandr Ostrovsky and the composer after Ostrovsky's comedy (subtitled *Son na Volge*, 'A Volga Dream') (Moscow, 1869).

V

Wachet auf, ruft uns die Stimme ('Awake, the Voice is Calling us'). J. S. Bach's cantata no. 140 (1731), based on a chorale by Philipp Nicolai (1599); one movement from it was transcribed for organ as the first (BWV645) of the *'Schübler' Chorales (1748). 'Wachet auf' is often translated as 'Sleepers, Awake'. 'Wach' auf' is the chorus in Act III of Wagner's *Die Meistersinger von Nürnberg*.

Waldscenen ('Woodland Scenes'). Set of nine piano pieces, op. 82 (1848–9), by Schumann.

'Waldstein' Sonata. Beethoven's Piano Sonata no. 21 in C major op. 53 (1803–4), so called because he dedicated it to his patron, Count Ferdinand von Waldstein (1762–1823).

Walk to the Paradise Garden, The. Intermezzo for orchestra before the final scene of Delius's opera *A *Village Romeo and Juliet* (the 'Paradise Garden' was the village inn); it was not in the original score but was added at Thomas Beecham's request to cover a scene change in the 1910 Covent Garden production. It is frequently played as a concert item.

Walküre, Die ('The Valkyrie'). Opera in three acts by Wagner to his own libretto, the 'first day' of *Der *Ring des Nibelungen*.

Wally, La. Opera (*dramma musicale*) in four acts by Catalani to a libretto by Luigi Illica after Wilhelmine von Hillern's novel *Die Geyer-Wally* (1875) (Milan, 1892).

'Wanderer' Fantasia. Nickname of Schubert's Fantasia in C major for piano, D760 (1822), so called because the Adagio is a set of variations on a theme from his song *Der Wanderer* D489 (1816). Liszt arranged it for piano and orchestra (*c*.1851).

Wand of Youth, The. Two orchestral suites by Elgar, opp. 1*a* (1907) and 1*b* (1908), arranged and orchestrated from material he wrote for a family play when he was 12; he reused some of the themes in his music for *The *Starlight Express* (1915).

War and Peace (*Voyna i mir*). Opera in 13 'lyrico-dramatic scenes' and a choral epigraph by Prokofiev to a libretto by the composer and Mira Mendelson (Prokof'yeva) after Lev Tolstoy's novel (1869); the opera has an extraordinarily complicated history and exists in five separate versions, of which four have been staged. The first major staging was in Leningrad in 1946 and the first relatively complete performance was in Moscow in 1959. *War and Peace* was chosen to open the Sydney Opera House (1974).

War Requiem. Choral work, op. 66 (1962), by Britten, for soprano, tenor, and baritone soloists, boys' choir, chorus, organ, and orchestra; settings of nine poems by the World War I poet Wilfred Owen (accompanied by a chamber orchestra) are interpolated into Britten's setting of the Latin Requiem Mass. It was written for, and first performed in, the rebuilt Coventry Cathedral.

Warsaw Concerto. Score for piano and orchestra by Richard Addinsell for the film *Dangerous Moonlight* (1941).

Wasps, The. Incidental music by Vaughan Williams, for tenor and baritone soloists, male chorus, and orchestra, composed for the 1909 Cambridge University production of Aristophanes' play; the same year Vaughan Williams arranged from it a five-movement orchestral suite, with an overture.

Water Carrier, The. *See* DEUX JOURNÉES, LES.

Water Music. 1. The popular name for three instrumental suites by Handel (in F, D, and G major), of which some or all of the movements were performed for a royal procession on the river Thames (17 July 1717); the well-known story that Handel wrote them to restore himself to favour with George I is unlikely to be true. Six of the movements became well known as a suite (1922) orchestrated by Hamilton Harty.
  2. Work (1952) by Cage for a pianist, who is required to pour water from pots, play cards, blow whistles under water, etc., while the score is displayed like a poster.

Waverley. Overture, op. 1, by Berlioz after Walter Scott's novel (1814); it was composed in 1826 but Berlioz revised it several times, reducing the enormous orchestral forces he originally required. The score is prefaced with two lines from Scott, 'Dreams of Love and Lady's charms / Give place to honour and to arms'.

We Come to the River. Opera ('actions for music') in two parts (11 scenes) by Henze to a libretto by Edward Bond (London, 1976).

Wedding, The. *See* NOCES, LES.

Wedding Day at Troldhaugen. Piano piece by Grieg, no. 6 of his *Lyric Pieces* (book 8) op. 65 (1897); it was later orchestrated. Troldhaugen was the name of Grieg's villa outside Bergen.

'Wedge' Fugue. Nickname for J. S. Bach's Fugue in E minor for organ, BWV548, so called because of the shape of the subject, the intervals of which gradually widen.

Weihe des Hauses, Die ('The Consecration of the House'). Overture by Beethoven, op. 124 (1822), to a play by C. Meisl given at the first night of the Josephstadt theatre in Vienna; the play was an adaptation of August von Kotzebue's *Die *Ruinen von Athen* (1812), for which Beethoven had written incidental music, so he adapted the earlier score and wrote a new overture.

Weise von Liebe und Tod des Cornets Christoph Rilke, Die ('The Lay of Cornet Christoph Rilke's Love and Death'). 'Operatic vision' by Siegfried Matthus to his own libretto after Rainer Maria Rilke's poem (1899) (Dresden, 1985).

Weisse Rose ('White Rose'). Opera in eight scenes by Udo Zimmermann to a libretto by Ingo Zimmermann (Dresden, 1967); it was revised, with a revised libretto by Wolfgang Willaschek (Hamburg, 1986).

Welcome songs. Cantatas by Henry Purcell written for the return to London on various occasions between 1680 and 1687 of Charles II and James II (one addressed to him as the Duke of York, before his accession); they include *Sound the Trumpet* (1687).

Wellingtons Sieg (*Wellingtons Sieg, oder Die Schlacht bei Vittoria*; 'Wellington's Victory, or The Battle near Vitoria'; *Battle Symphony*). Beethoven's op. 91 (1813), composed to celebrate the defeat of the French at Vitoria and incorporating English and French fanfares and patriotic songs (including 'Rule, Britannia!'). The second part was composed for Maelzel's panharmonicon but Beethoven later orchestrated the whole work for strings, wind bands, and artillery.

Well-Tempered Clavier, The (*Das wohltemperirte Clavier*). Title given by J. S. Bach to his two sets of 24 preludes and fugues in all the major and minor keys, BWV846–93 (1722, 1742), popularly known as the '48'; it demonstrates the range of keys that becomes possible using what were then relatively modern methods of tuning, or 'temperament', and has subsequently influenced the contrapuntal writing of countless composers and played a crucial role in teaching keyboard playing, composition, and analysis.

Werther. Opera (*drame lyrique*) in four acts by Massenet to a libretto by Édouard Blau, Paul Milliet, and Georges Hartmann after Johann Wolfgang von Goethe's novel *Die Leiden des jungen Werthers* ('The Sorrows of Young Werther', 1774) (Vienna, 1892).

Wesendonk-Lieder. Five songs (1857–8) by Wagner for voice and piano to poems by Mathilde Wesendonk; they were orchestrated by Felix Mottl under Wagner's supervision. They have been arranged for violin and piano (1872) by Hubert Léonard, and for high voice and chamber orchestra (1979) by Henze.

Western Wynde. 16th-century English secular song used as a cantus firmus in masses by Taverner, Tye, and Sheppard.

w

Whale, The. Dramatic cantata (1965–6) by Tavener, for narrator, mezzo-soprano, baritone, chorus, and orchestra, to his own text compiled from *Collins' Encyclopedia* and the Vulgate.

What Next? Chamber opera in one act by Elliott Carter to a libretto by Paul Griffiths (Berlin, 1999).

When I am laid in earth. *See* DIDO'S LAMENT.

Where the Wild Things Are. Fantasy opera in one act by Oliver Knussen to a libretto by Maurice Sendak after his children's book (1963) (preliminary version, Brussels, 1980; definitive version, London, 1984); it was followed by the companion-piece *Higglety Pigglety Pop!

White Man Sleeps. Work (1982) by Volans for two harpsichords, bass viol, and percussion, adapted in 1986 as his String Quartet no. 1.

Wildschütz, Der (*Der Wildschütz, oder Die Stimme der Natur*; 'The Poacher, or The Voice of Nature'). Opera (*komische Oper*) in three acts by Lortzing to his own libretto adapted from August von Kotzebue's comedy *Der Rehbock, oder Die schuldlosen Schuldbewussten* ('The Roebuck, or The Conscience-Stricken Innocents', 1815) (Leipzig, 1842).

William Tell. See GUILLAUME TELL.

Winter Daydreams. Nickname of Tchaikovsky's Symphony no. 1 in G minor op. 13; the first version was composed in 1866, the second later that year, and the third in 1874.

Wintermärchen ('Winter's Tale'). Opera in four acts by Philippe Boesmans to a libretto by Luc Bondy and Marie-Louise Bischofberger after Shakespeare's play (1610–11) (Brussels, 1999). John Harbison wrote an opera on the same subject (San Francisco, 1979).

Winter Music. Work (1957) by Cage for one to 20 pianos.

Winterreise ('Winter Journey'). Song cycle, D911 (1827), by Schubert, settings of 24 poems (1823–4) by Wilhelm Müller.

Winter Words. Song cycle, op. 52 (1953), by Britten, for soprano or tenor and piano, settings of eight poems by Thomas Hardy; the title is taken from Hardy's last published volume of poetry (1928).

Wise Virgins, The. Ballet in one act by Walton to a scenario based on the parable of the Wise and Foolish Virgins (Matthew 25), choreographed by Frederick Ashton (London, 1940). Walton's score is an arrangement of nine items selected by Constant Lambert from J. S. Bach's cantatas; he made an orchestral suite (1940) of six of the numbers.

Wohltemperirte Clavier, Das. See WELL-TEMPERED CLAVIER, THE.

Wolf Cub Village. Chamber opera in four scenes by Guo Wenjing to a libretto by Zeng Li and the composer after Lu Xun's story *Kuangren riji* ('Diary of a Madman', 1918) (Beijing, 1994).

Wonderful Widow of Eighteen Springs, The. Work (1942) by Cage for voice and closed piano to a text by James Joyce.

W

WoO. Abbreviation for *Werk ohne Opuszahl* (Ger.), 'work without opus number'. The term is especially common in references to Beethoven's music, since a number of his works were not published in his lifetime.

Wood Dove, The (*Holoubek*). Symphonic poem, op. 110 (1896), by Dvořák.

Wooden Prince, The (*A fából faragott királyfi*). Ballet in one act by Bartók to a scenario by Béla Balázs, choreographed by Otto Zöbisch (Budapest, 1917). Bartók arranged an orchestral suite (?1921–4) from the score.

Worldes Blis: Motet for Orchestra. Work (1969) by Maxwell Davies after the 13th-century English song of that title.

World's Ransoming, The. *See* TRIDUUM.

Wotquenne. Abbreviation for the standard thematic catalogue of the works of C. P. E. Bach drawn up by the Belgian bibliographer Alfred Wotquenne (1867–1939) and published in Leipzig in 1905. Bach's works are often referred to by Wotquenne number, usually further abbreviated to WQ.

Wozzeck. Opera in three acts by Berg to his own libretto after Georg Büchner's play *Woyzeck* (1836) (Berlin, 1925).

WQ. Abbreviation for *Wotquenne, used as a prefix to the numbers of C. P. E. Bach's works as given in the standard thematic catalogue of Alfred Wotquenne.

Wreckers, The (*Les Naufrageurs*; *Strandrecht*). Opera in three acts by Ethel Smyth to a libretto in French by the composer and Henry Brewster (Leipzig, 1906).

Writing to Vermeer. Opera in six scenes by Louis Andriessen to a libretto by Peter Greenaway (Amsterdam, 1999).

Wunderhorn, Des Knaben. *See* DES KNABEN WUNDERHORN.

Wuthering Heights. Opera in a prologue and four acts by Bernard Herrmann to a libretto by Lucille Fletcher after Emily Brontë's novel (1846) (Portland, OR, 1982). Carlisle Floyd wrote an opera on the same subject (Santa Fe, NM, 1958).

W

Xerxes. *See* SERSE.

Yankee Doodle. Popular American song dating from the late 18th century; its words and tune are of confused origin. Anton Rubinstein wrote piano variations on it, Henri Vieuxtemps's *Caprice burlesque* for violin and piano is based on it, and it appears in the last movement of Dvořák's Symphony no. 9, 'From the New World'.

Yan Tan Tethera. 'Mechanical pastoral' in one act by Birtwistle to a libretto by Tony Harrison (London, 1986).

Year 1905, The (*1905 god*). Subtitle of Shostakovich's Symphony no. 11 (1957), composed for the 40th anniversary of the Revolution; its movements ('Palace Square', 'Ninth of January', 'In Memoriam', and 'Tocsin') portray the events of the abortive 1905 revolution. *See also* 'YEAR 1917, THE'.

Year 1917, The (*1917 god*). Subtitle of Shostakovich's Symphony no. 12 ('Pamyati Lenina', 'To the memory of Lenin'; 1961); its movements ('Revolutionary Petrograd', 'Razliv', 'Aurora', and 'The Dawn of Mankind') portray elements of the Revolution of 1917. It forms a diptych with 'The *Year 1905'.

Yeomen of the Guard, The (*The Yeomen of the Guard; or, The Merryman and his Maid*). Operetta in two acts by Sullivan to a libretto by W. S. Gilbert (London, 1888).

Yevgeny Onegin. *See* EUGENE ONEGIN.

Yolanta. *See* IOLANTA.

Young Person's Guide to the Orchestra, The. Orchestral work, op. 34 (1946), by Britten, written for a documentary film *The Instruments of the Orchestra*; subtitled 'Variations and Fugue on a Theme of Henry Purcell', it illustrates the uses and characteristics of the instruments and sections of the orchestra in a set of variations on a theme from Purcell's incidental music to the play *Abdelazer* (1695), culminating in a fugue. It is sometimes performed with a narrator who speaks the original text, by Eric Crozier.

Youth's Magic Horn, The. *See* KNABEN WUNDERHORN, DES.

Zadok the Priest. Anthem by Handel, the first of four he composed for the coronation of George II in 1727 (*see* CORONATION ANTHEMS); it has been performed at every English coronation since.

Zaide (*Das Serail*). Singspiel in two acts by Mozart to a libretto by Johann Andreas Schachtner after Franz Josef Sebastiani's *Das Serail* (*c.*1778); it was composed in 1779–80, but was left untitled and unfinished, lacking an overture and finale. It was completed by Johann Anton André and first performed in Frankfurt in 1866 on Mozart's birthday.

Zaira. Opera (*tragedia lirica*) in two acts by Bellini to a libretto by Felice Romani after Voltaire's tragedy *Zaïre* (1732) (Parma, 1829).

Zampa (*Zampa, ou La Fiancée de marbre*; 'Zampa, or The Marble Fiancée'). Opera in three acts by Hérold to a libretto by Mélesville (Anne-Honoré-Joseph Duveyrier) (Paris, 1831).

Zarathustra. *See ALSO SPRACH ZARATHUSTRA.*

Zar und Zimmermann (*Czaar und Zimmermann, oder Die zwei [beiden] Peter*; 'Tsar and Carpenter, or The Two Peters'). Opera (*komische Oper*) in three acts by Lortzing to his own libretto after Georg Christian Römer's comedy *Der Bürgermeister von Saardam, oder Die zwei Peter*, itself based on Mélesville (Anne-Honoré-Joseph Duveyrier), E. Cantiran de Boirie, and J. T. Merle's play *Le Bourgmestre de Sardam, ou Les Deux Pierres* (1818) (Leipzig, 1837).

Zauberflöte, Die ('The Magic Flute'). Singspiel in two acts by Mozart to a libretto by Emanuel Schikaneder (Vienna, 1791).

Zazà. Opera (*commedia lirica*) in four acts by Leoncavallo to his own libretto after the play by Pierre Berton and Charles Simon (1898) (Milan, 1900).

Zeitmasze. Work (1955–6) by Stockhausen for flute, oboe, cor anglais, clarinet, and bassoon; it simultaneously combines different tempos.

Zelmira. Opera (*dramma*) in two acts by Rossini to a libretto by Andrea Leone Tottola after Dormont de Belloy's *Zelmire* (1762) (Naples, 1822).

Zémire et Azor ('Zémire and Azor'). Opera (*comédie-ballet mêlé de chants et de danses*) in four acts by Grétry to a libretto by Jean François Marmontel (Fontainebleau, 1771). Spohr wrote an opera, *Zemire und Azor*, to a libretto by Johann Jakob Ihlée after Marmontel's libretto (1819).

Zigeunerbaron, Der ('The Gypsy Baron'). Operetta in three acts by Johann Strauss (ii) to a libretto by Ignaz Schnitzer after Mór Jókai's novel *Sáffi* (1883) (Vienna, 1885).

Zigeunerlieder ('Gypsy Songs'). Brahms's op. 103 (1887), for soprano, alto, tenor, and bass, and piano, 11 settings of verses by Hugo Conrat adapted from prose versions of Hungarian folk poems by a Fräulein Witzl.

Zwerg, Der ('The Dwarf'). Opera in one act by Zemlinsky to a libretto by Georg Klaren after Oscar Wilde's novel *The Birthday of the Infanta* (1888) (Cologne, 1922).

Zwillingsbrüder, Die ('The Twin Brothers'). Opera (*Posse*, 'farce') in one act by Schubert to a libretto by Georg von Hofmann after a French vaudeville *Les Deux Valentins* (Vienna, 1820).

Zyklus ('Cycle'). Work (1959) by Stockhausen for percussionist; it may be begun on any page of the score, which is in graphic notation.

z

Index of composers

Abel, Carl Friedrich (*b* Cöthen, 22 Dec. 1723; *d* London, 20 June 1787)

Adam, Adolphe (Charles) (*b* Paris, 24 July 1803; *d* Paris, 3 May 1856)

Adam de la Halle [Adan le Bossu] (*b* Arras, 1245–50; *d* Naples, ?1285–8)

Adams, John (Coolidge) (*b* Worcester, MA, 15 Feb. 1947)

Addinsell, Richard (Stewart) (*b* London, 13 Jan. 1904; *d* London, 14 Nov. 1977)

Adès, Thomas (*b* London, 31 March 1971)

Aiblinger, Johann Kaspar (*b* Wasserburg, Bavaria, 23 Feb. 1779; *d* Munich, 6 May 1867)

Albéniz, Isaac (Manuel Francisco) (*b* Camprodón, Catalunya, 29 May 1860; *d* Cambô-les-Bains, 18 May 1909)

Albert, Eugen (Francis Charles) d' (*b* Glasgow, 10 April 1864; *d* Riga, 3 March 1932)

Albinoni, Tomaso Giovanni (*b* Venice, 14 June 1671; *d* Venice, 17 Jan. 1751)

Alfano, Franco (*b* Posillipo, nr Naples, 8 March 1875; *d* San Remo, 27 Oct. 1954)

Alpaerts, Flor (*b* Antwerp, 12 Sept. 1876; *d* Antwerp, 5 Oct. 1954)

Alwyn, William (*b* Northampton, 7 Nov. 1905; *d* Southwold, 11 Sept. 1985)

Anderson, Julian (David) (*b* London, 6 April 1967)

Anderson, Thomas Jefferson (*b* Coatesville, PA, 17 Aug. 1928)

André, Johann Anton (*b* Offenbach, 6 Oct. 1775; *d* Offenbach, 6 April 1842)

Andriessen, Louis (Joseph) (*b* Utrecht, 6 June 1939)

Anfossi, Pasquale (*b* Taggia, 15 April 1727; *d* Rome, ? Feb. 1797)

Antheil, George [Georg] (Johann Carl) (*b* Trenton, NJ, 8 July 1900; *d* New York, 12 Feb. 1959)

Aperghis, Georges (*b* Athens, 23 Dec. 1945)

Argento, Dominick (*b* York, PA, 27 Oct. 1927)

Arne, Thomas Augustine (*b* London, *bapt.* 28 May 1710; *d* London, 5 March 1778)

Ashley, Robert (Reynolds) (*b* Ann Arbor, MI, 28 March 1930)

Attwood, Thomas (*bapt.* London, 23 Nov. 1765; *d* London, 24 March 1838)

Auber, Daniel François Esprit (*b* Caen, 29 Jan. 1782; *d* Paris, 12 May 1871)

Auric, Georges (*b* Lodève, Hérault, 15 Feb. 1899; *d* Paris, 23 July 1983)

Austin, Frederic (*b* London, 30 March 1872; *d* London, 10 April 1952)

Babbitt, Milton (Byron) (*b* Philadelphia, 10 May 1916)

Bach, Johann Christian (*b* Leipzig, 5 Sept. 1735; *d* London, 1 Jan. 1782)

Bach, Johann Sebastian (*b* Eisenach, 21 March 1685; *d* Leipzig, 28 July 1750)

Bainbridge, Simon (Jeremy) (*b* London, 30 Aug. 1932)

Balakirev, Mily Alekseyevich (*b* Nizhniy Novgorod, 21 Dec. 1836/2 Jan. 1837; *d* St Petersburg, 16/29 May 1910)

Balfe, Michael William (*b* Dublin, 15 May 1808; *d* Rowney Abbey, Herts., 20 Oct. 1870)

Bantock, Sir **Granville (Ransome)** (*b* London, 7 Aug. 1868; *d* London, 16 Oct. 1946)

Barber, Samuel (*b* West Chester, PA, 9 March 1910; *d* New York, 23 Jan. 1981)

Barraqué, Jean (*b* Puteaux, 17 Jan. 1928; *d* Paris, 17 Aug. 1973)

Barry, Gerald (*b* Clare Hill, Co. Clare, 28 April 1952)

Bartók, Béla (Viktor János) (*b* Nagyszentmiklós, Hungary [now Sinnicolau Mare, Romania], 25 March 1881; *d* New York, 26 Sept. 1945)

Bax, Sir **Arnold (Edward Trevor)** (*b* Streatham, 8 Nov. 1883; *d* Cork, 3 Oct. 1953)

Bedford, David (Vickerman) (*b* London, 4 Aug. 1937)

Beethoven, Ludwig van (*b* Bonn, 16 Dec. 1770; *d* Vienna, 26 March 1827)

Bellini, Vincenzo (*b* Catania, Sicily, 3 Nov. 1801; *d* Puteaux, 23 Sept. 1835)

Benda, Georg (Anton) [Jiří Antonín] (*b* Staré Benátky, *bapt.* 30 June 1722; *d* Köstritz, 6 Nov. 1795)

Benedict, Sir **Julius** (*b* Stuttgart, 27 Nov. 1804; *d* London, 5 June 1885)

Benjamin, Arthur (Leslie) (*b* Sydney, 18 Sept. 1893; *d* London, 10 April 1960)

Benjamin, George (*b* London, 31 Jan. 1960)

Bennett, Sir **Richard Rodney** (*b* Broadstairs, 29 March 1936)

Berg, Alban (Maria Johannes) (*b* Vienna, 9 Feb. 1885; *d* Vienna, 24 Dec. 1935)

Berio, Luciano (*b* Oneglia, 24 Oct. 1925; *d* Rome, 27 May 2003)

Berkeley, Sir **Lennox (Randall Francis)** (*b* Oxford, 12 May 1903; *d* London, 26 Dec. 1989)

Berkeley, Michael (Fitzhardinge) (*b* London, 29 May 1948)

Berlioz, (Louis-)Hector (*b* La Côte-St-André, Isère, 11 Dec. 1803; *d* Paris, 8 March 1869)

Berners, (Gerald Hugh Tyrwhitt-Wilson, Baronet) Lord (*b* Apley Park, Bridgnorth, 18 Sept. 1883; *d* Faringdon, 19 April 1950)

Bernstein, Leonard (*b* Lawrence, MA, 25 Aug. 1918; *d* New York, 14 Oct. 1990)

Biber, Heinrich Ignaz Franz von (*b* Wartenberg, nr Reichenberg [now Liberec], Bohemia, Aug. 1644; *d* Salzburg, 3 May 1704)

Birtwistle, Sir **Harrison (Paul)** (*b* Accrington, 15 July 1934)

Bishop, Sir **Henry R(owley)** (*b* London, 18 Nov. 1786; *d* London, 30 April 1855)

Bizet, Georges (Alexandre César Léopold) (*b* Paris, 25 Oct. 1838; *d* Bougival, nr Paris, 3 June 1875)

Blacher, Boris (*b* Niu-chang, China, 19 Jan. 1903; *d* Berlin, 30 Jan. 1975)

Blake, David (Leonard) (*b* London, 2 Sept. 1936)

Bliss, Sir **Arthur (Drummond)** (*b* London, 2 Aug. 1891; *d* London, 27 March 1975)

Blitheman [Blytheman], John (*b c*.1525; *d* London, 23 May 1591)

Blitzstein, Marc (*b* Philadelphia, 2 March 1905; *d* Fort-de-France, Martinique, 22 Jan. 1964)

Bloch, Ernest (*b* Geneva, 24 July 1880; *d* Portland, OR, 15 July 1959)

Blockx, Jan (*b* Antwerp, 25 Jan. 1851; *d* Kapellenbos, nr Antwerp, 26 May 1912)

Blow, John (*b* Newark, Feb. 1649; *d* London, 1 Oct. 1708)

Boccherini, (Ridolfo) Luigi (*b* Lucca, 19 Feb. 1743; *d* Madrid, 28 May 1805)

Boesmans, Philippe (*b* Tongeren, 17 May 1936)

Boieldieu, (François-)Adrien (*b* Rouen, 16 Dec. 1775; *d* Jarcy, 8 Oct. 1834)

Boismortier, Joseph Bodin de (*b* Thionville, 23 Dec. 1689; *d* Roissy-en-Brie, 28 Oct. 1755)

Boito, Arrigo [Enrico] (*b* Padua, 24 Feb. 1842; *d* Milan, 10 June 1918)

Bolcom, William (Elden) (*b* Seattle, 26 May 1938)

Borodin, Aleksandr Porfir'yevich (*b* St Petersburg, 31 Oct./12 Nov. 1833; *d* St Petersburg, 15/27 Feb. 1887)

Bortnyansky, Dmitry Stepanovich (*b* Hlukhiv, Ukraine, 1751; *d* St Petersburg, 28 Sept./10 Oct. 1825)

Bose, Hans-Jürgen von (*b* Munich, 24 Dec. 1953)

Boughton, Rutland (*b* Aylesbury, 23 Jan. 1878; *d* London, 25 Jan. 1960)

Boulez, Pierre (*b* Montbrison, 26 March 1925)

Boyce, William (*b* London, *bapt.* 11 Sept. 1711; *d* Kensington, 7 Feb. 1779)

Brahms, Johannes (*b* Hamburg, 7 May 1833; *d* Vienna, 3 April 1897)

Brand, Max (*b* Lemberg [now L'viv, Ukraine], 26 April 1896; *d* Langenzersdorf, nr Vienna, 5 April 1980)

Braunfels, Walter (*b* Frankfurt, 19 Dec. 1882; *d* Cologne, 19 March 1954)

Brian, Havergal (*b* Dresden, Staffs., 29 Jan. 1876; *d* Shoreham, 28 Nov. 1972)

Bridge, Frank (*b* Brighton, 26 Feb. 1879; *d* Eastbourne, 10 Jan. 1941)

Britten, (Edward) Benjamin [Lord Britten of Aldeburgh] (*b* Lowestoft, 22 Nov. 1913; *d* Aldeburgh, 4 Dec. 1976)

Bruch, Max (Christian Friedrich) (*b* Cologne, 6 Jan. 1838; *d* Berlin, 2 Oct. 1920)

Bruckner, (Josef) Anton (*b* Ansfelden, 4 Sept. 1824; *d* Vienna, 11 Oct. 1896)

Bryars, (Richard) Gavin (*b* Goole, 16 Jan. 1943)

Bull, John (*b* Old Radnor, Radnorshire, *c*.1562; *d* Antwerp, 12 or 13 March 1628)

Bush, Alan (Dudley) (*b* London, 22 Dec. 1900; *d* Watford, 31 Oct. 1995)

Busnois [Busnoys], Antoine [Antonius] (*b c*.1430; *d* early Nov. 1492)

Busoni, Ferruccio (Dante Michelangiolo Benvenuto) (*b* Empoli, 1 April 1866; *d* Berlin, 27 July 1924)

Busser [Büsser], Henri (*b* Toulouse, 16 Jan. 1872; *d* Paris, 30 Dec. 1973)

Butterworth, George (Sainton Kaye) (b London, 12 July 1885; d Pozières, 5 Aug. 1916)

Buxtehude, Dietrich [Diderik] (b Oldesloe [now Bad Oldesloe], Holstein, c.1637; d Lübeck, 9 May 1707)

Byrd, William (b London, c.1540; d Stondon Massey, Essex, 4 July 1623)

Caccini, Giulio (b Rome, 8 Oct 1551; d Florence, Dec. 1618)

Cage, John (Milton) (b Los Angeles, 15 Sept. 1912; d New York, 12 Aug. 1992)

Campion [Campian], Thomas (b London, bapt. 12 Feb. 1567; d London, 1 March 1620)

Campra, André (b Aix-en-Provence, bapt. 4 Dec. 1660; d Versailles, 29 June 1744)

Canteloube (de Malaret), (Marie) Joseph (b Annonay, 21 Oct. 1879; d Paris, 4 Nov. 1957)

Caplet, André (b Le Havre, 23 Nov. 1878; d Neuilly-sur-Seine, 22 April 1925)

Cardew, Cornelius (b Winchcombe, Glos., 7 May 1936; d London, 12 Dec. 1981)

Carissimi, Giacomo (b Marini, nr Rome, bapt. 18 April 1605; d Rome, 12 Jan. 1674)

Carter, Elliott (Cook) (b New York, 11 Dec. 1908)

Casken, John (Arthur) (b Barnsley, 15 July 1949)

Catalani, Alfredo (b Lucca, 19 June 1854; d Milan, 7 Aug. 1893)

Catel, Charles-Simon (b Laigle, Normandy, 10 June 1773; d Paris, 29 Nov. 1830)

Cavalieri, Emilio de' (b Rome, c.1550; d Rome, 11 March 1602)

Cavalli [Caletti], (Pietro) Francesco (b Crema, 14 Feb. 1602; d Venice, 14 Jan. 1676)

Cavos, Catterino Al'bertovich (b Venice, 19/30 Oct. 1775; d St Petersburg, 28 April/ 10 May 1840)

Cesti, Antonio [Pietro] (b Arezzo, bapt. 5 Aug. 1623; d Florence, 14 Oct. 1669)

Chabrier, (Alexis-)Emmanuel (b Ambert, Puy-de-Dôme, 18 Jan. 1841; d Paris, 13 Sept. 1894)

Charpentier, Gustave (b Dieuze, Moselle, 25 June 1860; d Paris, 18 Feb. 1956)

Charpentier, Marc-Antoine (b Paris, 1643; d Paris, 24 Feb. 1704)

Chausson, (Amédée-)Ernest (b Paris, 20 Jan. 1855; d Limay, nr Mantes, Yvelines, 10 June 1899)

Cherubini, (Maria) Luigi (Carlo Zanobi Salvadore) (b Florence, 8 or 14 Sept. 1760; d Paris, 15 March 1842)

Chin, Unsuk (b Seoul, 14 July 1961)

Chopin, Fryderyk [Frédéric] (Franciszek) (b Żelazowa Wola, nr Warsaw, probably 1 March 1810; d Paris, 17 Oct. 1849)

Cilea, Francesco (b Palmi, Reggio Calabria, 23 July 1866; d Varazze, Savona, 20 Nov. 1950)

Cimarosa, Domenico (b Avera, nr Naples, 17 Dec. 1749; d Venice, 11 Jan. 1801)

Clarke, Jeremiah (b c.1674; d London, 1 Dec. 1707)

Clementi, Muzio (b Rome, 23 Jan. 1752; d Evesham, 10 March 1832)

Coates, Eric (b Hucknall, Notts., 27 Aug. 1886; d Chichester, 23 Dec. 1957)

Coleman, Charles (d London, bur. 8 July 1664)

Coleridge-Taylor, Samuel (b London, 15 Aug. 1875; d Croydon, 1 Sept. 1912)

Conti, Francesco Bartolomeo (b Florence, 20 Jan. 1682; d Venice, 20 July 1732)

Cooke, Henry (b ?Lichfield, c.1615; d Hampton Court, 13 July 1672)

Copland, Aaron (b Brooklyn, New York, 14 Nov. 1900; d Westchester, NY, 2 Dec. 1990)

Corelli, Arcangelo (b Fusignano, nr Faenza, 17 Feb. 1653; d Rome, 8 Jan. 1713)

Corigliano, John (Paul) (b New York, 16 Feb. 1938)

Cornelius, (Carl August) Peter (b Mainz, 24 Dec. 1824; d Mainz, 26 Oct. 1874)

Corsi, Jacopo (b Florence, 17 July 1561; d Florence, 29 Dec. 1602)

Couperin, François (b Paris, 10 Nov. 1668; d Paris, 11 Sept. 1733)

Croft, William (b Nether Ettington, Warwicks., bapt. 30 Dec. 1678; d Bath, 14 Aug. 1727)

Crosse, Gordon (b Bury, 1 Dec. 1937)

Crüger, Johannes (b Gross Breesen, nr Frankfurt an der Oder, 9 April 1598; d Berlin, 23 Feb. 1662)

Crumb, George (Henry) (b Charleston, WV, 24 Oct. 1929)

Cui, César [Kyui, Tsezar'] Antonovich (b Vilnius, 6/18 Jan. 1835; d Petrograd, 26 March 1918)

Drigo, Riccardo (*b* Padua, 30 June 1846; *d* Padua, 1 Oct. 1930)

Dufay, Guillaume (*b* c.1400; *d* Cambrai, 27 Nov. 1474)

Dukas, Paul (Abraham) (*b* Paris, 1 Oct. 1865; *d* Paris, 17 May 1935)

Dunstaple [Dunstable], John (*b* c.1390; *d* 24 Dec. 1453)

Duparc, (Marie Eugène) Henri (Fouques) (*b* Paris, 21 Jan. 1848; *d* Mont-de-Marsan, 12 Feb. 1933)

Dupré, Marcel (*b* Rouen, 3 May 1886; *d* Meudon, nr Paris, 30 May 1971)

Durand, Jacques (Massacrie) (*b* Paris, 22 Feb. 1865; *d* Bel-Ébat, nr Fontainebleau, 22 Aug. 1928)

Durey, Louis (Edmond) (*b* Paris, 27 May 1888; *d* Saint Tropez, 3 July 1979)

Duruflé, Maurice (*b* Louviers, 11 Jan. 1902; *d* Paris, 16 June 1986)

Dutilleux, Henri (*b* Angers, 22 Jan. 1916)

Dvořák, Antonín (Leopold) (*b* Nelahozeves, nr Prague, 8 Sept. 1841; *d* Prague, 1 May 1904)

Dykes, John Bacchus (*b* Hull, 10 March 1832; *d* Ticehurst, Sussex, 22 Jan. 1876)

Dzerzhinsky, Ivan Ivanovich (*b* Tambov, 27 March/9 April 1909; *d* Leningrad, 18 Jan. 1978)

Eaton, John C(harles) (*b* Bryn Mawr, PA, 30 March 1935)

Eccles, John (*b* c.1668; *d* Hampton Wick, 12 Jan. 1735)

Egk [Mayer], Werner (*b* Auchsesheim, Bavaria, 17 May 1901; *d* Inning, nr Munich, 10 July 1983)

Einem, Gottfried von (*b* Berne, 24 Jan. 1918; *d* Oberdürnbach, nr Maissau, 12 July 1996)

Eisler, Hanns (*b* Leipzig, 6 July 1898; *d* Berlin, 6 Sept. 1962)

Elgar, Sir **Edward (William)** (*b* Broadheath, Worcs., 2 June 1857; *d* Worcester, 23 Feb. 1934)

Enescu, George [Enesco, Georges] (*b* Leveni-Vîrnav [now George Enescu], nr Dorohoi, 19 Aug. 1881; *d* Paris, 4 May 1955)

Eötvös, Peter (*b* Székelyudvarhely, Transylvania, 2 Jan. 1944)

Erkel, Ferenc (*b* Gyula, county of Békés, 7 Nov. 1810; *d* Budapest, 15 June 1893)

Eybler, Joseph Leopold (*b* Schwechat, nr Vienna, 8 Feb. 1765; *d* Vienna, 24 July 1846)

Fabrizi, Vincenzo (*b* Naples, 1764; *d* ?after 1812)

Faccio, Franco [Francesco Antonio] (*b* Verona, 8 March 1840; *d* Monza, 21 July 1891)

Fall, Leo(pold) (*b* Olomouc, 2 Feb. 1873; *d* Vienna, 16 Sept. 1925)

Falla (y Matheu), Manuel de (*b* Cádiz, 23 Nov. 1876; *d* Alta Gracia, Argentina, 14 Nov. 1946)

Fanshawe, David (Arthur) (*b* Paignton, 19 April 1942)

Farnaby, Giles (*b c.*1563; *d* London, Nov. 1640)

Fauré, Gabriel (Urbain) (*b* Pamiers, Ariège, 12 May 1845; *d* Paris, 4 Nov. 1924)

Feldman, Morton (*b* New York, 12 Jan. 1926; *d* Buffalo, NY, 3 Sept. 1987)

Fenby, Eric (William) (*b* Scarborough, 22 April 1906; *d* Scarborough, 18 Feb. 1997)

Ferneyhough, Brian (*b* Coventry, 16 Jan. 1943)

Ferrabosco, Alfonso [i] (*b* Bologna, *bapt.* 18 Jan. 1543; *d* Bologna, 12 Aug. 1588)

Ferroud, Pierre-Octave (*b* Chasselay, nr Lyons, 6 Jan. 1900; *d* Debrecen, 17 Aug. 1936)

Fibich, Zdeněk [Zdenko] (Antonín Václav) (*b* Všebořice, Bohemia, 21 Dec. 1850; *d* Prague, 15 Oct. 1900)

Finck, Herman (*b* London, 4 Nov. 1872; *d* London, 21 April 1939)

Finger, Gottfried [Godfrey] (*b* ?Olmütz [now Olomouc], *c.*1660; *d* Mannheim, Aug. 1730)

Finnissy, Michael (*b* London, 17 March 1946)

Finzi, Gerald (Raphael) (*b* London, 14 July 1901; *d* Oxford, 27 Sept. 1956)

Floyd, Carlisle (Sessions) (*b* Latta, SC, 11 June 1926)

Förtsch, Johann Philipp (*b* Wertheim am Main, *bapt.* 14 May 1652; *d* Eutin, nr Lübeck, 14 Dec. 1732)

Foss [Fuchs], Lukas (*b* Berlin, 15 Aug. 1922)

Foster, Stephen (Collins) (*b* Lawrenceville, PA, 4 July 1826; *d* New York, 13 Jan. 1864)

Franchetti, Alberto (*b* Turin, 18 Sept. 1860; *d* Viareggio, 4 Aug. 1942)

Franck, César(-Auguste-Jean-Guillaume-Hubert) (*b* Liège, 10 Dec. 1822; *d* Paris, 8 Nov. 1890)

Fux, Johann Joseph (*b* Hirtenfeld, nr Graz, 1660; *d* Vienna, 13 Feb. 1741)

Gabrieli, Andrea (*b* Venice, *c*.1533; *d* Venice, 30 Aug. 1585)

Gabrieli, Giovanni (*b* Venice, *c*.1555; *d* Venice, Aug. 1612)

Gade, Niels (Wilhelm) (*b* Copenhagen, 22 Feb. 1817; *d* Copenhagen, 21 Dec. 1890)

Gagliano, Marco da (*b* Florence, 1 May 1582; *d* Florence, 25 Feb. 1642)

Galuppi, Baldassare (*b* Burano, nr Venice, 18 Oct. 1706; *d* Venice, 3 Jan. 1785)

García, Manuel (del Popolo Vicente Rodríguez) (*b* Seville, 21 Jan. 1775; *d* Paris, 10 June 1832)

Gasparini, Francesco (*b* Camaiore, nr Lucca, 5 March 1668; *d* Rome, 22 March 1727)

Gay, John (*b* Barnstaple, *bapt.* 16 Sept. 1685; *d* London, 4 Dec. 1732)

Gazzaniga, Giuseppe (*b* Verona, 5 Oct. 1743; *d* Crema, 1 Feb. 1818)

Geminiani, Francesco (Xaverio) (*b* Lucca, *bapt.* 5 Dec. 1687; *d* Dublin, 17 Sept. 1762)

Gerhard, Roberto (*b* Valls, Catalonia, 25 Sept. 1896; *d* Cambridge, 5 Jan. 1970)

German, Sir Edward [Jones, German Edward] (*b* Whitchurch, Shropshire, 17 Feb. 1862; *d* London, 11 Nov. 1936)

Gershwin, George [Gershvin, Jacob] (*b* Brooklyn, New York, 26 Sept. 1898; *d* Hollywood, CA, 11 July 1937)

Gesualdo, Carlo, Prince of Venosa (*b* ?Naples, *c*.1561; *d* Gesualdo, Avellino, 8 Sept. 1613)

Gibbons, Christopher (*b* Westminster, *bapt.* 22 Aug. 1615; *d* Westminster, 20 Oct. 1676)

Gibbons, Orlando (*b* Oxford, *bapt.* 25 Dec. 1583; *d* Canterbury, 5 June 1625)

Ginastera, Alberto (Evaristo) (*b* Buenos Aires, 11 April 1916; *d* Geneva, 25 June 1983)

Giordano, Umberto (Menotti Maria) (*b* Foggia, 28 Aug. 1867; *d* Milan, 12 Nov. 1948)

Glass, Philip (*b* Baltimore, MD, 31 Jan. 1937)

Glazunov, Aleksandr Konstantinovich (*b* St Petersburg, 29 July/10 Aug. 1865; *d* Paris, 21 March 1936)

Glière, Reinhold [Glier, Reyngol'd] Moritsevich (*b* Kiev, 30 Dec. 1874/11 Jan. 1875; *d* Moscow, 23 June 1956)

Glinka, Mikhail Ivanovich (*b* Novospasskoye [now Glinka], nr Smolensk, 20 May/ 1 June 1804; *d* Berlin, 15 Feb. 1857)

Gluck, Christoph Willibald Ritter von (*b* Erasbach, Upper Palatinate, 2 July 1714; *d* Vienna, 15 Nov. 1787)

Goebbels, Heiner (*b* Neustadt Weinstrasse, 17 Aug. 1952)

Goehr, (Peter) Alexander (*b* Berlin, 10 Aug. 1932)

Goldmark, Karl [Károly] (*b* Keszthely, 18 May 1830; *d* Vienna, 2 Jan. 1915)

Gomes, (Antônio) Carlos (*b* Campinas, 11 July 1836; *d* Belém, 16 Sept. 1896)

Goossens, Sir **(Aynsley) Eugene** (*b* London, 26 May 1893; *d* Hillingdon, 13 June 1962)

Górecki, Henryk (Mikołaj) (*b* Czernica, nr Rybnik, 6 Dec. 1933)

Gossec, François-Joseph (*b* Vergnies, Hainaut, 17 Jan. 1734; *d* Passy, 16 Feb. 1829)

Gounod, Charles (François) (*b* Paris, 17 June 1818; *d* Saint Cloud, 18 Oct. 1893)

Grainger, (George) Percy (Aldridge) (*b* Brighton, Melbourne, 8 July 1882; *d* White Plains, NY, 20 Feb. 1961)

Granados (y Campina), Enrique (*b* Lérida, 27 July 1867; *d* at sea, English Channel, 24 March 1916)

Graun, Carl Heinrich (*b* Wahrenbrück, nr Dresden, 1703 or 1704; *d* Berlin, 8 Aug. 1759)

Grétry, André-Ernest-Modeste (*b* Liège, 8 Feb. 1741; *d* Montmorency, Paris, 24 Sept. 1813)

Grieg, Edvard (Hagerup) (*b* Bergen, 15 June 1843; *d* Bergen, 4 Sept. 1907)

Griffes, Charles T(omlinson) (*b* Elmira, NY, 17 Sept. 1884; *d* New York, 8 April 1920)

Gruber, H(einz) K(arl) (*b* Vienna, 3 Jan. 1943)

Gubaidulina, Sofia (Asgatovna) (*b* Chistopol', Tatarstan, 24 Oct. 1931)

Guo Wenjing (*b* Chongquing, Sichuan, 1 Feb. 1956)

Gurney, Ivor (Bertie) (*b* Gloucester, 28 Aug. 1880; *d* Dartford, 26 Dec. 1937)

Hoffmann, E(rnst) T(heodor) A(madeus) [originally Wilhelm; Amadeus adopted in homage to Mozart] (*b* Königsberg [now Kaliningrad], 24 Jan. 1776; *d* Berlin, 25 June 1822)

Höller, York (*b* Leverkusen, 11 Jan. 1944)

Holliger, Heinz (*b* Langenthal, 21 May 1939)

Holloway, Robin (Greville) (*b* Leamington Spa, 10 Oct. 1943)

Holmboe, Vagn (*b* Horsens, Jutland, 20 Dec. 1909; *d* Ramløse, 1 Sept. 1996)

Holst, Gustav (Theodore) (*b* Cheltenham, 21 Sept. 1874; *d* London, 25 May 1934)

Holt, Simon (*b* Bolton, 21 Feb. 1958)

Honegger, Arthur (*b* Le Havre, 10 March 1892; *d* Paris, 27 Nov. 1955)

Horn, Charles Edward (*b* London, 21 June 1786; *d* Boston, 21 Oct. 1849)

Howells, Herbert (Norman) (*b* Lydney, Glos., 17 Oct. 1892; *d* London, 23 Feb. 1983)

Hudson, George (*d* London, 10 Dec. 1672)

Humperdinck, Engelbert (*b* Siegburg, nr Bonn, 1 Sept. 1854; *d* Neustrelitz, 27 Sept. 1921)

Ibert, Jacques (François Antoine Marie) (*b* Paris, 15 Aug. 1890; *d* Paris, 5 Feb. 1962)

Indy, (Paul Marie Théodore) Vincent d' (*b* Paris, 27 March 1851; *d* Paris, 2 Dec. 1931)

Ireland, John (Nicholson) (*b* Bowdon, Cheshire, 13 Aug. 1879; *d* Rock Mill, Washington, Sussex, 12 June 1962)

Isouard, Nicolas [Nicolò de Malte] (*b* Valletta, 18 May 1773; *d* Paris, 23 March 1818)

Ives, Charles (Edward) (*b* Danbury, CT, 20 Oct. 1874; *d* West Redding, CT, 19 May 1954)

Janáček, Leoš [Leo Eugen] (*b* Hukvaldy, Moravia, 3 July 1854; *d* Moravská Ostrava [now Ostrava], 12 Aug. 1928)

Janequin [Jannequin], Clément (*b* Châtellerault, nr Poitiers, *c.*1485; *d* Paris, 1558)

Jarnach, Philipp (*b* Noisy-le-Sec, nr Paris, 26 July 1892; *d* Börnsen, nr Bergedorf, 17 Dec. 1982)

Jeremiáš, Otakar (*b* Písek, 17 Oct. 1892; *d* Prague, 5 March 1962)

Jommelli [Jomelli], Nicolò (*b* Aversa, 10 Sept. 1714; *d* Naples, 25 Aug. 1774)

Joplin, Scott (*b* north-east Texas, July 1867 – mid-Jan. 1868; *d* New York, 1 April 1917)

Josquin des Prez [Jossequin Lebloitte] (*b* c.1450; *d* Condé-sur-Escaut, 27 Aug. 1521)

Kabalevsky, Dmitry Borisovich (*b* St Petersburg, 17/30 Dec. 1904; *d* Moscow, 14 Feb. 1987)

Kagel, Mauricio (Raúl) (*b* Buenos Aires, 24 Dec. 1931)

Kalkbrenner, Frédéric [Friedrich Wilhelm Michael] (*b* between Kassel and Berlin, Nov. 1785; *d* Enghien-les-Bains, 10 June 1849)

Karatïgin, Vyacheslav Gavrilovich (*b* Pavlovsk, 17 Sept. 1875; *d* Leningrad, 23 Oct. 1925)

Karetnikov, Nikolay Nikolayevich (*b* Moscow, 28 June 1930; *d* Moscow, 10 Oct. 1994)

Karg-Elert, Sigfrid (*b* Oberndorf am Neckar, 21 Nov. 1877; *d* Leipzig, 9 April 1933)

Ketèlbey, Albert W(illiam) (*b* Birmingham, 9 Aug. 1875; *d* Cowes, 26 Nov. 1959)

Khachaturian, Aram (*b* Tbilisi, 6 June 1903; *d* Moscow, 1 May 1978)

Khrennikov, Tikhon Nikolayevich (*b* Elets, 28 May/10 June 1913)

Knussen, (Stuart) Oliver (*b* Glasgow, 12 June 1952)

Kodály, Zoltán (*b* Kecskemét, Hungary, 16 Dec. 1882; *d* Budapest, 6 March 1967)

Koechlin, Charles (Louis Eugène) (*b* Paris, 27 Nov. 1867; *d* Le Canadel, Var, 31 Dec. 1950)

Korngold, Erich Wolfgang (*b* Brno, 29 May 1897; *d* Hollywood, CA, 29 Nov. 1957)

Krenek, Ernst (*b* Vienna, 23 Aug. 1900; *d* Palm Springs, CA, 22 Dec. 1991)

Kreutzer, Rodolphe (*b* Versailles, 16 Nov. 1766; *d* Geneva, 6 Jan. 1831)

Kuhnau, Johann (*b* Geising, Harz Mountains, 6 April 1660; *d* Leipzig, 5 June 1722)

Kunad, Rainer (*b* Chemnitz, 24 Oct. 1936)

Kurtág, György (*b* Lugoj, Transylvania, 19 Feb. 1926)

Lachenmann, Helmut (Friedrich) (*b* Stuttgart, 27 Nov. 1935)

Lalo, Édouard (Victoire Antoine) (*b* Lille, 27 Jan. 1823; *d* Paris, 22 April 1892)

Lambert, (Leonard) Constant (*b* London, 27 Aug. 1905; *d* London, 21 Aug. 1951)

Loewe, Carl (*b* Loebjuen, nr Halle, 30 Nov. 1796; *d* Kiel, 20 April 1869)

Lortzing, (Gustav) Albert (*b* Berlin, 23 Oct. 1801; *d* Berlin, 21 Jan. 1851)

Løvenskjold, Herman (Severin) (*b* 1815; *d* 1870)

Lully, Jean-Baptiste [Lulli, Giovanni Battista] (*b* Florence, 29 Nov. 1632; *d* Paris, 22 March 1687)

Lumbye, Hans Christian (*b* Copenhagen, 2 May 1810; *d* Copenhagen, 20 March 1874)

Lutosławski, Witold (*b* Warsaw, 25 Jan. 1913; *d* Warsaw, 7 Feb. 1994)

Lutyens, (Agnes) Elisabeth (*b* London, 6 July 1906; *d* London, 14 April 1983)

L'vov, Aleksey Fyodorovich (*b* Reval [now Tallinn, Estonia], 25 May/5 June 1798; *d* nr Kovno [now Kaunas, Lithuania], 16/28 Dec. 1870)

Lyadov, Anatoly Konstantinovich (*b* St Petersburg, 29 April/11 May 1855; *d* Polïnovka, Novgorod district, 15/28 Aug. 1914)

MacCunn, Hamish (*b* Greenock, 22 March 1868; *d* London, 2 Aug. 1916)

MacDowell, Edward (Alexander) (*b* New York, 18 Dec. 1860; *d* New York, 23 Jan. 1908)

Macfarren, Sir George (Alexander) (*b* London, 2 March 1813; *d* London, 31 Oct. 1887)

Machaut [Machault], Guillaume de (*b* ?Reims, *c*.1300; *d* ?Reims, 13 April 1377)

Machover, Tod (*b* New York, 24 Nov. 1953)

MacMillan, James (Loy) (*b* Kilwinning, Ayrshire, 16 July 1959)

Mahler, Gustav (*b* Kaliste, Bohemia, 7 July 1860; *d* Vienna, 18 May 1911)

Malipiero, Gian Francesco (*b* Venice, 18 March 1882; *d* Treviso, 1 Aug. 1973)

Marenzio, Luca (*b* Coccaglio, nr Brescia, *c*.1553; *d* Rome, 22 Aug. 1599)

Marschner, Heinrich (August) (*b* Zittau, 16 Aug. 1795; *d* Hanover, 14 Dec. 1861)

Martin, Frank (*b* Geneva, 15 Sept. 1890; *d* Naarden, 21 Nov. 1974)

Martinů, Bohuslav (Jan) (*b* Polička, Bohemia, 8 Dec. 1890; *d* Liestal, Switzerland, 28 Aug. 1959)

Martland, Steve (*b* Liverpool, 10 Oct. 1959)

Mascagni, Pietro (*b* Livorno, 7 Dec. 1863; *d* Rome, 2 Aug. 1945)

Mason, Benedict (*b* London, 21 June 1955)

Massenet, Jules (Émile Frédéric) (*b* Montaud, Saint Étienne, 12 May 1842; *d* Paris, 31 Aug. 1912)

Matthews, Colin (*b* London, 13 Feb. 1946)

Matthus, Siegfried (*b* Mallenuppen, East Prussia, 13 April 1934)

Maw, (John) Nicholas (*b* Grantham, 5 Nov. 1935)

Maxwell Davies, Peter. *See* Davies, Peter Maxwell.

Mayr, Simon (Johannes) (*b* Mendorf, Bavaria, 14 June 1763; *d* Bergamo, 2 Dec. 1845)

Medtner, Nicolas [Metner, Nikolay Karlovich] (*b* Moscow, 24 Dec. 1879/5 Jan. 1880; *d* London, 13 Nov. 1951)

Méhul, Étienne-Nicolas (*b* Givet, Ardennes, 22 June 1763; *d* Paris, 18 Oct. 1817)

Melani, Jacopo (*b* Pistoia, 6 July 1623; *d* Pistoia, 18 Aug. 1676)

Melani, Alessandro (*b* Pistoia, 4 Feb. 1639; *d* Rome, 3 Oct. 1703)

Mendelssohn(-Bartholdy), Felix Jakob Ludwig (*b* Hamburg, 3 Feb. 1809; *d* Leipzig, 4 Nov. 1847)

Menotti, Gian Carlo (*b* Cadegliano, 7 July 1911)

Mercadante, (Giuseppe) Saverio (Raffaele) (*b* Altamura, nr Bari, *bapt.* 17 Sept. 1795; *d* Naples, 17 Dec. 1870)

Messager, André (Charles Prosper) (*b* Montluçon, 30 Dec. 1853; *d* Paris, 24 Feb. 1929)

Messiaen, Olivier (Eugène Prosper Charles) (*b* Avignon, 10 Dec. 1908; *d* Paris, 27 April 1992)

Meyer, Krzysztof (*b* Kraków, 11 Aug. 1943)

Meyerbeer, Giacomo [Beer, Jakob Liebmann] (*b* Berlin, 5 Sept. 1791; *d* Paris, 2 May 1864)

Milhaud, Darius (*b* Aix-en-Provence, 4 Sept. 1892; *d* Geneva, 22 June 1974)

Millöcker, Carl (Joseph) (*b* Vienna, 29 April 1842; *d* Baden, nr Vienna, 31 Dec. 1899)

Minkus, Léon [Aloysius Ludwig] (*b* Vienna, 23 March 1826; *d* Vienna, 7 Dec. 1917)

Moeran, E(rnest) J(ohn) (*b* Heston, Middx., 31 Dec. 1894; *d* nr Kenmare, Co. Kerry, 1 Dec. 1950)

Moniuszko, Stanisław (*b* Ubiel, nr Minsk, 5 May 1819; *d* Warsaw, 4 June 1872)

Monk, Meredith (Jane) (*b* Lima, Peru, 20 Nov. 1942)

Montéclair, Michel Pignolet de (*b* Andelot, Haute-Marne, *bapt.* 4 Dec. 1667; *d* Aumont, 22 Sept. 1737)

Montemezzi, Italo (*b* Vigasio, nr Verona, 31 May 1875; *d* Vigasio, 15 May 1952)

Monteverdi, Claudio (Giovanni Antonio) (*b* Cremona, 15 May 1567; *d* Venice, 29 Nov. 1643)

Moore, Douglas S(tuart) (*b* Cutchogue, NY, 10 Aug. 1893; *d* Greenport, NY, 25 July 1969)

Morales, Cristóbal de (*b* Seville, *c.*1490–1500; *d* ?Málaga, 4 Sept.–7 Oct. 1553)

Morlacchi, Francesco (Giuseppe Baldassare) (*b* Perugia, 14 June 1784; *d* Innsbruck, 28 Oct. 1841)

Morley, Thomas (*b* Norwich, 1557 or 1558; *d* London, ? early Oct. 1602)

Moscheles, Ignaz (*b* Prague, 23 May 1794; *d* Leipzig, 10 March 1870)

Mosolov, Aleksandr Vasil'yevich (*b* Kiev, 29 July/11 Aug. 1900; *d* Moscow, 11 July 1973)

Mozart, Wolfgang Amadeus (*b* Salzburg, 27 Jan. 1756; *d* Vienna, 5 Dec. 1791)

Muldowney, Dominic (John) (*b* Southampton, 19 July 1952)

Müller, Wenzel (*b* Trnava, 26 Sept. 1767; *d* Baden, 3 Aug. 1835)

Musgrave, Thea (*b* Barnton, Midlothian, 27 May 1928)

Musorgsky, Modest Petrovich (*b* Karevo, Pskov district, 9/21 March 1839; *d* St Petersburg, 28 March 1881)

Myaskovsky, Nikolay Yakovlevich (*b* Novogeorgiyevsk, 8/20 April 1881; *d* Moscow, 8 Aug. 1950)

Mysliveček [Mysliweczek, Misliveček], Josef (*b* Prague, 9 March 1737; *d* Rome, 4 Feb. 1781)

Naumann, Johann Gottlieb (*b* Blasewitz, nr Dresden, 17 April 1741; *d* Dresden, 23 Oct. 1801)

Nielsen, Carl (August) (*b* Sortelung, nr Nørre Lyndelse, Fyn, 9 June 1865; *d* Copenhagen, 3 Oct. 1931)

Nono, Luigi (*b* Venice, 29 Jan. 1924; *d* Venice, 8 May 1990)

Nordheim, Arne (*b* Larvik, 20 June 1931)

Nørgård, Per (*b* Gentofte, 13 July 1932)

Persiani, Giuseppe (*b* Recanati, *c*.1799–1805; *d* Paris, 13 Aug. 1869)

Petrassi, Goffredo (*b* Zagarola, nr Palestrina, 16 July 1904; *d* Rome, 3 March 2003)

Pfitzner, Hans (*b* Moscow, 5 May 1869; *d* Salzburg, 22 May 1949)

Philidor, François-André Danican (*b* Dreux, 7 Sept. 1726; *d* London, 31 Aug. 1795)

Piazzolla, Astor (*b* Mar del Plata, 11 March 1921; *d* Buenos Aires, 5 July 1992)

Piccinni (Vito), Niccolò (Marcello Antonio Giacomo) (*b* Bari, 16 Jan. 1728; *d* Passy, 7 May 1800)

Pintscher, Matthias (*b* Marl, 29 Jan. 1971)

Pixis, Johann Peter (*b* Mannheim, 10 Feb. 1788; *d* Baden-Baden, 22 Dec. 1874)

Pizzetti, Ildebrando (*b* Borgo Strinato, nr Parma, 20 Sept. 1880; *d* Rome, 13 Feb. 1968)

Ponchielli, Amilcare (*b* Paderno, nr Cremona, 31 Aug. 1834; *d* Milan, 16 Jan. 1886)

Porpora, Nicola (Antonio) (*b* Naples, 17 Aug. 1686; *d* Naples, 3 March 1768)

Poulenc, Francis (Jean Marcel) (*b* Paris, 7 Jan. 1899; *d* Paris, 30 Jan. 1963)

Pousseur, Henri (Léon Marie Thérèse) (*b* Malmédy, nr Liège, 23 June 1929)

Praetorius, Michael (*b* Creuzburg an der Werra, 15 Feb. *c*.1571; *d* Wolfenbüttel, 15 Feb. 1621)

Prez, Josquin des. *See* Josquin des Prez.

Prokofiev, Sergey (Sergeyevich) (*b* Sontsovka, Ukraine, 11/23 April 1891; *d* Moscow, 5 March 1953)

Puccini, Giacomo (Antonio Domenico Michele Secondo Maria) (*b* Lucca, 22 Dec. 1858; *d* Brussels, 29 Nov. 1924)

Pugni, Cesare (*b* Genoa, 31 May 1802; *d* St Petersburg, 14/26 Jan. 1870)

Purcell, Daniel (*d* London, *bur.* 26 Nov. 1717)

Purcell, Henry (*b* Westminster, autumn 1659; *d* Westminster, 21 Nov. 1695)

Raff, (Joseph) Joachim (*b* Lachen, nr Zürich, 27 May 1822; *d* Frankfurt, 24 or 25 June 1882)

Rakhmaninov [Rachmaninoff], Sergey (Vasil′yevich) (*b* Semyonovo, 20 March/1 April 1873; *d* Beverly Hills, CA, 28 March 1943)

Somervell, Sir **Arthur** (*b* Windermere, 5 June 1863; *d* London, 2 May 1937)

Sorabji, Khaikosru Shapurji [Leon Dudley] (*b* Chingford, 14 Aug. 1892; *d* Wareham, Dorset, 14 Oct. 1988)

Sousa, John Philip (*b* Washington, DC, 6 Nov. 1854; *d* Reading, PA, 6 March 1932)

Spohr, Louis (*b* Brunswick, 5 April 1784; *d* Kassel, 22 Oct. 1859)

Spontini, Gaspare (Luigi Pacifico) (*b* Maiolati, nr Ancona, 14 Nov. 1774; *d* Maiolati, 24 Jan. 1851)

Stainer, Sir **John** (*b* London, 6 June 1840; *d* Verona, 31 March 1901)

Stanford, Sir **Charles Villiers** (*b* Dublin, 30 Sept. 1852; *d* London, 29 March 1924)

Steibelt, Daniel (Gottlieb) (*b* Berlin, 22 Oct. 1765; *d* St Petersburg, 20 Sept./2 Oct. 1823)

Steinberg, Maximilian (Oseyevich) (*b* Vilnius, 4 July 1883; *d* Leningrad, 6 Dec. 1946)

Stockhausen, Karlheinz (*b* Burg Mödrath, nr Cologne, 22 Aug. 1928)

Storace, Stephen (John Seymour) (*b* London, 4 April 1762; *d* London, 19 March 1796)

Straus, Oscar (*b* Vienna, 6 March 1870; *d* Bad Ischl, 11 Jan. 1954)

Strauss, Johann (Baptist) (i) (*b* Vienna, 14 March 1804; *d* Vienna, 25 Sept. 1849)

Strauss, Johann (Baptist) (ii) (*b* Vienna, 25 Oct. 1825; *d* Vienna, 3 June 1899)

Strauss, Richard (Georg) (*b* Munich, 11 June 1864; *d* Garmisch-Partenkirchen, Bavaria, 8 Sept. 1949)

Stravinsky, Igor (Fyodorovich) (*b* Oranienbaum [now Lomonosov], 5/17 June 1882; *d* New York, 6 April 1971)

Strungk, Nicolaus Adam (*b* Brunswick, *bapt.* 15 Nov. 1640; *d* Dresden, 23 Sept. 1700)

Suk, Josef (*b* Křečovice, 4 Jan. 1874; *d* Benešov, 29 May 1935)

Sullivan, Sir **Arthur (Seymour)** (*b* Lambeth, 13 May 1842; *d* London, 22 Nov. 1900)

Suppé, Franz von [Suppe, Francesco Ezechiele Ermenegildo de] (*b* Split, 18 April 1819; *d* Vienna, 21 May 1895)

Süssmayr, Franz Xaver (*b* Schwanenstadt, 1766; *d* Vienna, 17 Sept. 1803)

Sutermeister, Heinrich (*b* Feuerthalen, Schaffhausen, 12 Aug. 1910; *d* Vaux-sur-Morges, 16 March 1995)

Turnage, Mark-Anthony (b Corringham, Essex, 10 June 1960)

Tye, Christopher (b c.1505; d 27 Aug. 1571–15 March 1573)

Ullmann, Viktor (Josef) (b Teschen [now Česky Těšín], 1 Jan. 1898; d Auschwitz, 18 Oct. 1944)

Varèse, Edgard (Victor Achille Charles) (b Paris, 22 Dec. 1883; d New York, 6 Nov. 1965)

Vaughan Williams, Ralph (b Down Ampney, Glos., 12 Oct. 1872; d London, 26 Aug. 1958)

Vecchi, Orazio (Tiberio) (b Modena, 5 Dec. 1550; d Modena, 19 Feb. 1605)

Venturi del Nibbio, Stefano (fl 1592–1600)

Verdi, Giuseppe (Fortunino Francesco) (b Roncole, nr Busseto, 9 or 10 Oct. 1813; d Milan, 27 Jan. 1901)

Vieuxtemps, Henri (b Verviers, 17 Feb. 1820; d Mustapha, Algeria, 6 June 1881)

Villa-Lobos, Heitor (b Rio de Janeiro, 5 March 1887; d Rio de Janeiro, 17 Nov. 1959)

Vir, Param (b Delhi, 6 Feb. 1952)

Vivaldi, Antonio (Lucio) (b Venice, 4 March 1678; d Vienna, 28 July 1741)

Vivier, Claude (b Montreal, 14 April 1948; d Paris, 12 March 1983)

Volans, Kevin (b Pietermaritzburg, 26 July 1949)

Wagner, (Wilhelm) Richard (b Leipzig, 22 May 1813; d Venice, 13 Feb. 1883)

Waldteufel [Lévy], Émile (b Strasbourg, 9 Dec. 1848; d Paris, 12 Feb. 1915)

Wallace, (William) Vincent (b Waterford, 11 March 1812; d Château de Haget, Vieuzos, Hautes-Pyrénées, 12 Oct. 1865)

Walton, Sir **William (Turner)** (b Oldham, Lancs., 29 March 1902; d Ischia, 8 March 1983)

Ward, Robert (Eugene) (b Cleveland, OH, 13 Sept. 1917)

Warlock, Peter [Heseltine, Philip (Arnold)] (b London, 30 Oct. 1894; d London, 17 Dec. 1930)

Weber, Carl Maria (Friedrich Ernst) von (b Eutin, 18 Nov. 1786; d London, 5 June 1826)

Webern, Anton (Friedrich Wilhelm von) (b Vienna, 3 Dec. 1883; d Mittersill, 15 Sept. 1945)

Oxford Paperback Reference

The Oxford Dictionary of Dance
Debra Craine and Judith Mackrell

Over 2,500 entries on everything from hip-hop to classical ballet,
covering dancers, dance styles, choreographers and composers,
techniques, companies, and productions.

'A must-have volume ... impressively thorough'
Margaret Reynolds, *The Times*

Who's Who in Opera
Joyce Bourne

Covering operas, operettas, roles, perfomances, and well-known
personalities.

'a generally scrupulous and scholarly book'
Opera

The Concise Oxford Dictionary of Music
Michael Kennedy

The most comprehensive, authoritative, and up-to-date dictionary of
music available in paperback.

'clearly the best around ... the dictionary that everyone should have'
Literary Review